Spoonful

Devotions for Reading Through the Bible in a Year

Pat Bullock

by
Patrick W. Bullock, Sr.

II Timothy 3:16-17

ISBN-13: 978-1508998884
ISBN-10: 1508998884

Cover design by Jonna Feavel

Images used with permission
Stock Photo ID: 56084561 African elephant female and her baby elephant balancing on a blue balls. Copyright: Kletr

Stock Photo ID: 75024328 Old Silver Spoon Isolated On White Background
Copyright: urfingus

Unless otherwise identified, all scripture quotations in this publication are taken from *The Holy Bible, New International Version®*, NIV, Copyright © 1973, 1978, 1984, by International Bible Society. Used by permission.

Scripture references identified by AMP are taken from taken from the Amplified® Bible, Copyright © 1954, 1958, 1962, 1964, 1965, 1987 by The Lockman Foundation. Used by permission. (www.Lockman.org)

Scripture references identified by KJV are taken from the King James Version, a public domain work.

Dedication

I dedicate this book to my wife, Nancy, and our three children Bill, Tamah, and Cindi. Nancy did all the typing and some editing for which I am very grateful. May this book draw people to the Word of God, which brings people closer to the Lord of Life: Jesus the Resurrected King of Kings.

Pat Bullock

Table of Contents

Forward

I've known Pat Bullock for twenty seven years and during that time he has urged people to read the entire Bible. This devotion book is designed to get people to read God's Word. Reading the Bible is more important than reading his devotions even though they will bless You. I agree with David Limbaugh in his book *Jesus on Trial* that "God is actually present with us and communicates His Words to us through the Holy Spirit" when we read the Bible. This book is written with that purpose in mind.

If You follow the designated passage each day You will read the entire Bible from Genesis to Revelation. The devotions speak briefly to a portion of the assigned passages and will bless You by making an application of that portion to Your life.

I recommend this book as a blessing to Your spiritual walk.

Terry Fox, Senior Pastor of Summit Church
Wichita, Kansas and co-host of the
Answering the Call Radio Program

Spoonful

Introduction

How do you eat an elephant? According to the old saying, you do it "one spoonful at a time." People often feel like reading the Bible all the way through in a year is as daunting a task as trying to eat an elephant. Yet, if you take it spoonful by spoonful, it can be done.

The goal and purpose of this book of devotions is to help people read the Bible from Genesis straight through to Revelation. The assigned passages will assure your completion of the goal to read the entire Bible in one year if you read the passages daily. Two weeks a year can be set aside for sickness or other emergency and yet still stay on track to complete the entire Bible. The most important result of reading these devotions is to get people to read the Bible for themselves. The devotions reflect and elaborate on the passage that you read that day.

Spoonful

Yearly Devotions – Week 1

Day 1: Doing Nothing is Dangerous

Read GENESIS Chapters 1-3

Adam stood idly by while Eve ate from the tree of the knowledge of good and evil. "She also gave some to her husband, who was with her, and he ate it." (3:6) [NIV] "...she took of the fruit thereof, and did eat, and gave also unto her husband with her; and he did eat." [KJV] What a tragedy when men refuse to be the spiritual leader of their home. Adam should have kindly told Eve that God's instruction and commandment would not allow them to eat the fruit. He should have refused to eat it in spite of what she did.

Adam loved Eve more than he loved God or he would have obeyed the Lord. Jesus said, "If ye love Me, keep My commandments" (John 14:15). We can praise the Lord because Jesus loved us enough to shed His blood to pay the penalty for our sin and restore our relationship with the Father.

My prayer: It is my desire and request that You teach me how to love You more and give me the strength to obey You.

Day 2: God Intends Good for All Men

Read GENESIS Chapters 4-6

God warned Cain to try to keep him from sinning. "...if You do what is right will You not be accepted? But if You do not do what is right, sin is crouching at Your door; it desires to have You, but You must master it" (4:7). [NIV] This comment from God was before Cain killed Abel. God replaced Abel with Godly Seth.

Lamech recognized God blessing the world by sending Noah. "He named him Noah and said, 'He will comfort us in the labor and painful toil of our hands caused by the ground the Lord has cursed." (5:29) [NIV]

He prepared a way for mankind to survive the coming flood. He told Noah "...make Yourself an Ark of cypress wood" (6:14). Over and over God provides man a way of escape. He warns, sends men and instructs on how to live through His judgment. That is why Jesus came! "For God so loved the world {mankind} that He gave His only begotten Son..." (John 3:16).

My prayer: Thank You for revealing Your will is to bless us and give us Your kind of life.

Day 3: God Gives Fresh Starts

Read GENESIS Chapters 7-10

In these passages, we see that man is a complete moral failure. God removed all living creatures off of the earth and gave man a fresh start through Noah.

- God established new conditions for man's existence after the flood.
- God again tells man to "...multiply on the earth and be fruitful and increase in number." (8:17)
- God promised never to destroy life on earth with a flood again. (8:21)
- God demanded murderers to be executed. (9:6)
- God established meat as a part of man's diet. (9:3)
- God made animals to fear humans. (9:2)

When God gives man a fresh start, He demands that the new start encompass a new lifestyle. A Christian is a changed person. Jesus changes the heart of a person. "...therefore, if anyone is in Christ, he is a new creation;..." (II Cor. 5:17).

My prayer: Thank You for removing my sin and my desire for sin. Keep me close so that all my desires will be pleasing to You.

Day 4: From a Liar to a Leader
Read GENESIS Chapters 11-14

The only perfect man to walk on the earth was Jesus. No matter who God uses, he or she will have failed morally at some time in their life. Abram failed the honesty test when he told a half-truth to Pharaoh. Abram's faith faltered when he acted out of fear with Pharaoh. In spite of these failures, he became a fierce military leader when Lot was captured by the coalition of Mesopotamian Kings.

Not only did he become a successful soldier, but he also remained a faithful follower of Jehovah-God by tithing to Melchizedek. God can always use a person whose heart's desire is to please Him. He can use any person even after they fail Him.

My prayer: Lord, my desire is to please You and to remain faithful to Your calling in my life. I ask for Your strength and wisdom to honor You by my actions.

Day 5: Conversations with Jesus
Read GENESIS Chapters 15-18

This first conversation is an amazing occurrence because Jesus appears in person to Abraham and Sarah as a man before He was born of a virgin. Jesus asked Sarah why she laughed when she heard she was to give birth. She argued with Jesus and lied to Him. She said, "'I did not laugh;' Jesus corrected her and said, 'Yes, You did laugh'" (18:15). Are we like Sarah and think we can fool God by lying to Him and ourselves?

The amazing thing about the second conversation was that God let Abraham in on His plans to destroy Sodom and Gomorrah. The infinite God let the finite man know what He was preparing to do. Abraham felt comfortable enough with the Lord to attempt to interfere in His plans and attempt to forestall judgment.

Prayer is holding a conversation with God. Praying includes praising, pleading and challenging God. It also includes listening to Him and letting Him instruct us. A conversation takes place when both parties participate.

My prayer: Thank You for allowing me, Your creation, to talk to You and seek Your wisdom and will. Thank You for answering prayer and for not answering some prayers.

Day 6: Old Habits Are Hard to Quit
Read GENESIS Chapters 19-21

Oops! Abraham does it again. He let fear overpower his faith. He lied in Egypt, and he lied again about the same thing. He was afraid that men would lust after his beautiful ninety year old wife and kill him for her. He could not conquer that fear even though God had spared him in Egypt. God had promised him success wherever he went. He had talked to Jesus and two angels. He had seen God's power in destroying Sodom and Gomorrah. God had spared Lot and his daughters. It seems that Abraham should have been confident that God would take care of him and that Sarah would not be a problem because of God's protection.

Abraham was a lot like us today. We have God's blessings and presence in our lives and we still revert to worldly methods to survive. Abraham could not know fully that God's real purpose for his life was to establish a nation to track the human ancestry of His Son. God has a purpose for all of His children in like manner.

My prayer: Lord, please keep me on Your course for my life and help me to reject my old habits.

Day 7: Praying Servants

Read GENESIS Chapters 22-24

Abraham's servant had seen God work in a marvelous way in Abraham's life. He had seen God defeat Kings, expand Abraham's wealth and give Abraham and Sarah a child in their old age. That must have convinced him God was real and answered prayer. His praying got immediate results. "Before he had finished praying..." Rebekah appeared (24:15). He believed God answers prayer and God honored that.

Jesus encouraged us to pray believing God answers prayer. He said, "...Your Father knoweth what things ye have need of, before ye ask Him" (Matt. 6:8). The prophet Isaiah believed God answers prayer. "And it shall come to pass, that before they call, I will answer; and while they are yet speaking, I will hear." (Isaiah 65:24). God desires to reveal Himself to His children through prayer.

We must approach God with a believing heart. Why should He bless unbelief?

My prayer: Thank You for answered prayer when we come to You through Jesus.

Spoonful

Yearly Devotions – Week 2

Day 1: Family Features

Read GENESIS Chapters 25-28

Every family has its own dynamics. There is an atmosphere and lifestyle unconsciously passed on to each generation. Abraham lied to Abimelech about Sarah being his wife in Genesis 20. Years later Isaac lied to another Abimelech about Rebekah being his wife. Abraham and Isaac both feared for their lives. The weakness of Abraham was repeated by his son Isaac.

God's blessing Abraham and Isaac with wealth caused problems with the pagan world. "Abimelech...said to Abraham; 'God is with You in everything You do'" (21:22). Another Abimelech, the son of the first Abimelech, said to Isaac, "move away from us; You have become too powerful for us" (26:16). The family had a reputation of having God's blessings.

Esau and Jacob came into conflict over their father's wealth and became enemies. Ishmael and Isaac also became enemies over the inheritance from Abraham.

As parents we must be careful what family features we leave our children.

My prayer: Lord, bless my children with Your favor and protect them from the evil one. Cause them to reject my weaknesses and inherit any good features found in our home.

Day 2: God—The Provider

Read GENESIS Chapters 29-31

Even scheming Laban recognized God provided Jacob with wealth and prosperity. God was involved in Jacobs's life even though he had a dysfunctional family. Laban said, "...I have learned by divination that the Lord has blessed me because of you (Jacob)" (30:27). Laban, the schemer, tried to out-do Jacob the trickster. When I say dysfunctional family, I am referring to the jealousy between Jacob's wives as they competed for his love. Also, his wives did not trust their father. They said, "...not only has he sold us, but he has used up what was paid for us..." (31:15).

In spite of the family discord, God still worked in their lives. He provided for their emotional well-being and their physical needs. When Rachel was barren, God intervened. "Then God remembered Rachel; He listened to her and opened her womb" (30:22). God protected Jacob by warning Laban. "Then God came to Laban...and said, 'Be careful not to say anything to Jacob, either good or bad'" (31:24).

God provides for us not because we deserve it but because He loves us.

My prayer: I praise You, the creator of all things, for continuing to watch over us finite human beings. Thank You for loving us and caring about us. Thank You for working to bring only good into our lives.

Day 3: Facing Past Behavior

Read GENESIS Chapters 32-34

Our son begged us to let him play football in high school. We reluctantly agreed, knowing the danger. He did well until he injured his knee. Now in his fifties, he has had four surgeries. The last surgery was to replace his knee. He experienced tremendous pain because he is allergic to pain medication. He made the comment that young people cannot grasp the possible consequences of their behavior until it is too late.

Jacob could say the same thing. He had participated in deception and dishonesty to cheat his brother Esau. When it came time to face his brother after twenty years, he was filled with fear. He prayed, "...Save me, I pray, from the hand of my brother Esau, for I am afraid he will come and attack me..." (32:11). He tried to protect himself with fanfare and gifts. "...I will pacify him with these gifts I am sending ahead..." (32:20). His past behavior also involved his family in the danger of facing Esau. As the danger appeared to be imminent, he did turn to God to protect him from his past behavior.

My prayer: I beseech You, Lord, to protect me from my past, present and future behavior. Guide me as I make choices to choose those that are Your will.

Day 4: Buried gods

Read GENESIS Chapters 35-37

God told Jacob to build an altar to worship Him. To worship God correctly, Jacob was told the place of worship. This was a sacred place because of Jacob's former participation in a supernatural experience there. Preparation to worship meant the people had to put away their idols. Jacob told them to "Get rid of the foreign gods You have with You...so they gave Jacob all the foreign gods...and Jacob buried them under the Oak at Shechem" (35:2-4). God wants us to bury our gods at the foot of Calvary's Tree.

The problem with Jacob's family is that they kept digging the idols up and returning to them. This is seen in Joseph's brothers digging up the idols of jealousy, lying, and hearts of murder. False gods can only bring heartache. Jacob's heart was broken when he was lied to about Joseph. When false gods are buried beneath the blood of Christ and Jesus is Lord in our lives, honesty and openness are present and people are blessed.

My prayer: Please reveal the idols in my life so I can bury them and have them removed from me forever. Give me the power to remain faithful in what I worship.

Day 5: Judah and Joseph

Read GENESIS Chapters 38-40

One brother was disobedient and one was dedicated. One brother let his fleshly appetite control him and one let God control his future. Judah lived out of fear while Joseph lived by faith. Judah feared his last son would die. Joseph believed God would bless him in spite of the circumstances. Even though Joseph was betrayed by his brothers and lied about by Potiphar's wife, he remained faithful to the Lord. He was forgotten by the cup-bearer and experienced the continued loss of freedom and yet he was really free from the bondage of sin.

Joseph remained faithful to the only one who could control events in his life. Amazingly he didn't whine and question God. He easily could have said, "God, I've remained faithful to You and I have ended up a slave in prison." He did what is very difficult. He trusted God when nothing seemed to turn out right. His reaction to adversity demonstrated his conviction that God controlled the events in his life. It wasn't easy to remain faithful to the Lord, but it was God-honoring and rewarding.

My prayer: Lord, I praise You that You are in control of all of life and that You are blessing my life even when circumstances appear otherwise.

Day 6: God Chooses Who He Uses

Read GENESIS Chapters 41-43

Joseph is a picture of the treatment of Christ on earth. Joseph was despised by his brothers and loved by his father. The brothers rejected the idea that Joseph would be over them. His brothers could not comprehend the disciplined life he lived. He refused to sin against God in adultery. Joseph declared his dependence upon God for the ability to interpret dreams. "Joseph replied to Pharaoh, 'But God will give Pharaoh the answer he desires" (41:16). Jesus said, "I tell You the truth, the Son can do nothing by Himself; he can do only what He sees the Father doing" (John 5:19). God chose the despised, disciplined, and dependent to serve Him.

Just like Joseph, we cannot earn our salvation. We are dependent upon God to give it to us through Jesus and His shed blood. To be a disciple means we allow God to discipline us. A disciple will be despised by the world because of their desire to obey the heavenly Father. The world cannot comprehend that disciples of Christ have value. It is a privilege to be despised so God can be glorified.

My prayer: Thank You for choosing to use me. Thank You for using the foolish, weak, lowly things to do Your work so I could be included.

Day 7: Carts of Affirmation

Read GENESIS Chapters 44-46

Jesus said, "...I am come that they might have life. And that they might have it more abundantly" (John 10:10). Joseph had been gone almost fifteen years. Jacob had believed his sons when they indicated Joseph was dead. Jacob could not believe Joseph was alive until he saw the supplies and transportation sent by Joseph. Joseph "...sent to his father ten donkeys loaded with the best things of Egypt..." (45:23). "...When he saw the carts Joseph had sent to carry him back, the spirit of their father Jacob revived" (45:27).

Jesus is alive and arose bodily from the grave. Like Jacob, we know He is alive because of the gift of salvation and the gifts of the Spirit He sent. A Christian is supplied with "...love, joy, peace, long-suffering, gentleness, goodness, faith, meekness, temperance..." (Galatians 5:22-23). A life filled with these treasures confirms that God is real and Jesus is Lord. The world cannot deliver these supplies. Jesus said, "...The thief cometh not, but for to steal, and to kill and to destroy..." (John 10:10). Satan, the thief, tries to rob us of an abundant life. Thank God, we've seen the cart of God's love.

My prayer: Thank You for the certainty of the hope of heaven because of Your word You sent to supply our hearts with the truth. Thank You for the gift of salvation and the Fruit of the Spirit.

Yearly Devotions – Week 3

Day 1: God's Goodness is Unstoppable

Read GENESIS Chapters 47-50

Did God get Joseph's brothers to sell him into slavery? God cannot be a part of jealousy and hatred. Therefore, He could not be a part of evil behavior. This story shows that no matter what evil Joseph's brothers or the world did to him, God's goodness through him could not be stopped. God redirected their evil actions to carry out His will.

God indicated in Joseph's dreams that he was to rule. How God was originally going to make Joseph a ruler cannot be known because his brother's actions interfered. God overcame their evil intent and completed His will for Joseph and Israel. Joseph understood and believed God's hand had protected him through all the events in his life. He said to his brothers, "...You intended to harm me, but God intended it for good to accomplish what is now being done, the saving of many lives..." (50:19) Just as men meant evil for Jesus, God's goodness came through to bring salvation.

My prayer: I can only praise You and thank You for Your goodness by sending Your Son Jesus to bring us Your words, work and will by dying on the cross.

Day 2: God's Agenda – Rescue the Perishing

Read EXODUS Chapters 1-3

Pharaoh's daughter named Moses after rescuing him from the river. The name "Moses" sounds like the Hebrew for "drawn out." Moses mother believed God would rescue her son from drowning in the river. Moses rescued a fellow Hebrew from the abusive treatment of an Egyptian. Moses rescued Jethro's daughters who were kept away from a well. "…Moses got up and came to their rescue and watered their flock." (2:17) Moses' nature was to rescue the helpless.

God chose Moses to rescue the entire nation of Israel from their cruel oppressors. God told Moses, "…I have come down to rescue them from the hand of the Egyptians and to bring them out of that land…" (3:8). God said, "So I will stretch out my hand and strike the Egyptians with all the wonders that I will perform among them…" (3:20).

God has always been in the rescue business. Jesus came to rescue all men from sin, death, and hell and then deliver us safely to the Father.

My prayer: Thank You for rescuing me from myself and my sin. I pray that I might be a part of Your rescue team by telling everyone that Jesus saves.

Day 3: Chosen to Serve

Read EXODUS Chapters 4-6

Moses' failure to help free Israel from slavery humbled him and caused him to doubt God could use him. He was surprised when God called him to serve. This call of God caused him to struggle the rest of his life. His first struggle was to submit to God's will. He felt unqualified to face Pharaoh and his own people. His second struggle was to solicit Israel's support by convincing them he was authorized by God to gain their liberty. He faced resistance from everyone. His third struggle was to surrender the results of his obedience to God. The greatest test in his struggles was when he finally stood before Pharaoh and asked permission to worship his God.

Much of Moses' struggle was that he could not see the complete picture of God's work nor his part in it. Like Moses, every Christian is called to serve and must leave the results to Him. Every Christian will have the same struggles when they attempt to obey the Lord.

My prayer: Lord increase my faith through Your word so that I can trust You with every aspect of my life. Thank You for allowing me to serve You.

Day 4: Christianity is Based on the Miraculous

Read EXODUS Chapters 7-9

A naturalist denies miracles exist. "For a naturalist, the universe is analogues to a closed box. Everything that happens inside the box is caused by, or is explicable in terms of, other things that exist within the box. Nothing (including God) exists outside the box; therefore, nothing outside the box we call the universe or nature can have any casual effect within the box.[1]" Christians believe God created the world freely and out of nothing. God, who created the Laws of the cosmos, can circumvent those laws to perform a miracle.

Christians believe God miraculously conceived Jesus in Mary by the Holy Spirit. Christians believe Jesus overcame nature and healed the sick and raised the dead. Christians believe Jesus bodily rose from the dead. Without God performing miracles, there is no salvation or Christianity. The miracles in Exodus demonstrate that only Jehovah-God controls nature and uses it for His purpose among His created beings called "humans."

---

[1] The Apologetics Study Bible, 2007. Holman Bible Publisher, Nashville, TN, Pg. 96

My prayer: I praise You Lord for being all powerful and all good at the same time. I praise You for being in control of all creation and my life. I praise You for giving Your Son to overcome death, sin, and hell.

Day 5: Pagan gods Exposed

Read EXODUS Chapters 10-12

God says, "You shall have no other gods before Me" (Exodus 20:3). It is the nature of man to have a god he can control or cajole. Men "...changed the glory of the incorruptible God into an image made like corruptible man, and to birds, and four-footed beasts, and creeping things" (Romans 1:23). Jehovah-God of the Bible cannot be controlled or cajoled into obeying man's desires.

God had to strengthen Pharaoh to be able to fully demonstrate how He could destroy and defeat all their petty gods. God's goal was to "...bring judgment on all the gods of Egypt" (12:12). God hardened Pharaoh's heart to have enough time to expose and defeat all the false gods of Egypt. God exposed the worship of snakes, the Nile, cows, the sun, and Pharaoh himself. When Pharaoh's resistance weakened, God strengthened him and hardened his heart. When God had another god He wanted to judge, He would send another plague.

We in America must forsake our gods of pleasure, money, power, abortion, sports, sex and many others. God will judge them all.

My prayer: Lord God have mercy on me and the country where I live. We have forsaken You. Please send a revival of Your Word and the work of Your Holy Spirit.

Day 6: Reverence's Source

Read EXODUS Chapters 13-15

Stewart Hamblin wrote the song "It Is No Secret" after witnessing to the actor John Wayne. One part of the song says, "What He has done for others He can do for You." That is true in two ways. He can save anyone who repents and believes or He can judge anyone who rejects Jesus as Savior.

When Israel saw God's powerful judgment as He drowned the Egyptian army, it caused them to fear God. If He could do that to Egypt, He could do that to Israel also. "And when the Israelites saw the great power the Lord displayed against the Egyptians the people feared the Lord and put their trust in Him and in Moses His servant" (14:31). The source of reverence is the fear of displeasing God and acknowledging His right to judge us. Reverence comes when man realizes he must give an account of his life to God. Reverence comes when man knows there is a judgment day. "For we must all appear before the judgment seat of Christ, that each one may receive the things done in the body, according to what he has done, whether good or bad" (II Cor. 5:10). Jesus is man's only advocate. "The fear of the Lord is the beginning of wisdom."

My prayer: Lord help me to live and strengthen me to behave in such a way that I never have to dread facing You at the Judgment Seat.

Day 7: God Consistently Blesses

Read EXODUS Chapters 16-18

God continued to placate and provide for Israel in spite of their murmuring and unthankful attitude. They had seen God defeat the Egyptian army and yet they refused to believe God would take care of them. They said to Moses, "…You have brought us out into this desert to starve this entire assembly to death" (16:4). God said, "I have heard the grumbling of the Israelites" (16:11). God then sent quail and manna to feed them. Their next complaint was that they were thirsty. They said, "Why did You bring us up out of Egypt to make us …die of thirst?" (17:3). God then gave them water.

God consistently blesses His people when they follow Him. God blesses His leaders who are faithful to His call. God gave Israel victory over the Amalekites and advice to judge His people. Paul states God's goodness, pointing out the truth that God wants to bless all people. He wrote, "…do You show contempt for the riches of His kindness, tolerance and patience, not realizing that God's kindness leads You toward repentance" (Romans 2:4). A believer should, by faith anticipate God's blessings not His punishment.

My prayer: Thank You for a life filled with Your blessings. Thank You for a future filled with Your blessings.

Yearly Devotions – Week 4

Day 1: Life with God

Read EXODUS Chapters 19-21

Israel had lived as slaves while under Pharaoh. Now, they were free of Egypt's mastery but not free of their own fallen nature. Now, they had to face the tyrant living within themselves called the "sinful nature." God dealt with that monster with His laws and commandments. God regulated every aspect of their life. Those regulations were designed to insure humane relationships between individuals. Their entire national life was to be founded upon the holy Jehovah-God as the foundation of their social structure.

Moses transmitted God's holy laws for a holy life to his people Israel. "Moses said to the people, 'Do not be afraid, God has come to test You, so that the fear of God will be with You to keep You from sinning'" (20:20). God's entire design of life is to give men peace, joy, and happiness through His righteousness. The only secure, fulfilling life comes from following the Lord Jesus and His instructions.

My prayer: Lord, help me to submit to Your will and follow the Lord Jesus with all my possessions, heart and soul.

Day 2: GPS

Read EXODUS Chapters 22-24

Today we think of the global positioning satellite when we see the letters GPS. In Moses' time, it could stand for God's presence separates. What does His presence separate? It separated Israel from all other nations. It separated Godly Moses from the elders. It separated the multitude of Israelites from Moses. In the Garden of Eden, God met with Adam and

Eve anywhere, anytime. In Moses' time, to meet with God was an extraordinarily special time. "When Moses went up on the mountain, the cloud covered it, and the glory of the Lord settled on Mount Sinai...Then Moses entered the cloud..." (24:15, 18).

Today, since Christ's shed blood pays for man's sin, man can enter His presence anytime, anywhere. Jesus said, "...I will send Him (the Holy Spirit) to You... when He, the Spirit of truth comes, He will guide You into all truth" (John 16:7, 13). His presence separates men again. "Therefore, come out from them and be separate, says the Lord" (II Corinthians 6:17).

My prayer: Lord, I praise You for sending Jesus to pay for my sin. I praise Jesus for sending the Holy Spirit to teach Your truth. Give me strength to separate from the world's lifestyle.

Day 3: Blood is Red

Read EXODUS Chapters 25-27

God chose to use Israel as the nation to trace the human side of Jesus from Abraham. Jesus' ancestry can be identified from Abraham to David to Mary. No imposter Satan sent could have engineered that. No person claiming to be the Messiah could fulfill prophecy concerning it.

The description of the Tabernacle is a reflection of what heaven is like and God's Son's mission. The colors blue, purple, and scarlet point to the beauty of heaven. Gold, silver and bronze show the richness of heaven. The main attraction of Israel's camp was the tabernacle. All the tents in Israel's camp were dark or black goat's hair. There were hundreds of black tents erected in a square pattern around the Tabernacle. The Tabernacle stood out at the center of the camp because God told Moses to "Make for the tent a covering of rams skin dyed red..." (26:14) In the very center of their camp stood the

Tabernacle which had been dyed red as a picture of Christ's shed blood for all men's sin. Christ's blood is the center piece in heaven. That is what keeps us saved.

My Prayer: Lord, I praise You that I'm saved by grace through faith in the blood of Jesus.

Day 4: Bells of Life

Read EXODUS Chapters 28-29

Israel's priests were to be mediators between Israel and God. Their job was to lead people to worship Jehovah-God. Their task was to join the hearts of Israel to God's heart. United to God, there would be joy in their journey. If they approached God without dealing with their sin, they would die. They had to be ceremonially cleansed and anointed with oil to approach the creator of the universe.

The priests could approach God after seven days of preparation. They wore bells on their garments so the people would know they had been accepted by God and were alive. "The sound of the bells will be heard when he enters the Holy Place before the Lord and when he comes out, so that he will not die" (28:35). Believers get the bells of life when they receive Jesus. Those bells are the joy that comes from the presence of the Holy Spirit in their life. It is a joy knowing we can enter God's presence anywhere any time. "Let us therefore come boldly unto the throne of grace, that we may obtain mercy, and find grace to help in time of need" (Hebrews 4:16).

My prayer: Thank You Father, for Your mercy and grace that allows me to tell You all my troubles and to know that You hear me.

Day 5: Chosen but Not Cherubs

Read EXODUS Chapters 30-32

God chose Abraham to be the head of Israel. God chose Israel to be the means to trace Christ's birth. Israel had done nothing to earn or deserve that privilege. They were chosen by God's sovereign will. They were a stubborn and sinful people. They weren't better than any other nation. They could only approach God through sacrificing animals and sprinkling their blood on the altar to cover their sin. "When You take a census of the Israelites to count them, each one must pay the Lord a ransom for his life at the time he is counted" (30:11).

The only way God can accept any man is by the ransom paid for by Christ and His shed blood. Jesus said, "For even the Son of Man came not to be ministered unto, but to minister, and to give His life a ransom for many" (Mark 10:45). "For there is one God, and one mediator between God and men, the man Christ Jesus; who gave Himself a ransom for all, to be testified in due time" (I Timothy 2:6). Salvation cannot be earned. It is a gift. "And if by grace (a gift), then is it no more of works: otherwise grace is no more grace. But if it be of works, then is it no more grace" (Romans 11:6).

My prayer: Again, I praise You and honor You and worship You, Father, for Your mercy toward me a sinner. Your goodness and care and blessings are more than I deserve. Thank You for saving me and calling me to serve You. Thank You for covering my sins with Christ's blood. Keep me pure so I can fellowship with You.

Day 6: A Little Talk with God Reveals Big Truths

Read EXODUS Chapters 33-35

Moses conversation with God helps us today. Here is what I learned by eavesdropping on their conversation. First, any Godly success comes from Him not man. God said, "I will send an angel before You and drive out..." the nations (33:2). Secondly, the people God helps usually are stubborn. God said, "Tell the Israelites, 'You are a stiff-necked people. If I were to go with You even for a moment, I might destroy You" (33:5). Thirdly, men must see God's glory and learn His ways to follow Him. Moses said, "...teach me Your ways so I may know You..." (33:13). "Then Moses said, 'Now show me Your glory" (33:18). Fourthly, God's full glory would slay any man in His presence. God said, "...You cannot see My face, for no one may see Me and live" (33:20). Fifthly, if Israel worshipped correctly, God would shield them from disaster. God said, "...no one will covet Your land when You go up three times each year to appear before the Lord Your God" (34:24). I learned I need to listen and then obey.

My prayer: Lord, I desire a conversation with You where I can hear what You say and know Your will. Give me the wisdom to understand what I hear You say and give me the strength to obey.

Day 7: Grateful Giving
Read EXODUS Chapters 36-38

The people of Israel were finally free and living without being mistreated by cruel masters. Now God was their master. He was gracious and kind. All He asked was to be worshipped. Therefore, when He told them to build a tabernacle to worship Him, they gave freely out of gratitude. Everything they owned came through God causing the Egyptians to give them their back pay. Their gratitude to God is reflected in their giving. The skilled craftsman said, "The people are bringing more than enough for doing the work the Lord commanded to be done" (36:4). Moses ordered that "No man or woman is to make anything else as an offering for the sanctuary" (36:6).

A grateful heart gives generously through the church today. Tithing to the Lord is an act of worship. It is an act of obedience and shows dependence upon the Lord. Everything a person has comes from God. All He asks is for ten percent to be used in His work. Jesus said to the scribes and Pharisees, "...ye pay tithe of mint and anise and cumin, and have omitted the weightier matters of the law, judgment, mercy, and faith: these OUGHT ye to have done (tithe) and not to leave the other undone" (Matthew 23:23, KJV).

My prayer: Thank You for freeing me from the bondage of sin and the punishment of Hell. Please bless my giving and thank You for Your generosity to my family. Help me to have a grateful and giving heart.

Yearly Devotions – Week 5

Day 1: Obedience Brings God's Glory

Read EXODUS Chapters 39-40

"Moses could not enter the tent of meeting because the cloud had settled upon it, and the glory of the Lord filled the Tabernacle" (40:35). The glory of God that had rested on Mt. Sinai was transferred to the Tabernacle. The visible glory revealed God's presence in Israel. God dwelled in the midst of Israel and was the center of their life. Why did God dwell in Israel's midst? What allowed Him to display His glory among them? Sixteen times in Chapters thirty nine and forty it says, "...as the Lord commanded Moses." It wasn't until Moses completed the building of the tabernacle exactly as God said that His glory came down. It says, "...Moses finished the work" (40:33).

Moses could have tried to adapt the building of the Tabernacle to his ideas. He could have tried to improve the Tabernacle and the utensils for his benefit, but he didn't. He made it exactly the way God said. His obedience allowed God to put His glory in the Tabernacle. God is not fully glorified until people are completely obedient. Complete obedience allows God to display His glory.

My prayer: Lord, Your Word is perfect and helps me to obey it. Your glory is my desire to experience in ministry.

Day 2: The Only Approach

Read LEVITICUS Chapters 1-4

Landing at a large, busy airport can be a nerve-wracking experience for a pilot. He is told from what direction to approach the airport and which runway to use. He is to announce his position to the airport at each phase of his approach. He must declare his position when on final approach. God gives all men His instructions when they approach Him. There is only one approach to God and that is through the shed blood for sin. As it says in Hebrews 9:22, "without shedding of blood is no remission (punishment for sin)."

The priests had to cut the animal's throat correctly and clean its intestines correctly and cut it up correctly and catch its blood correctly and then properly place all the pieces on the altar correctly. The most important part of those sacrifices was their attitudes while performing these acts of worship. These offerings were the means by which God's people could officially recognize their sins, experience God's forgiveness, and remain secure within His covenant. Jesus fulfilled every aspect of the sacrificial requirements. Just as Israel was to approach God on His terms, so men today can approach only on His terms.

My prayer: Thank You for providing a safe approach to You and heaven through Jesus. Thank You for the gift of salvation through Jesus. Thank You that my name has been written down in the Lamb's Book of Life. Thank You for the certainty of heaven and eternal life. Thank You for shedding Your blood as payment for my sin.

Day 3: Perpetual Fellowship

Read LEVITICUS Chapters 5-7

Fellowship with God is possible because of His grace. That fellowship can be interrupted by sin. Restoring fellowship with God brings joy. When King David sought God's forgiveness, he sought that joy that comes with fellowshipping with God. He prayed, "...restore unto me the joy of thy salvation" (Psalms 51:12, KJV). He didn't lose his salvation when he sinned, he lost his fellowship with God. What did he do to regain fellowship? He confessed his sin. He had to agree with God that he had sinned. David said, "for I acknowledge my transgression…" (Psalms 51:3). He said, "…I have sinned, and done this evil in thy sight" (Psalms 51:4, KJV). God required this from all Israelites. God told Moses, "Where anyone is guilty in any of these ways, he must confess in what he has sinned…" (5:5).

The people sinned continually so God said, "The fire on the altar must be kept burning; it must not go out" (6:12). Our Savior is our sacrifice and shields us from God's wrath. "For there is one God, and one mediator between God and men, the man Christ Jesus…" (I Timothy 2:5).

My prayer: Again, we praise You Lord for giving us the privilege to fellowship with You. Thank You for removing our sin with Christ's blood. Thank You for providing a way for forgiveness and the certainty of our eternal fellowship with You.

Day 4: Set Aside for Service

Read LEVITICUS Chapters 8-10

The greatest privilege in life is to be set aside by God for His use. A man called of God has purpose and meaning in life. He will be fulfilled in life when he knows he is doing what God created him for. Christian boldness, confidence and humility accompany the knowledge and obedience of God's will.

Moses, led by God, emphasized the sacredness of the priests' tasks by a consecration process. That process included a ceremonial cleansing and an anointing with oil and blood. To have a special place in God's service is a special blessing that carries a special responsibility. That responsibility is to display God's holiness. "This is what the Lord spoke of when He said, 'Among those who approach Me I will show Myself holy; in the sight of all the people I will be honored'" (10:3). "You must distinguish between the holy and the common, between the unclean and the clean, and You must teach the Israelites all the decrees the Lord has given them through Moses" (10:10-11).

My prayer: Thank You for the privilege of ministering to Your people in a local church. Give me Your wisdom and grace to fulfill the task You set me aside for.

Day 5: Creation Reveals God's Holiness
Read LEVITICUS Chapters 11-13

How does creation reveal God's holiness? God designed man's bodies to live forever. After Adam and Eve sinned, God expelled them from the Garden of Eden so man would not live forever in his fallen state. Because of their disobedience, man lost the ability to be holy like God. Had they chosen to obey God and eat of the tree of life, man's body would never deteriorate and die. God said, "He must not be allowed to reach out his hand and take also from the tree of life and eat, and live forever" (Genesis 3:22). When Adam lost God's holiness, he lost his life.

In Leviticus, God is continually giving object lessons of His holiness. Anything that is not of God, is not holy." He illustrates over and over that there is "clean" and "unclean". "Unclean" is unacceptable to God and "clean" is acceptable to Him. Being unholy is the opposite of God's being. Israel is reminded of this every time they chose an animal, bird, fish, or insect to eat.

My prayer: Help me to make choices that reveal Your holiness and that honor Your sinless nature.

Day 6: Pasteurized Believers

Read LEVITICUS Chapter 14-15

Louis Pasteur, 1822-1895, was a French chemist who discovered that bacteria caused people to become sick. He exploded the myth of spontaneous generation. Pasteurization is the method used today to treat food, especially milk, to make them free from disease-causing bacteria.

God knew about bacteria and diseases before Louis Pasteur ever existed. He devised a system to combat diseases in Israel before scientist ever thought about it. God demanded His people to be physically, ceremonially, and morally clean at all times. They had to be clean to approach Him.

Christ came to wash and cleanse all of us from our disease of sin. Sin is to miss the mark of God's standards. Only Jesus met that standard and He became the sacrifice, instead of the doves, to pay for our sin. His blood cleanses us from all sin and unrighteousness. "...the blood of Jesus Christ His Son cleanseth us from all sin" (I John 1:7, KJV). "...though Your sins are like scarlet, they shall be as white as snow..." (Isaiah 1:18).

My prayer: Again, I praise You for providing a way of escape from Your judgment of my sin. Thank You for covering my sin with Christ's blood and giving me His righteousness as a gift.

Day 7: Cleanliness is Next to Godliness

Read LEVITICUS Chapters 16-18

The cleansing in Leviticus is not so much a bodily cleansing but a soul cleansing. The ceremonial cleansing with water magnified the idea that men are dirty before God if they don't deal with their sin. No priest could approach God in the

Tabernacle without first cleansing himself through washing with water, wearing special garments, and sprinkling blood on the altar and the mercy seat.

Not only did the priests have to cleanse themselves and have their sins covered by blood, but they had to do all these things in the exact place God demanded. "Any Israelite who sacrifices an ox, a lamb or a goat in the camp or outside of it instead of bringing it to the entrance of the tent of meeting...that man shall be...cut off from his people" (17:4). In like manner the only place we attain salvation is in Jesus alone. "Salvation is found in no one else, for there is no other name under heaven given to men by which we must be saved" (Acts 4:12). Jesus' blood alone is able to cleanse us. Jesus plus nothing!

My prayer: I praise You Lord for providing the cleansing agent that washes away all my sin. Thank You that You forgive me for the sins I confess and for those I can't remember. You said, "If I confess my sins, You are faithful and just and will forgive me of my sins and purify me from all unrighteousness," even the ones I can't remember (I John 1:9).

Yearly Devotions – Week 6

Day 1: Your Behavior Reveals Your God

Read LEVITICUS Chapters 19-20

Every commandment of God was given to reveal who He is and man's proper attitude and what our behavior should be toward Him and others. Since Adam and Eve lost their direct access to God, their descendants drifted away from Godly attitudes and behaviors. Their behavior became distorted and destructive. Without a holy God to guide man, death became the regular result among men. Men became pagan (idolaters and worshippers of false gods) which caused them to kill their children as a form of worship. They lost the concept of a holy God who brings life. Their false gods brought death. Pagan thinking believes gods need to be appeased because of their arbitrary and mischievous moods. They do not know God is love and loves man.

God told Israel that He is not like the false gods of the pagan nations. He said, "Speak to the entire assembly of Israel and say to them: 'be holy because I, the Lord Your God, am holy" (19:2). God's instructions to Israel are to reveal to them and to the nations what a holy God is like. A holy God brings life and honors life. He does not bring death and destruction.

My prayer: Thank You for revealing Yourself as the giver of life. Thank You for making life worth living. Thank You for allowing me to be alive and to serve You and through that service, You give meaning to my life. Thank You, Jesus, for conquering death, hell, Satan, and the world. Give me Your strength to stand and live for You: the holy God.

Day 2: Spiritual Food

Read LEVITICUS Chapters 21-23

There is good spiritual food and bad spiritual food. Behind every book, play, movie, T.V. program, or lecture there is a religious philosophy that produces it. All the spiritual food of the world is junk food. For example, a movie that makes light of homosexuality, adultery, and fornication teaches a religious belief that there is no judgment coming from a holy God. They deny the truth of God's Word and promote the philosophy that there are no consequences from such behavior.

God told Israel not to eat certain things because it could defile them and keep them from His presence. He said, "...He must not eat anything found dead or torn by wild animals, and so become unclean through it. I am the Lord" (22:8). Any belief not based upon God's Word is dead and has been torn from the truth. It is unclean and detestable to the Lord.

My prayer: Lord, help me keep my spiritual diet according to Your menu. Help me to see the dead spiritual food of the world that has been cooked by Satan so I can avoid it.

Day 3: God's Welfare Program

Read LEVITICUS Chapters 24-25

God designed Israel's society to make individuals responsible for their livelihood and finances. They were not to depend upon a government to take care of their debt problems. God's plan kept people from being homeless and jobless. They could sell their livestock, property or themselves to get out of debt.

God demanded that every fiftieth year a man would be set free from his slavery or he could get his property back and start his life over. A man's relative could also buy his debt and redeem him or his property or both. Boaz redeemed Naomi and Ruth by this law.

This plan pictures what God provides for all of mankind who were sold into sin by Adam. Christ redeems us from our debt of sin. The great song sung in heaven is, "…Thou art worthy to take the book, and open the seals thereof: For thou wast slain, and hast redeemed us to God by thy blood out of every kindred, and tongue, and people, and nation…" (Revelation 5:9 KJV).

My prayer: I can do nothing but praise You for loving me while still a sinner with nothing to offer You but a filthy life. Thank You for purchasing me with Your shed blood so I could be set free from my sin debt.

Day 4: Obedience Brings Blessings

Read LEVITICUS Chapters 26-27

These two chapters illustrate what Paul wrote in Galatians 6:7-8. God said through him, "Be not deceived; God is not mocked: For whatsoever a man soweth, that shall he also reap. For he that soweth to his flesh shall of the flesh reap corruption; but he that soweth to the Spirit shall of the Spirit reap life everlasting. (KJV)" We see this principle in Leviticus. "But if You will not listen to me and carry out all these commands, and if You reject my decrees…I will bring upon You sudden terror, wasting diseases and fever that will destroy Your sight and drain away Your life" (26:14). This pictures "the flesh" in control of people.

Those who sow obedience to the Lord and seek to be led by the Holy Spirit reap life. "If You follow my decrees and are careful to obey my commands, I will send You rain in its season…" (26:30). He also promises 1) good crops; 2) they will eat all the food they want; 3) they will live in safety; 4) there will be peace in the land; 5) they will be victorious in battle; 6) their population will increase. This principle is true for America and every other country also.

My prayer: Thank You for the promises that You keep and the blessings You give. Thank You for loving us even when we sow to the flesh. I plead for mercy and grace to yield myself to the Spirit's control.

Day 5: Godliness Brings Orderliness

Read NUMBERS Chapters 1-2

The Apostle Paul urged the Corinthians to, "Let all things be done decently and in order" (I Corinthians 14:40). God who created physics, math, biology, DNA, and geometry is a God of formulas and mathematical exactness. He cannot tolerate chaos. We see this in the book of Numbers where God designed Israel's camp in a precise manner. God's presence and place of worship was the center of everything. Solomon expressed this when he said, "Where there is no vision (God's revelation), the people perish (are confused): but he that keepeth the Law, happy is he" (Proverbs 29:18 KJV).

God arranged Israel's camp in an exact pattern. He had three tribes assigned in the four directions of the compass.

1) East - Judah, Issachar, and Zebulon;
2) South - Ruben, Simeon, and Gad;
3) West - Ephraim, Manasseh, and Benjamin;
4) North - Dan, Asher, and Naphtali.

"So the Israelites did everything the Lord commanded Moses; that is the way they encamped under their standards, and that is the way they set out, each with his clan and family" (2:34). Godly living will have direction and order.

My prayer: My prayer is for my life to be ordered by You Lord, so that it will be organized to effectively serve You.

Day 6: Everyone Has a Part

Read NUMBERS Chapters 3-5

God chose the Levite tribe to carry and maintain the Tabernacle. Each family in that tribe was given a specific assignment to transport the "tent". Aaron's sons and descendants were to offer the sacred sacrifices. When everyone carried out their assigned tasks the Tabernacle was moved quickly and efficiently. Each assigned task was important and contributed to a successful move.

In like manner, the church is a body of believers working together to carry out God's assigned mission. That mission is to take the good news of salvation through Christ to the world. Every church member is assigned a part in completing that task. Paul said, "The body is a unit, though it is made up of many parts...now the body is not made up of one part but of many...now You are the body of Christ, and each one of You is a part of it" (I Corinthians 12:12, 14, 27). It may not seem like much when we give our tithe, or invite someone, or attend Bible study and worship, or teach, or greet people at church, or witness but when everyone does it together the gates of hell cannot stop the church.

My prayer: Thank You for letting me have a part in Your work. Give me the patience and endurance to be faithful to the end.

Day 7: Commitment's Price

Read NUMBERS Chapters 6-7

Commitment in every area of life is the great need today. Marriages last because of commitment to the Lord and each other. A church's strength is dependent on the Lordship of Jesus and the member's commitment to Him. There is no perfect church, but a commitment of the members to Jesus and the church make it a great church.

The Nazarite vow was taken to demonstrate a person's commitment to the Lord. An Israelite could take a temporary vow that must last thirty days or more. There were only three men in the Bible who were lifetime Nazarites: 1) Samuel, 2) Samson, and 3) John the Baptist. A Nazarite vowed to abstain from wine to place his appetite on the altar. He abstained from dead bodies to place his affections on the altar. He abstained from cutting his hair to place his appearance on the altar. We are to be spiritual Nazarites. "I beseech You therefore, brethren, by the mercies of God, that ye present Your bodies a living sacrifice, holy, acceptable unto God, which is Your reasonable service" (Romans 12:1).

My prayer: I commit myself to serve You at all cost. I ask for Your grace to carry out Your will. Lord bless me and keep me: make Your face shine on me, and be gracious to me and lift up Your countenance on me and give me peace.

Yearly Devotions – Week 7

Day 1: Spiritual Leaders are God's Gifts

Read NUMBERS Chapters 8-9

Every Godly pastor is a gift from God. "But to each one of us grace has been given as Christ apportioned it....it was He who gave some to be...pastors and teachers, to prepare God's people for works of service, so that the body of Christ may be built up..." (Ephesians 4:7, 11-12). God has always chosen individual men to be used as spiritual leaders.

God had planned to dedicate the firstborn son as a priest for each family until the events in Exodus 32. Then He chose the Levites to serve the priests in the Tabernacle. God said, "...they are the Israelites who are given wholly to Me. I have taken them as My own in place of the firstborn, the first male offspring from every Israelite woman" (8:16).

Since God gave His first and only Son as a sacrifice, every believer is a priest. "But You are a chosen people, a royal priesthood, a holy nation, a people belonging to God..." (I Peter 2:9). Each believer has access to God through Jesus. "...Jesus lives forever, He has a permanent priesthood" (Hebrews 7:24).

My prayer: I praise You for the privilege of being able to enter Your presence through Jesus.

Day 2: God's People are Never Alone

Read NUMBERS Chapters 10-11

One of the great benefits of belonging to the Lord is that we are never alone. God instructed Israel to sound trumpets to give notice of God's presence directing their lives. He provided a cloud by day and fire by night. He told Moses He would distribute his burdens on others to help him. God said, "...I will take of the Spirit that is on you and put the Spirit on them. They will help you carry the burden of the people so that you will not have to carry it alone" (11:17). God let His presence be known by sending fire to punish and quail to feed the people.

When Christ is the Lord of Your life He never lets you go through life alone. When He was preparing to die He said, "...I tell you the truth: it is for your good that I am going away. Unless I go away, the Counselor will not come to you; but if I go, I will send Him (the Holy Spirit) to you" (John 16:7). Whatever you're going through You are not alone when Jesus is Your Savior.

My prayer: Thank You for not letting us face the trials of life alone. Thank You for going away so You could send the Holy Spirit as my comforter. I pray for those who are all alone in life that they might come to know You and Your love.

Day 3: What Does the Lord Hear?

Read NUMBERS Chapters 12-14

We know for certain that He hears complainers complaining. Miriam and Aaron used Moses' wife as an excuse to complain that they weren't as important as Moses. They said, "Has the Lord spoken only through Moses? ...Hasn't He also spoken through us? 'And the Lord heard this" (12:2). The spies who gave a negative report said, "We can't attack those people, they are stronger than we are" (13:31). The people said, "Why is the Lord bringing us to this land only to let us fall by the sword..." (14:3)? Listen to God's response: "How long will this wicked community grumble against Me? I have heard the complaints of these grumbling Israelites" (14:27).

What the Israelites were saying by their complaints was that God didn't care about them and that He wasn't all powerful to take care of them. They were saying they didn't believe God nor trust Him. God heard Caleb's and Joshua's words of faith and rewarded them. Jesus said, "...by Your words You will be acquitted, and by Your words You will be condemned" (Matthew 12:37).

My prayer: Lord, I need Your help and strength to make sure I am not speaking against You with complaints of my place in life and ministry. Help guard my mouth to be a channel of encouragement and faith.

Day 4: God-Resistant Flesh

Read NUMBERS Chapters 15-16

Bacteria and viruses can build immunity to medicine. In like manner, the fallen nature of man resists a holy God. God offers fallen man many opportunities to learn the joy of being with Him and obeying His will. Paul said, "For to be carnally minded is death: but to be spiritually minded is life and peace. Because the carnal mind is enmity against God: for it is not subject to the Law of God, neither indeed can be. So then they that are in the flesh cannot please God" (Romans 8:6-8).

Israel's behavior in chapters fifteen and sixteen is a good illustration showing how rebellious man's heart is. It's our nature to resist God. The people of Israel see Korah, Dathan, and Abiram and their families destroyed by God because of their rebellion and they still defy God. "The next day the whole Israelite community grumbled against Moses and Aaron. 'You have killed the Lord's people,' they said" (16:41). Their rebellion brought death. "....14,700 people died from the plague..." (16:49). God sent in judgment.

My prayer: Thank You for providing an antidote to my sin. Give me the wisdom to see when my flesh is resisting You and show me how to please You. I praise You for Your mercy.

Day 5: Dead Things Defile

Read NUMBERS Chapters 17-19

"Whoever touches the dead body of anyone will be unclean for seven days." (19:11) Those dead bodies remind us that what the world offers without God will eventually kill us. The world's attitude and activities are temporal and worthless. Since life is fleeting, all men are dead men walking. The moment a person is born, he begins to die. The only cure for this deadness is to deal with its cause, sin, and be cleansed from it. "Just as man is destined to die once, and after that to face judgment, so Christ was sacrificed to take away the sins of many people..." (Hebrews 9:27).

Sacrificing the red heifer made cleansing available for Israelites who had touched a dead body. That is a picture of Christ's crucifixion being the cure for all men's sin. The heifer was sacrificed outside the camp just as Jesus was crucified outside Jerusalem. The heifer's ashes were used to purify Israelites after touching a dead body like Christ's crucifixion purifies us from sin. "In fact, the Law requires that nearly everything be cleansed with blood, and without the shedding of blood there is no forgiveness" (Hebrews 9:22).

My prayer: Again, I praise You for providing eternal life and the removal of my sin. Give me the boldness to share this good news to all I come in contact with.

Day 6: Consequences Can Be Costly

Read NUMBERS Chapters 20-21

Our attitude towards life affects the consequences of our actions. A person can choose a lifestyle where nothing matters as long as he can have fun, but there are consequences. There are consequences from having a negative attitude. Instead of Israel being grateful for being set free from slavery, they complained. "Why did You bring us up out of Egypt to this terrible place? ...There is no water to drink!" (20:5-6). God gave them water but Moses paid a high price in the process. There were consequences for not honoring God in getting the water.

King Arad attacked Israel and paid a high price. The consequence of his action was his destruction. Israel, "...completely destroyed them and their towns..."(21:2). Israel, "...spoke against God and Moses..." (21:3). "Then the Lord sent venomous snakes among them...and many Israelites died" (21:26). Sihon...mustered his army and marched out into the desert against Israel" (21:23). "Israel, however, put him to the sword and took over his land..." (21:24). Og, King of Bashan attacked Israel and was destroyed. A person can do what he wants but there are consequences.

My prayer: I praise You for the mercy You have shown me even when I've made bad choices. Thank You for the grace of Your forgiveness! I ask for mercy on America that is making bad choices about abortion, immorality and greed. Help us turn to the Cross of Christ again.

Day 7: Money People
Read NUMBERS Chapter 22-24

The truth of I Timothy 6:10 is seen in the life of Balaam. "For the love of money is the root of all evil:..." This is true for all mankind, including preachers. God disclosed to Balaam that Israel was His chosen people. Even though he accurately gave

God's message to a pagan King, he did not value his position as a prophet of God as much as he did money. "…Balaam the son of Bosor, who loved the wages of unrighteousness; But was rebuked for his iniquity: the dumb ass speaking with man's voice forbade the madness of the prophets" (II Peter 2:15-16 KJV). Balaam deliberately taught King Balak and his people how to pervert Israel so that God would fight against them. Jesus said to the church at Pergamos, "…thou hast there them that hold the doctrine of Balaam, who taught Balak to cast a stumbling block before the children of Israel, to eat things sacrificed unto idols, and to commit fornication" (Revelation 2:14). "Money people" are those that put making money before anything else including morals, family or spiritual values.

My prayer: Lord, help me to place more value on Your Word and commands than making money. Keep me honest in all business transactions and purchases. May I seek to please You above any appetite or desire in this life.

Yearly Devotions – Week 8

Day 1: Satan's Strategy

Read NUMBERS Chapters 25-26

The prophet Balaam, lover of money, could hear from God and speak His truth but then be used of Satan to hurt Israel. Satan still uses the same strategy. If he can use a godless man like Hitler, he will, but he will also use a Christian or a preacher of the gospel if they let him.

King Balak was a descendant of Lot and his daughter. They had become debased which reflected their heritage. They lived close to where Sodom and Gomorrah had been destroyed and continued their immoral lifestyle.

Balaam saw that he could not get God to curse Israel so he devised a plan to get Israel to anger God and bring His judgment on them. Satan used sexual perversion in worship to try to destroy Israel. "The Lord said to Israel's judges, 'Take all the leaders of these people, kill them and expose them in broad daylight before the Lord, so that the Lord's fierce anger may turn away from Israel" (25:4). Twenty-four thousand Israelites died because of Satan's strategy. Every Christian must be aware of this strategy. Satan can use anyone.

My prayer: Help me recognize when Satan is trying to use me and help me to seek You above everything else through Your word and through prayer.

Day 2: God Interrupts the Routine

Read NUMBERS Chapters 27-29

Moses was removed as the leader because he disobeyed and dishonored God. Israel's leadership was interrupted and God's holiness was demonstrated by Moses death. God interrupted Israel's daily life by requiring offerings. There were numerous celebrations and offerings yearly. God designed their worship so they would have to go to the Tabernacle often. Worship involved daily offerings, Sabbath offerings, monthly offerings, the Passover, Feast of weeks, Feast of trumpets, Day of Atonement, and Feast of Tabernacles.

Daily life revolved around worship. Every offering and sacrifice was to remind them that Israel was made to worship Jehovah-God. Every animal and every crop was a potential offering and should make them think of God. When they observed their livestock they should have looked to see if it qualified as a holy sacrifice. Everything they owned and cared for was a potential offering and was to focus their lives on God. Our worship today should interrupt the routine of our life and focus on Jesus.

My prayer: Thank You for a life filled with many blessings and a hope that anticipates the future here on earth and in eternity. Help me to see what I am to present as a sacrifice in my life.

Day 3: Corporate Responsibility

Read NUMBERS Chapters 30-32

God designed society to be responsible to each other. He designed life to be based on men working together in harmony. Relationships are the foundational force of God's plan for man. This is seen in the marriage relationship. Israel's society placed the woman in total dependence on the man for security and sustenance. To keep harmony in the home, God gave the man the veto power over a wife's vows. God made the man to be the head of the home to protect and care for his wife.

Working together, a nation can accomplish anything it attempts. The Reubenites and Gadites were not exempt from working toward Israel's complete victory over the Canaanites. Everyone working together guaranteed God would give them the land.

A church united and working together cannot be stopped by the devil, the world or the flesh. "The body is a unit, though it is made up of many parts; and though all its parts are many, they form one body. So it is with Christ" (I Corinthians 12:12).

My prayer: Please send unity and a cooperative spirit to our nation, churches and homes through Jesus and the Holy Spirit. We must have Your Spirit to accomplish Your goal.

Day 4: Exchange gods for God

Read NUMBERS Chapters 33-34

What the world worships can't compare to God. The world worships with its senses. It isn't wrong to use Your senses unless it causes You to worship the world. God redirects our attention away from them when we worship the world's gods. Anything that controls You is Your god. Your priorities can be Your god.

All the plagues in Egypt were to show Israel and the Egyptians, "who were burying all their firstborn, whom the Lord had struck down among them; for the Lord had brought judgment on their gods" (33:3-4).

After God destroyed their gods and freed the Israelites He gave them their inheritance. After God removes our sin through Christ we receive our inheritance. "Blessed be the God and Father of the Lord Jesus Christ...who...has begotten us...to an inheritance incorruptible and undefiled and that does not fade away, reserved in heaven for You..." (I Peter 1:3, 4 KJV).

My prayer: Lord, I seek to worship You and not the things of this world. Show me the gods I need to bury so I can be free to worship You.

Day 5: Christ is Our Refuge

Read NUMBERS Chapters 35-36

The cities of refuge protected those who accidently killed someone. They also were cities that held court to decide whether a person was guilty of murder. God designed this Law to protect life. "The avenger of blood shall put the murderer to death..." (35:19). Without organized government in Israel, the closest of kin became the avenger of blood. Only God has the right to take life. God hates violence. "...bloodshed pollutes the land, and atonement cannot be made for the land on which blood has been shed, except by the blood of the one who shed it" (35:33). God designed capital punishment.

Sin kills our relationship with the Lord. Sin's penalty is the second death unless a sinner can get to his refuge. "Blessed and holy are those who have part in the Resurrection. The second death has no power over them...the Lake of Fire is the second death" (Revelation 20:6, 14). Jesus is our refuge that we can flee to and escape the second death. "Blessed is the man to whom the Lord will not impute sin." (Romans 4:8)

My prayer: I praise You for providing a way of escape from being punished for my sin. Thank You that I have escaped hell and the Lake of Fire.

Day 6: Remembering Can Be Good and Bad

Read DEUTERONOMY Chapters 1-2

Moses is about to die and wants the people he has led for forty years to remember what they have been through. Remembering the past brought good memories and bad ones. The good memories are how God cared for them and the bad memories are how they failed to trust and obey God.

- Good - God said, "See, I have given You this land." (1:8)
- Bad - The people said, "The Lord hates us; so He brought us out of Egypt to deliver us into the hands of the Amorites to destroy us. (1:27)
- Good - Moses said, "The Lord Your God, who is going before You, will fight for You..." (1:30)
- Bad - Moses reminds them, "...You did not trust the Lord Your God..." (1:32)
- Good - God said, "...Do not go up and fight, because I will not be with You." (1:42)
- Bad - The people, "...rebelled against the Lord's command..." (1:43)

Their behavior is an example of the Scripture that says, "...there is none righteous, no, not one" (Romans 3:10). Remembering is good when we remember God's grace. It is bad when we remember our condition. "For by grace are ye saved through faith..." (Eph. 2:8 KJV).

My prayer: Your grace is an overwhelming gift that amazes me and I thank You for Your forgiveness and mercy. Help me to trust You no matter what the circumstances are. Give me strength and wisdom to know when You are leading and I should follow.

Day 7: God is Reliable

Read DUETERONOMY Chapters 3-4

Our flesh has a tendency to doubt God even when He has proven He can be trusted by His previous actions. Moses is about to die and reminds Israel of God's faithfulness. He reminds them how God provided and protected them for forty years. He reminds them of the two Kings, Sihon and Og, that God defeated for them. "You have seen with Your own eyes all that the Lord Your God has done to these two Kings..." (3:21).

Moses reminds them that God had entered into their pilgrimage by guiding them audibly. "Then the Lord spoke to You out of the fire. You heard the sound of words but saw no form; there was only a voice" (4:12). "...do not become corrupt and make Yourselves an idol, an image of any shape..." (4:16).

The point that Moses made was that if God has proven His faithfulness in taking care of Israel in the past they could trust Him to take care of them in the future. A believer's future is secure and safe because God is faithful. We won't see a visible image nor hear an audible word but we know by faith God takes care of our future.

My prayer: Lord, help me keep my eyes on You and not the circumstances. I praise You for how You have provided for me and thank You for Your watch-care in the future.

Yearly Devotions – Week 9

Day 1: God's Priority

Read DEUTERONOMY Chapters 5-7

It seems drastic for God to destroy the nations in Canaan. God told Israel to "...wipe out their names from under heaven...You will destroy them" (7:24). Why was God so harsh? He was harsh because of His priority. His priority is to be the only object of man's worship. Canaan's great sin is described by Paul. "For although they knew God, they neither glorified Him as God nor gave thanks to Him, but their thinking became futile and their foolish hearts were darkened. Although they claimed to be wise, they became fools and exchanged the glory of the immortal God for images made to look like mortal man and birds and animals and reptiles" (Romans 1:21-23). God commanded that "the images of their gods You are to burn in the fire" (7:25).

God has the right to demand total allegiance to Him because He created man. There is no other God but Jehovah-God of the Bible. For anyone to worship anything other than Him means they are worshipping a non-existent god. Worshipping that which is false is harmful to man. Men become like what they worship. False gods tarnish the image of God in man.

My prayer: I praise You for opening my eyes and heart to the truth of who You are through Your Holy Word. Thank You for saving me through grace. Guide me to share the truth of Jesus so others can be rescued from worshipping false gods.

Day 2: God's Classroom

Read DEUTERONOMY Chapters 8-10

God's classroom was a desert. His class lasted forty years. "Remember how the Lord Your God led You all the way in the desert these forty years" (8:12). God's curriculum included a humbling activity, a test, and then a teaching time. It included a disciplining exercise. It took forty years "...to humble You and to test You..." (8:12). Moses said to Israel. He continued reminding them that "...the Lord Your God disciplines You" (8:5).

When a teacher has to leave a classroom, he will warn the class to behave while he is gone. He may assign someone to take names. God warned Israel He was taking names when Moses left in death. If they didn't obey Him they would be "...like the nations the Lord destroyed before You, so You will be destroyed for not obeying the Lord God" (8:20).

God always tests first and then He teaches. He lets them know they will be tested first and then they will be taught what the test was to teach them. God's objective is to teach them they are to obey Him or they will fail the course.

My prayer: Thank You Lord for giving me salvation by grace. Thank You that my salvation is not dependent upon me. Thank You for disciplining me so that I will become more like my Savior. Forgive me as I fail life's test from time to time. Help me to learn from the testing I go through.

Day 3: God's Place of Worship

Read DEUTERONOMY Chapters 11-12

Does it make a difference where You worship? It made a difference to God where Israel worshipped. "But You are to seek the place the Lord Your God will choose from among all Your tribes to put His Name there for His dwelling" (12:5). "Then to the place the Lord Your God will choose as a dwelling for His Name – there You are to bring everything, I command You: ..." (12:11).

Israel had to worship exactly where God told them to. Today, the presence of the Holy Spirit allows believers to worship privately or with a group. God established the New Testament church as a place for public worship.

Only Satan would fight organized and vibrant local churches. God tells believers to meet regularly. "Not forsaking the assembling of ourselves together, as the manner of some is; but exhorting one another: and so much the more, as ye see the day approaching" (Hebrews 10:25 KJV).

What place has God chosen for present day believers to worship? He has chosen one of the places to be a church where people believe the Bible. He has chosen a place where the Bible is preached and taught. It is a place where Jesus is lifted up and the Holy Spirit works.

My prayer: Thank You Lord for providing a place where I have a spiritual family that I belong to. Thank You for a church that seeks to follow the leadership of the Holy Spirit. Thank You for a pastor who believes Your word.

Day 4 Watered-down Worship

Read DEUTERONOMY Chapters 13-14

What is watered-down worship? It is any worship that takes the focus off of Jesus and places it on anything else. Genuine worship is when people acknowledge Jehovah-God as the only God worthy of worship. Biblical worship acknowledges Jesus as the only way to know God. God told Israel that when anyone said, "Let us follow other gods and let us worship them; You must not listen to the words of that prophet or dreamer" (13:2-3).

Paul warned of watering down the gospel. "But even if we or an angel from heaven preach a gospel other than the one we preached to You, let him be eternally condemned!" (Galatians 1:8). A watered-down gospel is one that says that Jesus was a good man but there are other ways to gain salvation. A watered-down gospel avoids the fact that man is a sinner and will go to hell if he rejects Jesus as his Savior. A watered-down gospel is one that says the blood of Christ is not necessary for salvation. A watered-down gospel says You have to do something plus believe in Jesus. It denies that salvation is a free gift.

My prayer: I can only praise You for giving us salvation as a gift of love and is paid for by Christ's crucifixion and shed blood.

Day 5: Celebration is Worship Also

Read DEUTERONOMY Chapters 15-17

God is generous. He wants His followers to be generous. He designed Israel's economic system to be generous. A person can truly celebrate when they are free from indebtedness. "...there should be no poor among You, for the land the Lord Your God is giving You to possess as Your inheritance will richly bless You..." (15:4). "There will always be poor people in the land. Therefore I command You to be open-handed toward Your brothers and toward the poor..." (15:11).

God caused the Israelites to celebrate enthusiastically every seven years by demanding that all debts be canceled. That caused the rich to be generous and the poor to genuinely celebrate their new freedom from debt. "Be joyful at Your Feast..." (16:14). "For seven days celebrate the Feast to the

Lord Your God...for the Lord Your God will bless You in all Your harvest...and Your joy will be complete" (16:15). Followers of Jesus can celebrate their salvation every day because their sin-debt has been paid for by Christ's shed blood.

My prayer: Your salvation is so great that it is hard to comprehend how You Lord could be so generous to a wretched sinner like me. Thank You for removing ALL my sin. Thank You for eternal life. Thank You that my name is written down in the Lamb's book of life.

Day 6: Godly Decision-Making

Read DEUTERONOMY Chapters 18-20

There comes a time in life for everyone when a life-changing decision must be made. Where You seek council before making that decision is very important. God directed Israel to be sure their decisions were not made on superstition or demonic activity. "Let no one be found among You who sacrifices his son or daughter in the fire, who practices divination or sorcery, interprets omens, engages in witchcraft, or casts spells, or who is a medium (physic) or spiritist or who consults the dead" (18:10).

All decisions should be based upon the principles found in God's Word. Decisions should be made with the Holy Spirit's leading. God seeks to be a part of every decision a person makes. The Apostle Paul depended on the Holy Spirit to lead him. Paul and Silas "...were forbidden of the Holy Ghost to preach the word in Asia...after he had seen the vision...assuredly gathering that the Lord had called us for to preach the gospel unto them (Macedonians)" (Acts 16:6-10). If Paul needed God's guidance surely we need it today also.

My prayer: Thank You for being involved in my life. Thank You for caring about my well-being and my future. I ask for the Holy Spirit to show me Your plans and will as I attempt to make the right decisions.

Day 7: God's Work Means Caring for the Helpless

Read DEUTERONOMY Chapters 21-24

How a man treats others reflects on his belief of who God is. God demanded Israel to watch out for the helpless. "Do not deprive the alien or the fatherless of justice, or take the cloak of the widow as a pledge..." (24:17). When harvesting, "...leave the remains for the alien, the fatherless and the widow..." (24:19-20).

What does God use to motivate the Israelites to care for each other? He reminds them over and over that they are to remember they were helpless at one time and God intervened to rescue them. "Remember that You were slaves in Egypt and the Lord Your God redeemed You from there. That is why I command You to do this" (24:18).

All men are helpless to free themselves from the bondage and penalty of sin. God has compassion on all men and offers to deliver them from sin and death. Once a person has been set free through faith in the blood of Jesus he becomes an alien in a hostile country and is helpless in his own strength. God provides His followers protection. Jesus said, "...I will pray the Father, and He shall give You another Comforter, that He may abide with You forever..." (John 14:16).

My prayer: Thank You for saving me and for providing the Holy Spirit to be my Comforter and strength. I yield to His control and *ask to be filled again today. Help me to help the helpless. Give me Your compassion for the lost and the rebellious. I rejoice that You cared enough to send someone to my home to tell us of Jesus.*

Spoonful

Yearly Devotions – Week 10

Day 1: Lagging Behind is Dangerous

Read DEUTERONOMY Chapters 25-27

The Amalekites, who hated Israel, attempted to destroy Israel when they first came out of Egypt. Amalek was the grandson of Esau (Genesis 36:12). Because of their cruelty towards Israel, God told Israel to blot out their memory from under the sun. They were the ones who hired Balaam to curse Israel. "Remember what the Amalekites did to You along the way when You came out of Egypt. When You were weary and worn out, they met on Your journey and cut off all who were lagging behind; they had no fear of God" (25:17).

Satan is worse than Amalek or the Amalekites. He will attempt to cut off anyone who lags behind in prayer, worship, and church attendance, tithing or soul-winning. It is imperative that each believer be committed to stay close to the Lord and focus on Him. When a believer becomes lax in their spiritual walk and lags behind he will be cut off from the joy of his salvation.

My prayer: Keep me close to the cross and the Resurrection. Help me keep up with what You do through me and follow You with a whole heart.

Day 2: Obedience Honors God

Read DEUTERONOMY Chapters 28-29

God made it very plain that He chose Israel to be an example to all other nations. They could be a good example or a bad one. God's blessings on Israel when they remained faithful to Him demonstrated that the God of Israel was the only true

God. God's judgments on Israel when they were unfaithful to Him demonstrated again that God is the only true God. "If You fully obey the Lord Your God and carefully follow all His commands I give You today, the Lord Your God will set You high above all the nations on earth" (28:1).

There were no atheistic secular nations during Moses' time. They all worshipped something. God chose Israel to be the instrument through which He revealed Himself as the only God. God said that their faithfulness to Him and His blessings on their faithfulness would display His authenticity. "I did so that You might know that I am the Lord Your God" (29:6). In like manner Christians are to demonstrate the true God of the Bible by the way they live. Jesus said, "...let Your light shine before men, that they may see Your good deeds and praise Your Father in heaven" (Matthew 5:16).

My prayer: Thank You for giving us the light to know You are real and the blessings of obedience so we can experience Your presence. Give me the strength to be obedient and faithful so that You will be honored.

Day 3: God is in the Restoration Business

Read DEUTERONOMY Chapters 30-31

We were gone out of town for several days and arrived back home to find our basement flooded. We called the insurance company and they paid for a restoration service to dry-out the floor and fix the walls. God told Israel that if they would return to worshipping Him he would restore their nation to its former great strength and prosperity. "...when You and Your children return to the Lord Your God and obey Him with all Your heart and with all Your soul...then the Lord Your God will restore Your fortunes and have compassion on You..."

(30:2-3). Israel's basement wasn't flooded but its heart was corrupted.

God is prepared and ready to restore anyone who will return to Him as the Lord of their life. No one could be any worse than Israel when it turned its back on God and practiced immoral worship along with idols. The individual has a choice that only he can make. God said, "See, I set before You today life and prosperity, death and destruction" (30:15). God's desire for everyone is to choose life and prosperity.

My prayer: Thank You Lord for restoring my life to a place of victory in trials and security in troubled times. I pray for America that it will return to God so You can restore its greatness and bring glory and honor to Your name.

Day 4: The Song God Wrote

Read DEUTERONOMY Chapters 32-34

Songs affect the emotions of people. That effect can be good or bad. God's songs have a good effect. I can be transported back to East Texas immediately when I hear the songs entitled "Tennessee Waltz" or "I Found My Thrill on Blueberry Hill" or "Cross over the Bridge." The emotional attachment to those songs refreshes my memory of my teenage years.

God designed us and knows what stays with us. He knows our spiritual life can be easily derailed. He wrote a song to help Israel remain faithful to Him. This song was to help keep Israel from worshipping false gods.

1. His song reminds them of who He is. "A faithful God who does no wrong, upright and just is He"(32:14).

2. His song reminds Israel of what He has done for them. "He shielded him and cared for him; he guarded him as the apple of His eye" (32:10).
3. His song reminds them He is their only security. He says of Israel's enemies that, "it is mine to avenge; I will repay" (32:35). Only the love of Jesus can give us a song of comfort and hope.

My prayer: Refresh my mind daily with how You have blessed me and help me remember how You have given Your grace freely to my family. I praise You and honor You and Your holiness and goodness. Please bless my memory with Your goodness, and power, and glory.

Day 5: Preachers Should Be in the River

Read JOSHUA Chapters 1-3

Israel's priests were to lead the army and the nation into the swollen river and remain there until everyone crossed over. The Ark was the instrument that displayed God's presence. The river is a picture of the pagan force in the world. It would terrify the Canaanites that Israel's God could control their god, Baal. They believed Baal; the mighty storm god and fertility deity had defeated the god Yam, the sea god. For Jehovah-God to create a dry path through the raging river, demonstrated that Jehovah-God was superior and the only true God.

For the priests to put their feet in the river took obedience based upon their faith in who God is. Their act brought a stop to the powerful flow of the river. What is needed today are preachers who will step into the flow of the secular force raging in America. They need to step in under the direction of the Holy Spirit with confidence and boldness in the Word of God and the gospel of Jesus Christ.

My prayer: God, please, give me boldness to witness and preach in power. Give insight into what is really taking place in my country, family and heart. Thank You for Your truth that sets us free.

Day 6: Glory Belongs to God

Read JOSHUA Chapters 4-6

The monument built out of the stones from the river reminded Israel that God got the glory for their successful entrance into Canaan. It reminded all the pagan cities and nations that God was all powerful. "He did this so that all the peoples of the earth might know that the hand of the Lord is powerful and so that You might always fear the Lord Your God" (4:24). God will not share His glory because He alone deserves glory. For example Herod died instantly because he tried to share God's glory. "Immediately, because Herod did not give praise to God, an angel of the Lord struck him down" (Acts 12:23). Paul said, "he who glories, let him glory in the Lord" (I Corinthians 1:29). "...let no one glory in men..." (I Corinthians 3:21). David said, "Declare His glory among the nations..." (Psalms 96:3). Again, Paul said, "But God forbid that I should glory except in the cross of our Lord Jesus Christ..." (Galatians 6:14).

Our lives are to be living monuments of God's glory. "...You also, like living stones, are being built into a spiritual house..." (I Peter 2:5).

My prayer: Thank You for every victory and success in the ministry, family and church. Help me to always give You the glory for my healing and health. I praise You for Your kindness.

Day 7: Sin Hurts More Than the Sinner

Read JOSHUA Chapters 7-8

The funeral I watched on T.V. yesterday illustrated the pain sin and abuse cause. It hurts more than the person involved in it. The person who says, "It's my life and I can live it any way I want to and it's nobody's business what I do," has no idea the trouble he can cause people who care about him. The drug addict and the alcoholic can cause their family thousands of dollars in bills and medical care. Sin causes suffering and anxiety and is dangerous in many other ways.

Achan was overcome with greed and lust for money and clothes that had been dedicated to God. What he did was done in secret. No one could have known his sin until thirty-six men paid with their lives. God knew and told Joshua there had to be an accounting. "Israel has sinned; they have violated my covenant, which I commanded them to keep" (7:11).

It is imperative that every believer strive to be faithful and obedient to the Lord. What we do as individuals can affect the entire church and the name of Christ. "...the one who is in You is greater than the one who is in the world" (I John 4:4).

My prayer: Keep my heart stayed on You and let me see how I can be a blessing to others and not a hindrance.

Yearly Devotions – Week 11

Day 1: Israel's Name – God's Fame

Read JOSHUA Chapters 9 – 10

When nations heard the name Israel in Joshua's time they thought of Jehovah-God and His power. The Gibeonites lied because they were convinced God's power was going to destroy them. "Your servants have come from a very distant country because of the FAME of the LORD Your GOD. For we have heard reports of Him: all that He did in Egypt..." (9:9). The Gibeonites acted on what they believed. They were convinced of the invincibility of Israel's God. They believed they were doomed unless they could make a deal with Israel and were willing to take a great risk to try to protect themselves.

These pagans had more faith in God's power than a lot of professing Christians today. They acted on what they believed. Real faith always produces works. Salvation is a gift that is received by faith in Christ alone and then works follow. Our faith in Christ justifies us before God and our works justify us before man. "Wilt thou know O vain man that faith without works is dead?" (James 2:20 KJV). It would bring megreat joy if my name brought God fame because of His work in my life.

My prayer: May my work in Your field honor You and bless others. It is my desire to be used of You as a servant that brings glory to Your name. It is my sincere desire to let You live Your life through me.

Day 2: The Battle is Already Won

Read JOSHUA Chapters 11 – 13

What battle is already won? The battle between good and evil has already been won. Aleksander Solzhenitsyn said, "the line dividing good and evil… passes through all human hearts.[2]" Just as Israel could not conquer Canaan in their own power, neither can man conquer evil in his heart in his own power. Joshua was faced with a fierce group of kings and their armies. Then, "the Lord said to Joshua, 'Do not be afraid of them, because by this time tomorrow I will hand all of them over to Israel, slain" (11:6). God is the source of all good in the world. The real power and presence of good is God and it is Him that overcomes evil. Jesus triumphed over evil at the cross and the Resurrection.

Many times it appears evil has won as it appeared at the cross. It appears that way because people are impatient to see justice immediately. God's justice is done on His schedule, which is perfect. "…We know that in all things God works for the good of those who love Him…" (Romans 8:28).

My prayer: I praise You for letting us know that good does ultimately triumph and that evil will be done away with. Thank You for the hope that all believers have in Christ.

Day 3: The Whole Heart is Needed

Read JOSHUA Chapters 14 – 16

There are two contrasting results seen as Israel conquered Canaan. In one scenario there was complete obedience activated by faith that brought victory. In other attempts to conquer pagan nations other tribes weren't completely

---

[2] http://www.goodreads.com/author/quotes/10420.Aleksandr_Solzhenitsyn

successful. They did not carry out the task of conquering their part of the land with a whole-hearted effort.

Caleb was successful. "So Hebron has belonged to Caleb son of Jephunneh the Kenizzite ever since, because he followed the Lord, the God of Israel, wholeheartedly" (14:14).

Two tribes were not able to possess all God gave them. Those two tribes were Judah and Ephraim. "Judah could not dislodge the Jebusites, who were living in Jerusalem; to this day the Jebusites live there with the people of Judah" (15:63). "They (Ephraim) did not dislodge the Canaanites living in Gezer; to this day the Canaanites live among the people of Ephraim..." (16:10). Great grief awaited those who were half-hearted in their obedience.

My prayer: Lord, it is my desire and commitment to serve You with all my heart. Please help me to yield to Your control and leadership so that You can live through me.

Day 4: God Oversees Small Things Too

Read JOSHUA Chapters 17 – 19

Listed in the towns divided among Israel is the exactness of God's knowledge. In that listing, the town of Bethlehem is mentioned. "Included were Kattath, Nahalal, Shimron, Idalah and Bethlehem." (19:15) "This Bethlehem is Beth Lalm, east of Mt. Carmel-not to be confused with Bethlehem in Judah.[3]" Since there were two Bethlehems, God pin-pointed which Bethlehem His Son Jesus would be born in. Micah prophesied, "But You, Bethlehem Epharathah, though You are small

---

[3] NIV Archaeological Study Bible: An Illustrated Walk Through Biblical History and Culture, 2005, Zondervan Corporation.

among the clans of Judah, out of You will come for me One who will be ruler over Israel…" (Micah 5:2).

David's ancestors, Ruth and Boaz met in Bethlehem. David was born there. This Bethlehem was in the district of Ephrathah in Judah. God kept His eye on this Bethlehem because it had been set aside to be the place for His Son, Jesus, to be born. The Roman Emperor Justinian built a church building over the spot where Jesus was supposedly born and it still stands today as one of the most ancient church buildings in existence.

My prayer: I praise You Lord that I serve a God who knows the beginning and the ending of all things. Thank You that You know the length of my life and the journey that I make. You are an awesome God.

Day 5: Everyone Pays in Some Way

Read JOSHUA Chapters 20-22

After Achan and his followers were destroyed for disobeying the Lord, the ten Tribes were fearful God would judge them if the tribes in Gilead worshipped a false god. They believed that everyone would pay if a few turned away from God. "If You rebel against the Lord today, tomorrow He will be angry with the whole community of Israel" (22:18). "When Achan son of Zerah acted unfaithfully regarding the devoted things, did not wrath come upon the whole community of Israel? He was not the only one who died for his sin" (22:20).

There is linkage between a church member's behavior and the church he attends. There is linkage to all Christians when a professing believer sins and behaves in an ungodly manner. All believers are painted with the broad brush of hypocrisy when believers sin. Christians give Satan ammunition to ridicule the church when they sin. Christians should listen to Joshua. He said we are "...to love the Lord Your God, to walk in all His ways, to obey His commands, to hold fast to Him and to serve Him with all Your heart and all Your soul" (22:5).

My prayer: Help me to be mindful that I am the ambassador of Christ and that all my actions reflect on my Savior and church. Thank You for Your mercy and forgiveness when I do sin.

Day 6: Lives that Shape a Generation

Read JOSHUA Chapters 23-24

Each generation must determine for itself whether it will believe in the God of the Bible. Those who go before each generation leave a legacy of righteousness or ungodliness. The writer of Joshua says, "Israel served the Lord throughout the lifetime of Joshua and of the elders who outlived him and who had experienced everything the Lord had done for Israel" (24:31).

Those who had seen what God did in Egypt were only children when they saw God's miracles. They grew up in the desert. The only leaders they knew were Moses, Joshua, Aaron and Caleb. They had experienced what it was like to have Godly leadership. Their models helped them decide to continue obeying the Lord. Joshua warned the next generation that "...if You turn away...these nations... will become snares and traps for You, whips on Your backs and thorns in Your eyes, until You perish from this good land..." (23:12-13).

This applies to any nation, especially America as it was founded on Biblical principles. God's protection has been removed and we have been attacked with planes, debt, and disunity.

My prayer: Lord, I lift up our churches and our government to You and plead for a spirit of repentance and revival in our nation. I pray for all of our leaders that they will turn to You with all their heart. I pray especially for the pastors who preach the Word of God that they will be anointed and bold in all their stands.

Day 7: Tried and Tested

Read JUDGES Chapters 1-3

God knows everything and no one needs to explain anything to Him. Why then did He test Israel? God said to Israel, "...I will no longer drive out before them any of the nations Joshua left when he died. I will use them to test Israel and see whether they will keep the way of the Lord and walk in it as their forefathers did" (2:21-22). These tests must be teaching tools rather than information gathering.

Jesus always tested the disciples before He taught them and He is our model. Jesus fed 5000 men once and 4000 men on another occasion. He used these tests of the disciples to teach them about a spiritual truth. Jesus warned the disciples about the Pharisees doctrines referring to them as "yeast". The disciples thought Jesus was talking about not having bread. He rebuked them, "You of little faith, why are You talking among Yourselves about having no bread? ...Don't You remember the five loaves for the five thousand...or the seven loaves for the four thousand...how is it You don't understand that I was not talking about bread" (Matthew 16:8-12). If God knew what Pharaoh would do, He knew what Israel would do, so these tests were to show Israel their true nature.

My prayer: Lord, keep my eyes focused on You that my faith may always be in You and not waver because of circumstances.

Yearly Devotions – Week 12

Day 1: Faith Can Grow

Read JUDGES Chapters 4-6

First, faith that grows must hear from the Lord. "The Angel of the Lord" spoke to Gideon. That conversation revealed his lack of faith. "The Angel of the Lord" in the Old Testament is considered to be the pre-incarnate Logos (Word). The Lord said to Gideon, "The Lord is with You, mighty warrior" (6:12). The Lord saw Gideon as a mighty warrior when empowered by God. Gideon lacked the faith at first to see himself as a "mighty warrior". He said, "How can I save Israel? My clan is the weakest in Manasseh, and I am the least in my family" (6:15).

Secondly, faith must act on what faith it has. Gideon sneakingly obeyed the Lord's command to tear down an idol at night. "…because he was afraid of his family and the men of the town, he did it at night rather than in the daytime" (6:27).

Thirdly, faith makes sure God is leading. Gideon placed a fleece out twice to confirm God's leading. His faith finally grew to the point of complete obedience and victory. "So then faith cometh by hearing, and hearing by the Word of God" (Romans 10:17). Jesus said, "If ye have faith as a mustard seed…nothing shall be impossible unto You" (Matthew 17:20).

My prayer: I believe, help thou my unbelief. I invite You to be in charge of my life. Let me see what You can do through me. Thank You for growing my faith with Your faithfulness.

Day 2: Danger Follows Victory

Read JUDGES Chapters 7-9

Great victories can be followed by great failures. Gideon had a great victory by following the Lord's instructions and by relying on His power and assurance of victory. Gideon's army of three hundred men had defeated the Midianites. "...a force of about fifteen thousand men, all that were left of the armies of the eastern peoples; a hundred and twenty thousand swordsmen had fallen" (8:10).

Gideon turned down the power of being a King and told Israel to let God be their King. Gideon said, "I will not rule over You...the Lord will rule over You" (8:23). He was a humble man that did not seek power for his own benefit.

After his great victory, he did something that seemed innocent enough but turned into a disaster. It may have been a memorial to his victory. He made an ephod. He could have made it to help discover God's will like the Priest's ephod. He had a great legacy until he left this stumbling block that became an object of worship. We must be vigilant after a victorious event. Paul said when we restore a fallen brother we should "...watch Yourself, or You also may be tempted" (Galatians 6:1).

My prayer: *Keep my heart from judging anyone and help me to be careful to not let my guard down after experiencing Your presence and power. Guide my words to not only say You gave the victory but believe it in my heart.*

Day 3: God Chooses Who He Uses

Read JUDGES Chapters 10-11

It is interesting as well as mystifying why God uses certain people. The mystery is explained in first Corinthians. "Where is the wise? Where is the scribe? Where is the disputer of this age? Has not God made foolish the wisdom of this world? For since, in the wisdom of God, the world through wisdom did not know God, it pleased God through the foolishness of the message preached to save those who believe" (I Corinthians 1:20-21).

This is seen in the life of Jephthah. Jephthah was an illegitimate son who was an outcast. He was not received in respectable society. "His father was Gilead; his mother was a prostitute" (11:1). He gathered unsavory men around him. "So Jephthah fled from his brothers and settled in the land of Tob, where a group of adventurers gathered around him and followed him" (11:3). When Israel faced danger they asked him for help. "...we are turning to You now; come with us to fight the Ammonites..." (11:8). "Then Jephthah went out to fight the Ammonites, and the Lord gave them into his hands" (11:32). Why? The Lord "...could bear Israel's misery no longer" (10:16).

My prayer: _Thank You for using a foolish instrument like me. Thank You for being in charge and using who You want to and doing what You sovereignly want to._

Day 4: Undisciplined

Read JUDGES Chapters 12-14

Samson had to be a highly anticipated baby to be announced by a divine being. The "Angel of the Lord" gave instructions indicating he was going to be very special. It became apparent as he matured that he was an undisciplined person. He lived for the moment without regard for the future. He had great potential to be a mighty servant of God. "...the boy will be a

Nazarite of God from birth until the day of his death" (13:7). He was a chosen instrument of God.

The Bible indicates Samson was self-willed and demanding. He appears to have been denied nothing he wanted by his parents. His first selfish act was to choose a pagan woman. He said, "...I have seen a Philistine woman in Timnah; now get her for me as my wife" (14:2). He could have been much more effective if he had been dedicated and disciplined to follow the Lord. God used him anyway. "His parents did not know that this was from the Lord, who was seeking an occasion to confront the Philistines..." (14:3). If he had Paul's understanding he would have been more effective. Paul said, "For I am not seeking my own good but the good of many..." (I Corinthians 10:33).

My prayer: My prayer is that I live in such a way that I will not "seek my own good but the good of many." Lead me to be a blessing to others and bring glory to Christ.

Day 5: Comfortable Before Capture

Read JUDGES Chapters 15-17

Men attempt to see how close they can get to the danger of sin without being captured by it. They become complacent about a sin when it appears it didn't harm them. One drink of an alcoholic beverage or one hit of cocaine and a person is deluded into believing they can handle it without becoming addicted. They believe it won't hurt to do it again. Many people have gone down that slippery slope. That trip was taken by Samson thousands of years ago.

Samson became comfortable among the Philistine's lifestyle. He sought their pagan women. He became so comfortable he let a pagan woman charm the secret of his strength from him.

He adjusted to her trickery. His comfort caused him to wake up with no knowledge that he was powerless over his situation. "He awoke from his sleep and thought; I'll go out as before and shake myself free" (16:20). Paul urged Timothy to "Flee the evil desires of Youth, and pursue righteousness, faith, love and peace, along with those who call on the Lord out of a pure heart" (II Timothy 2:22).

My prayer: Thank You for the grace and power of the Holy Spirit to resist temptation. Thank You for making me uncomfortable with sin. Please forgive me where I fail You and give me strength to continue to strive for Your standards.

Day 6: Compassion Comes from God

Read JUDGES Chapters 18-20

The value of a life is determined by how close a person is to Jehovah-God. The murder and rape of the Levite's concubine is the most horrible story in the Bible. However, the murder and rape is not the most horrible part. The most horrible part is the lack of compassion on the part of the Levite and the old man. Their idol worship led them away from a holy God to loathsome gods. A society and its culture reflect the God they worship. Israel quit worshipping Jehovah-God and engaged in idolatry. Women became property and instruments to be used. To offer our daughter and your wife to perverts to save your own life reveals callousness beyond belief. The old man said, "Look, here is my virgin daughter, and his concubine" (19:24). The concubine is raped all night and dies on the old man's doorstep. The Levite says to her dead body, "Get up; let's go." Godlessness saps men of compassion.

Christians serve a God who cares about the individual. "For we do not have a high priest who is unable to sympathize with our weaknesses, but we have one who has been tempted in every way, just as we are – yet was without sin" (Hebrews 4:15).

My prayer: Lord, teach us to care more and love more like You.

Day 7: A Break in the Clouds

JUDGES Chapters 21-RUTH 1

Storms can be scary and dark. There is a sense of anxiety and fear the storm might hurt someone or do great damage. But when the black boiling clouds finally pass over and there is a break in the clouds a rainbow can appear. A shaft of light strikes and illuminates the sky. The book of Ruth is like that light of hope breaking through the clouds. Ruth pictures a family that had a great loss but was finally restored to wealth and a bright future. The fighting and turmoil of the book of Judges is over and God is seen restoring a family that had lost so much. We see God's mercy and care.

Ruth herself shows loyalty and love for her new mother like the church should love the Savior. Her words to Naomi should be the church's words to Jesus. "...Where You go I will go, and where You stay I will stay. Your people will be my people..." (Ruth 1:16). Ruth abandoned her old life to live a new one in a new place and in a new way. "Therefore, if anyone is in Christ, he is a new creation; old things have passed away; behold, all things have become new" (II Corinthians 5:17).

My prayer: Thank You for giving the family I grew up with a new life. I praise You for the kind of life You gave us. I thank You for the kind of life You give us in eternity.

Yearly Devotions – Week 13

Day 1: Divine Attraction

Read RUTH Chapters 2-4

Ruth is on mission to care for her new adopted mother. Her commitment is admirable and honored her mother-in-law. Boaz was a responsible committed man with a benevolent heart. These two committed people are attracted to each other instantly. He had heard of her but had not seen her until he saw her in the field. They had no idea at that moment the part God had planned for them. They were to become the great grandparents of the great King David. They would become a part of the lineage of God's Son. That lineage was unique and unusual. "Salmon the father of Boaz, whose mother was Rahab (the harlot), Boaz the father of Obed, whose mother was Ruth, Obed the father of Jesse, and Jesse the father of King David" (Matthew 1:5-6).

Their relationship is a picture of Christ and the church. Jesus is man's Kinsman-Redeemer who purchased the church by paying for their sin with His shed blood. John the Baptist accurately proclaimed "...Behold the Lamb of God, which taketh away the sin of the world" (John 1:29 KJV).

My prayer: Thank You Lord for having everything planned and prepared for all who seek the truth. Thank You for sending Your Son to remove my sin!

Day 2: The Right Start

Read I SAMUEL Chapters 1-3

Hannah longed to fulfill her role as a mother. She went to the right place to cure her barrenness. She prayed to the Lord. The right start for any child is to have a praying mother. After having her son she concentrated her attention on preparing him for God's use.

She prayed and carried out her commitment to surrender Samuel to God's work. "So now I give him to the Lord" (1:28). She left her beloved baby boy with Eli at the age of three or four. Her faith in the Lord must have been enormous to trust her son to an aged Priest. Her impact on Samuel is seen in his obedience and attitude to listen to Eli and the Lord. Her trust had to be in the Lord because Eli had failed to give his sons a right start. "Eli's sons were wicked men; they had no regard for the Lord" (2:12).

What caused Eli's sons to be so wicked? God said, "For I told him that I would judge his family forever because of the sin he knew about; his sons made themselves contemptible, and he failed to restrain them" (3:13). The right start for any child is to prepare them so God can use them.

My prayer: Thank You for having mercy on my children and forgive me where I failed to love them and restrain them. I pray for their children and our great grandchildren. I pray that they will be used of God.

Day 3: You Can't Put God in a Box

Read I SAMUEL Chapters 4-6

The Philistines thought they had captured Israel's God and could keep him in a safe place. "After the Philistines had captured the Ark of God...they carried the Ark into Dagons Temple and set it beside Dagon" (5:1, 2).

You can't put God in a box or compare Him to anything. "...There was Dagon, fallen on his face on the ground before the Ark of the Lord" (5:3)! No pagan religion can stand up to the true God and His Word. The Philistines couldn't keep their god propped up. God's presence will heal or hurt depending on one's relationship with Him. The gospel is offensive to the unbeliever.

The Philistines chose to separate from the presence of God rather than worship Him. They could not help but recognize the super natural results of God's presence. They reverenced Jehovah-God out of fear instead of love. Even the Israelites learned to reverence the Lord. The Israelites said, "Who can stand in the presence of the Lord, this holy God" (6:20)? Jesus said, "the work of God is this: to believe in the one He has sent" (John 6:29).

My prayer: Thank You for giving of Yourself and then giving me Your life. You have given my wife and me a wonderful time here on earth. You have given us many blessings and surprises. Please give me the wisdom and strength to testify to Your almighty presence.

Day 4: Committed Again – Another Battle Begins

Read I SAMUEL Chapters 7-9

God knows men have a tendency to stray away from Him. Nations and individuals wander away from Him. Man is constantly seeking to get right with God. When people return to God they encounter Satanic resistance. Samuel said, "If You are returning to the Lord with all Your hearts, then rid Yourselves of the foreign gods…and commit Yourselves to the Lord…" (7:3). "So the Israelites put away their Baal's and Ashtoreth's, and served the Lord only" (7:4).

After they returned to the Lord they did not have peace and security. Just the opposite was true. When people commit to serve the Lord it stirs Satan and his demons up. As soon as Israel met together to serve the Lord, "...the Philistines came up to attack them" (7:7). Satan never changes his tactics. As soon as Jesus was baptized He had to face Satan. "Then Jesus was led by the Spirit into the desert to be tempted by the devil" (Matthew 4:1). We should be encouraged when we are attacked that our commitment is worthy of Satan's notice. John said, "...the one who is in You is greater than the one who is in the world" (I John 4:4).

My prayer: Thank You that the Holy Spirit is more powerful than any circumstance or enemy of the gospel. I pray now for Pastor Yousef in Iran that the enemy will be defeated and he will be set free.

Day 5: Be Careful What You Pray For

Read I SAMUEL Chapters 10-12

We need to be careful what we pray for because God may give it to us. Israel asked God for a King. God gave them a King. "Then Samuel took a flask of oil and poured it on Saul's head and kissed him, saying, 'Has not the Lord anointed You leader over His inheritance" (10:1). God knew He had been rejected and yet He gave them what they asked for. God said to Samuel, "...it is not You they have rejected but they have rejected ME as their King" (8:7).

God told them their answered prayer would ultimately not be good for them. God said the King would eventually make their children servants for his use and pleasure. He said the King would burden them with heavy taxes. Israel did not listen to God and said, "...then we will be like all the other nations..." (8:20).

God allowed Israel to make the wrong choice. God has a permissive will and a perfect will. Every believer should seek God's perfect will. Since the consequences of making wrong choices can be devastating we must yield to the Word of God and His will. God said to Israel, "Yet if You persist in doing evil both You and Your King will be swept away" (12:25).

My prayer: Lord, it is my earnest desire to follow Your perfect will. Give me wisdom and bless me as I seek to follow Your will. I ask what Jabez asked "Oh that thou wouldst bless me indeed, and enlarge my coast, and that thine hand might be with me, and that thou wouldst keep me from evil, that it may not grieve me!" (I Chronicles 4:10 KJV)

Day 6: Godly Discernment Leads to Godly Decisions

Read I SAMUEL Chapters 13-14

The meaning of the word "discern" is to see or understand differences;" "one who knows and judges" and is able to distinguish the truth. The Apostle Paul talks about Godly discernment. "The man without the Spirit does not accept the things that come from the Spirit of God...and he cannot understand them because they are spiritually discerned" (I Corinthians 2:14).

King Saul lacked spiritual discernment. He offered an unauthorized burnt-offering only to be offered by Samuel. He did not want to wait on God or the priest. Samuel said, "You acted foolishly...You have not kept the command the Lord Your God gave You..." (13:13). Then King Saul made a foolish vow not to have his men eat until there was victory in battle. His lack of discernment limited Israel's victory. In contrast, his son Jonathan had Godly discernment. His faith in God was expressed when he said to his armor-bearer "Nothing can hinder the Lord from saving, whether by many or few" (14:6). Jonathan's spiritual discernment led him to know when to rely on the Lord to singlehandedly attack the enemy and win a great victory.

My prayer: Lord, may I see what You see and live according to Your directions and truth. Thank You for leaving the Comforter to guide us into all truth to make the right decisions in life.

Day 7: Qualified for God's Use

Read I SAMUEL Chapters 15-17

Is it a good education that qualifies a person to be used of God? Education is good. Is it physical strength and a brilliant mind? Is it to have the right up-bringing and the correct pedigree? What qualification does God look for? Saul had qualities men look for. He was tall, handsome and modest. He appeared humble at first. Samuel said of him "...You were once small in Your own eyes..." (15:17).

Saul's true character became evident as he acquired more power. He was never fully committed to follow the Lord. His disobedience revealed that he had "...rejected the Word of the Lord" (15:23). What was God demanding of Saul? He demanded obedience without reservation. Samuel asked Saul, "Why did You not obey the Lord? ...to obey is better than sacrifice...for rebellion is like the sin of divination, and arrogance like the evil of idolatry" (15:22-23). What qualities is God looking for? The two main qualities are obedience and a pure heart. God said, "The Lord does not look at the things man looks at. Man looks at the outward appearance, but the Lord looks at the heart" (16:7). A committed heart is the greatest quality.

My prayer: Lord, I yield to Your way and will. Help my stubbornness to surrender to Your word and give me the spirit of obedience. Thank You for directing my life so that You can bless me. I pray for our governmental leaders to obey You and seek to honor You.

Spoonful

Yearly Devotions – Week 14

Day 1: God's Blessing Secures Success

Read I SAMUEL Chapters 18-20

God chose David to replace Saul. With God's blessing David had God's protection. That protection did not prevent David from experiencing trials. It did mean God would go with him through the trials.

God prepared David to be a King by using his tribulations to mature him. God used King Saul as an instrument to train David to depend totally on Him. David's life became a life of turmoil. His relationship with Saul is ruined by jealousy. His life is threatened by Saul's hatred. David's relationship with Michal, his wife, and Jonathan, his best friend, is attacked by Saul. David became an outcast and was unjustly treated.

But in all of that adversity David remained faithful to the Lord. Michal helped him escape from her father. Jonathan warned him of danger and he got to safety. God's Spirit at Ramah neutralized Saul and his soldiers. God's blessing overcame every attack. That is why David said, "But You are a shield around me, O Lord; You bestow glory on me and lift up my head" (Psalms 3:3).

My prayer: I praise You for Your blessings in my life and thank You for the many times You protected me from danger and at times from myself.

Day 2: Cross-fires Can Hurt Everyone

Read I SAMUEL Chapters 21-23

The object of any army in battle is to get their enemy in a crossfire. That situation occurs when an opposing force is trapped between two units of an army. The enemy is shot at from two directions.

When Saul rebelled against God those caught between him and God were destroyed or in hiding. When people rebel against God they should remember they can put everyone around them in jeopardy. Ahimelech, the priest of Nob, was caught in the crossfire of David, God's man, and Saul, the rebel fighting God. Ahimelech did nothing disloyal nor did he dishonor God or the King. He was caught between two forces opposing each other. Even though he was innocent of any wrong doing King Saul killed him and his family in defiance of God. The town of Keilah refused to be caught in this crossfire.

We must remember that all rebellion can put others who are innocent in the crossfire of our struggle with God.

My prayer: Lord, please keep my heart in tune with Your will and I surrender to You and ask for Your protection from the evil-one.

Day 3: Trust God for Justice

Read I SAMUEL Chapters 24-26

America's justice system is troubled when a person with lots of money can get away with murder. Only in God's court will true justice be done. David was convinced God would bring about justice in King Saul's life. Since David trusted God to make things right he didn't attempt to take things into his own hands. David's confidence in God to bring about justice revealed he had an intimate relationship with Him. This was unusual for such a Young man. David made sure he was on God's side before entering battle.

We see David's confidence in God to make things right when he said, "As surely as the Lord lives...the LORD HIMSELF will strike him (Saul); either his time will come and he will die, or he will go into battle and perish. But the Lord forbid that I should lay a hand on the Lord's anointed." (26:10-11) God says, "It is mine to avenge; I will repay...the Lord will judge His people. It is a dreadful thing to fall into the hands of the living God" (Hebrews 10:30-31). Jesus death brought justice for all the sin of mankind.

My prayer: Lord, I thank You for Your mercy and that I'm not going to get justice in my own life because of Jesus' death and resurrection. Thank You that my name is written down in the Lamb's Book of Life even though I don't deserve to be there.

Day 4: Who Does God Talk To?

Read I SAMUEL Chapters 27-30

David and his men came back from the battlefield to find their city had been attacked and plundered. David and his men were in great despair. David did what every believer should do in times of desperation. "But David found strength in the Lord his God" (30:6). David then asked the priest if God would give him victory if he pursued the ones who had taken all of the valuable objects of his city. God answered, "Pursue them...You will certainly overtake them and succeed in the rescue" (30:8). David's obedience and dependence upon God allowed God to continue to talk to him.

King Saul is not able to hear from God during his crisis. The Philistines are about to attack him and he needed God's assurance of victory. God refused to talk to a rebellious king. Saul reverts to a pagan practice of talking to the dead. The Priest and prophet Samuel appeared and told him why God won't talk to him. "Because You did not obey the Lord or carry out His fierce wrath against the Amelekites, the Lord has done this to You today" (28:18). Why should God talk to someone who won't listen or obey?

My prayer: It is my desire to listen for Your leadership and direction. Help keep my heart open to hear when You speak and then to obey what I know and hear.

Day 5: An Element Needed for God's Blessing

Read I SAMUEL Chapters 31-II SAMUEL 2

King Saul did not reverence the Lord and love Him with all his heart. How do we know that? He did not value the worship of God. He performed what only the priest Samuel was anointed to do. He disobeyed God by not destroying the entire enemy and blamed others for his actions. He became corrupted by his power and became self-willed. His life ended badly and concluded with suicide.

God replaced King Saul with a man who had that one element God could bless even though he had flaws. That one element that set him apart from Saul was that he reverenced God and loved him with all his heart. His reverence is seen by the question he asked the man who claimed to have ended Saul's life. "Why were You not afraid to lift Your hand to destroy the Lord's anointed" (II Samuel 1:14)? Because he reverenced God he reverenced God's anointed no matter what he did. David became corrupted by power also and sinned but truly repented. David cried out, "For I know my transgressions and my sin is always before me. Against You, You only, have I sinned and done this evil in Your sight" (Psalms 51:3-4).

My prayer: I come to worship You today in Spirit and in truth. I come as a sinner that has all my sins removed by the blood of Jesus who died on the cross. "Cleanse me with hyssop, and I will be whiter than snow...create in me a pure heart, O Lord."

Day 6: Principles Are to Live By

Read II SAMUEL Chapters 3-5

There are many who attend church who are practicing atheist during the week. They go to church on Sunday but do not live by the principles taught there. They separate their job and other activities from what is preached and taught from God's Word. David lived by his principles daily which is evident by how he responded to the challenges he faced in these three chapters.

David was willing to bring about peace and forgive those who had been his enemies. He was outraged at the murder of his opposing general by his own general Joab. He demonstrated his genuineness during Abner's funeral by honoring his old enemy. When Nancy and I visited Abner's tomb, the guide spoke again how David honored Abner. His true feelings of respect and honor for Abner displayed David's integrity and his principled behavior.

David put into practice what he believed when he executed the two men who murdered his arch-enemy in cold blood. He believed God should deal with His anointed King, not man.

My prayer: Lord, keep my heart committed to walk the way I talk.

Day 7: Service Follows Worship

Read II SAMUEL Chapters 6-8

When people attend church they hold what is called "worship services." A person must experience worship before he can effectively serve the Lord. David displayed what real worship is. When they brought the Ark of the Covenant to Jerusalem David spontaneously praised God.

Real worship is to be abandoned to the praise of God with an uninhibited expression of love for the Lord. "David, wearing a linen ephod, danced before the Lord with all his might while he and the entire house of Israel brought up the Ark of the Lord with shouts and the sound of trumpets" (6:14). God responds to this kind of worship. God told David, "the Lord declares to You that the Lord Himself will establish a house for You" (7:11).

The world and the flesh does not like real worship. Real worship is humiliating to the flesh. Michal, David's wife, was repulsed by David's enthusiastic worship.

David served the Lord with victory and joy after he worshipped.

My prayer: Lord, teach me to worship like David. Like David I say, "How great You are, o sovereign Lord. There is no one like You, and there is no God but You..." I yield to Your will and seek to immerse in Your protection and love.

Yearly Devotions – Week 15

Day 1: Sin is Like Yeast

Read II SAMUEL Chapters 9-12

How is sin like yeast? Yeast makes dough expand and rise to a size much larger than any flour could do on its own. Yeast is put in perfectly good dough and then begins its work in the flour. David had just treated Jonathan's son with kindness and generosity. That was a picture of King Jesus letting man in on the riches of heaven even though he had been crippled by sin. David was not perfect like Jesus and sin was fixing to expand into terrible consequences in his life.

David, with his many wives, wanted information about Bathsheba. Lust set in. The next step of his sin was to ignore her marital status. He invited her to his palace. He committed adultery with her. She got pregnant. To cover up his sin he sent for her husband and lied to him. David had him murdered. Sin's trail keeps getting longer and more vicious.

Nathan, the prophet, confronts David. David learns the price of his sin. David pronounces his own judgment. "He must pay four times over..." (12:6). God said to David, "Before Your very eyes I will take Your wives and give them to one who is close to You..." (12:11). "Now, therefore, the sword will never depart from Your house..." (12:10).

My prayer: Lord, please keep me from the evil-one and keep him from me. Help me not to yield to temptation.

Day 2: Bringing Back the Banished

Read II SAMUEL Chapters 13-14

One of the vilest characters in the Bible is Amnon who raped his half-sister and sent her away in disgrace. The Bible does not condone such behavior but exposes it as sin. The Bible always reveals sin as a devastating act that hurts the sinner along with the innocent victims. God warned David after his terrible sin that judgment would be severe. God said, "Out of Your own household I am going to bring calamity upon You" (12:11). Amnon had seen his father lust, commit adultery, lie and murder. He followed his father's example.

After Amnon satisfied his lust he had nothing but contempt for his half-sister. In like manner, the lost world has contempt for those who abandoned their convictions. Sin's result never ceases affecting those who get caught in its web. Absalom kills Amnon and becomes an outcast from his father's kingdom. Joab's charade brings Absalom home. Joab made a statement here in the Old Testament that is fulfilled in the New. "But God does not take away life; instead, he devises ways that a banished person may not remain estranged from Him (14:14).

My prayer: Thank You for Your grace and restoration through Your Son Jesus. Thank You that when I was banished to hell You brought me back through Christ's shed blood.

Day 3: Answered Prayer – God's Man

Read II SAMUEL Chapters 15-17

Absalom's rebellion blossomed into civil-war with his father. Absalom had the advantage over his father. He had the advantage of surprise, preparation for war, he had built rapport with the people, he had chosen a wise counselor, and he had Youth and ambition to do what was necessary to capture the kingdom. There was one important thing he lacked. He lacked God's anointing and blessing. He faced a seasoned father who had faith in a holy God.

David prayed, "O Lord, turn Ahithophel's counsel into foolishness (15:31). David's prayer was answered almost immediately when Hushai the faithful counselor was there to meet him at the Mt. of Olives. David trusted him to "...help me by frustrating Ahithophel's advice" (15:34). David had been humiliated and humbled to the point that he would not retaliate when Shimei cursed him. David had cast all of his care upon the Lord and God protected him. Absalom and all his men of Israel said, "The advice of Hushai the Arkite is better than Ahitophel. For the Lord had determined to frustrate the good advice of Ahithophel..." (17:14).

My prayer: Lord, teach me to listen to the person You send into my life to help during tough times. Your word is the wisdom I need to live in a way that brings You honor.

Day 4: Pride is Always Present With Sin

Read II SAMUEL Chapters 18-19

Satan's rebellion against God was based on pride. Satan said, "...I will ascend to heaven; I will raise my throne above the stars of God" (Isaiah 14:13). Eve wanted to be a goddess instead of a gardener's wife. Satan told her she would "...be like God, knowing good and evil" (Genesis 3:5). Absalom's actions revealed a man full of pride. "In all Israel there was not a man so highly praised for his handsome appearance as Absalom...there was no blemish in him" (14:25). He had long beautiful hair that weighed five pounds when it was cut.

Absalom's hair is an accurate picture of how the source of pride is where a person can be caught in its trap. Interestingly, a mule was the usual mount of a prince or king. When he caught his hair in a tree he lost his royal seat. He became vulnerable as he hung in mid-air. He was powerless to defend himself or a nation. The hardest part of fulfilling II Chronicles 7:14 is to obey the admonition where God says, "...if my people, who are called by my name, will humble themselves...then..."

My prayer: I come to You O Lord to ask for a spirit of humility.

Day 5: Vows Are Sacred

Read II SAMUEL Chapters 20-22

God takes people's vows very seriously. "When You make a vow to God, do not delay in fulfilling it. He has no pleasure in fools; fulfill Your vow. It is better not to vow than to make a vow and not fulfill it" (Ecclesiastes 5:4). When a couple gives vows in marriage to each other and to the Lord they should realize the gravity of it. When imminent danger is avoided after a vow to God is given and then forgotten there could be serious consequences. Signatures on contracts are vows and should be honored if humanly possible.

This truth is illustrated in II Samuel. "During the reign of David, there was a famine for three successive years; so David sought the face of the Lord. The Lord said, 'it is on account of Saul and his blood-stained house; it is because he put the Gibeonites to death" (21:1). These were the Gibeonites that deceived Joshua into believing they were from outside the Holy Land. Joshua said, "We have given our oath by the Lord...We cannot touch them now" (Joshua 9:19). Because one man broke that oath all of Israel paid the price.

My prayer: Lord, I need Your strength to keep commitments to You and to my fellow man. Like David I pray and praise You Lord, "In my distress I called to the Lord; I called out to my God. From his temple he heard my voice; my cry came to His ears" (22:7).

Day 6: Jesus – A King Without Sin

Read II SAMUEL Chapters 23-24

Jesus did not possess one ounce of pride. He humbly came as a servant to do exactly what the heavenly Father told him to do. He had all the power of heaven and remained humble. Before His crucifixion He said, "Do You think I cannot call on My Father, and He will at once put at My disposal more than twelve legions (12,000) of angels" (Matthew 26:53)?

David, a man after God's own heart, could not be a king without pride and sin. He praised God in chapter twenty three and listed all the mighty men in his army. In chapter twenty four he fell off the humble wagon and took a census. God permitted David to do what he wanted to do. God said, "You want a census take it!" God then punished Israel and humbled David for their wayward behavior.

God loved David because he genuinely repented after falling into sin. David gives a preview of Jesus, the sinless king, when he says, "I am the one who has sinned and done wrong...Let Your hand fall upon me and my family" (24:17). He purchased Araunah's threshing floor to offer a burnt-offering to stop the plague. That threshing floor was Mt Moriah where Solomon built the Temple. The perfect King Jesus came and cleansed it centuries later. "God made Him who had no sin to be sin for us, so that in Him we might become the righteousness of God" (II Corinthians 5:21).

My prayer: Lord, my prayer is that I will remain faithful no matter what the future holds. Just as David said, Jesus..."is like the light of morning at sunrise on a cloudless morning, like the brightness after rain..." (23:4).

Day 7: Satan's Most Used Weapon

Read I KINGS Chapters 1-2

Paul wrote, "For our struggle is not against flesh and blood, but against the rulers, against the authorities, against the powers of this dark world and against the spiritual forces of evil in the heavenly realms" (Ephesians 6:12). Those spiritual beings cannot make anyone do anything. What they can do is make people want to disobey God.

It was common knowledge that David had chosen Solomon as the next king. There was rebellion in Adonijah's heart because his father never restrained him. "His father never interfered with him by asking, 'Why do You behave as You do'" (1:6)? A rebellious spirit results in disobedience. Adonijah attempted another coup by trying to marry Abishag. His disobedience cost him his life which is Satan's goal.

Satan used disobedience in Shemei's life. He promised Solomon he would never leave Jerusalem. He disobeyed Solomon. It cost him his life. He had been warned by Solomon, "...You can be sure You will die; Your blood will be on Your own head" (2:37). Satan's goal for everyone is to disobey and die like Adam and Eve.

My prayer: Lord, I yield to Your will and seek to obey You. Give me wisdom and strength from above to be like Solomon and David who were blessed and "remain secure before the Lord forever."

Yearly Devotions – Week 16

Day 1: The Great Exception

Read I KINGS Chapters 3-5

The difference between David and Solomon was one exception. Solomon tolerated what David never did. "...Solomon loved the Lord...EXCEPT that he sacrificed and burned incense at the high places" (1:3). His prayer to God at Gibeon "...was the great high place..." (1:4). His prayer was answered but he had to tolerate pagan worship to be there. What was wrong?

"In Canaan these "high places" had become the scenes of orgies and human sacrifice connected with the idolatrous worship of these imaginary gods..." (Pictorial Bible Dictionary). God had commanded Israel "....to drive out all the inhabitants of the land from before you, destroy all their engraved stones, destroy all their molded images, and demolish all their high places" (Numbers 33:52). God heard Solomon's prayer here and granted him surpassing wisdom in spite of this exception. It brought his ruin in later life. His tolerance allowed his wives to lead him from "high places" to "low practices." "...his wives turned his heart after other gods; and his heart was not loyal to the Lord his God..." (I Kings 11:4). When a believer says, "this one exception won't hurt anything," remember Solomon.

My prayer: Thank You Lord for the Holy Spirit who leads us into all truth and cleanses us on our journey in life on earth. I truly need You "every hour."

Day 2: Building Silently

Read I KINGS Chapters 6-7

God is a God of detail. Those who believe God started creation and then abandoned it to let it run its course have not read much of the Bible. God recorded in detail every aspect of the Temple including the decorations.

The engineering of the Temple was amazing. It was prepared before any of the materiel was brought to the building site. Huge stones were chiseled to the exact specifications needed to assemble them together without the sound of a hammer being heard during construction. "In building the Temple, only blocks dressed at the quarry were used, and no hammer, chisel or any other iron tool was heard at the Temple sight while it was being built" (6:7).

That silent work is like the Holy Spirit working in individuals privately to prepare individuals to be fitted together for the work of the ministry through the church. "Now you are the body of Christ, and each one of you is a part of it" (I Corinthians 12:27).

My Prayer: Lead me to know my part of your work so that I will fit into Your scheme of things. You are the contractor of my life to build Your church for Your glory.

Day 3: God is The Focus

Read I KINGS Chapters 8-9

The Ark was brought into the Temple after its completion. Israel worshipped the only true God and the Ark symbolized His presence. When the priests left, God's presence arrived around the Ark. Neither the priests nor Solomon were in charge of God's arrival. God came when He chose to come. God chose to bless Israel with His presence in such a way that all activity stopped and concentrated on Him. "When the priests withdrew from the Holy Place, the cloud filled the Temple of the Lord. And the priests could not perform their service because of the cloud, for the glory of the Lord filled His Temple" (8:10).

Every time God is the focus of worship men are overwhelmed. When God appeared to Jacob he thought, "...surely the Lord is in this place...he was afraid and said, 'How awesome is this place" (Genesis 28:16-17)! When God showed up in power in the early church "suddenly a sound like the blowing of a violent wind came from heaven and filled the whole house..." (Acts 2:2). The people were amazed and perplexed but they recognized a supernatural presence.

My prayer: I beseech You Lord to visit our church service in such power all human effort will be overwhelmed and unnoticed.

Day 4: Compromise Led to Corruption

Read I KINGS Chapters 10-12

God had warned Israel not to let their sons marry women from pagan nations. God knew that "...when You choose some of their daughters as wives...and those daughters prostitute themselves to their gods, they will lead Your sons to do the same" (Exodus 34:16).

Solomon compromised this command and lost his kingdom for his son. His wealth and wisdom could not stop God's judgment. His compromise caused him to lose what the queen of Sheba had seen. She said, "Indeed, not even half was told me; in wisdom and wealth You have far exceeded the report I heard" (10:7). In fact, "the whole world sought audience with Solomon to hear the wisdom God had put in his heart" (10:24). His wealth is seen when he made five hundred shields out of almost three thousand pounds of gold. "All King

Solomon's goblets were gold and all the household articles..." (10:21). His compromise of marrying pagan women led to half-hearted worship. Solomon's compromise brought him to the condition that his "...heart was not fully devoted to the Lord" (11:4).

My prayer: Lord protect me from the sin of compromising with the world's lifestyle and philosophy. Thank You for the truth of Your word.

Day 5: Blind Ahijah's Sight Was Good

Read I KINGS Chapters 13-15

"Now Ahijah could not see; his sight was gone because of his age" (14:4). But he saw more with God than the world could with healthy eyes without God. He could see the future because he had a relationship with the One who knows the future – Jehovah-God. The writer of Hebrews voices it best. "Now faith is being sure of what we hope for and certain of what we do not see" (Hebrews 11:1). Like Moses who "...left Egypt, not fearing the kings anger; he persevered because he saw him who is invisible" (Hebrews 11:27). To have Ahijah's sight You must have a relationship to the God of all insight.

Jeroboam and his wife could not fool a blind prophet because God kept him informed. Ahijah destroyed her pretense when he said, "Come in wife of Jeroboam" (14:6). He informed Jeroboam and his wife their son would die. He saw into the future and shared with them that God was removing Jeroboam as king and removing Israel from the Promised Land. It takes a relationship with God through Jesus to have the correct perspective of the events of life.

My prayer: Keep me so in tune to You Lord that I see what You see. Help keep Your word in front of me so I can see things according to a Biblical perspective.

Day 6: God Worship vs. Satan Worship

Read I KINGS Chapters 16-18

God had Elijah challenge the god Baal by stopping any rain for three years. "If the Lord withheld the rain, rendering Baal – considered the god of fertility and Lord of the rain clouds – powerless, He would be proven the true God and Elijah the true prophet of His word." (Arch. Study Bible)

All worship is either of Jehovah-God or Satan! There is no middle ground. Satan loves religion and religious worship. Satan had eight hundred fifty prophets of Baal and Ashtoreth against one prophet of God. The false prophets resorted to all sorts of ritualistic activity. God had one prophet with a simple prayer. The choice of who to worship has always been, "if the Lord is God, follow Him; but if Baal is God, follow him" (18:21).

True Biblical worship is powerful and productive. Israel was attracted to the worthless worship of idols and Satan's brand of worship. Like the world today Israelites were reluctant followers of the true God. Since God's fire of judgment fell on Mt. Calvary everyone must choose who they will worship.

My prayer: All I can do is praise You for Your mercy by saving me and letting me participate in the true worship of God.

Day 7: God is Longsuffering

I KINGS Chapters 19-21

"There was never a man like Ahab, who sold himself to do evil in the eyes of the Lord, urged on by Jezebel his wife" (21:25). He partnered with someone as wicked as himself. Ahab disobeyed God by marrying outside the nation of Israel and by worshipping Baal. He supported Jezebel when she sought to kill Elijah. She had Naboth killed to get his property and satisfy Ahab's lust. She encouraged Ahab to do evil and worship falsely. Ahab was a weak man who had no strength of character.

What is astounding is God's response of mercy to Ahab's repentance. God said to Ahab, "...because you have sold yourself to do evil in the eyes of the Lord...I am going to bring disaster on you" (21:20-21). "When Ahab heard these words, he tore his clothes, put on sackcloth and fasted. He...went around meekly" (21:27). God's longsuffering and mercy is seen when He told Elijah, "...Have you noticed how Ahab has humbled himself before Me? Because he has humbled himself I will not bring disaster in his day..." (21:29).

My prayer: Again, Lord, I praise You that I have already received Your mercy and not Your judgment. Like the Psalmist said, "But I, by Your great mercy, will come into Your house; in reverence will I bow down toward Your Holy Temple" (Psalms 5:7).

Yearly Devotions – Week 17

Day 1: Bad Companies Are Dangerous

Read I KINGS Chapter 22

How many innocent, unsuspecting people have been arrested or seriously hurt by being with the wrong person or persons at the wrong time. Bad things can happen unexpectedly and quickly.

Jehoshaphat, a Godly good King of Judah, was such a person. "In everything he walked in the ways of his father Asa and did not stray from them; he did what was right in the eyes of the Lord." (22:43) Jehoshaphat should not have associated with Ahab even though they were at peace with each other.

He almost made a fatal mistake by being with Ahab and his war with Aram (Syria). He should have known the prophets of Baal were unreliable. He should have listened to Micaiah, the Godly prophet. He should have known when God's prophet told Ahab that God had sent a lying spirit to the false prophets to give him what he wanted to hear. He should have known when Ahab disguised himself. What was he thinking? "...You must not associate with anyone who calls himself a brother but is sexually immoral or greedy, an idolater or a slanderer, a drunkard or a swindler" (I Corinthians 5:11).

My prayer: Lord, help me to love the unlovely and those determined to rebel against You. Show me how to minister to them without being involved in their activities. I lift up Jesus' prayer to You: Jesus said, "My prayer is not that You take them out of the world but that You protect them from the evil one." (John 17:15)

Day 2: God's Handouts

Read II KINGS Chapters 1-3

God displayed His sufficiency in four incidents. Four different needs were met in four different ways. God provides for man, not government.

1. King Ahaziah sent men to arrest Elijah because he didn't like his prophecy. "...pagan people of the time thought that magical power of curses could be nullified either by forcing the pronouncer of the curse to retract the statement or by killing the prophet." (Arch. Study Bible) God provided Elijah protection with a blast of fire. God handed out protection to His servant.
2. God handed out a new prophet to replace Elijah. Elijah's ministry was doubled through Elisha. Elisha's request for a double portion of anointing is the amount of inheritance for the first born child when the father dies.
3. God provided water and victory for Israel and Judah when they faced a fierce enemy. God handed out water to bring about a victory and His glory.
4. God purified the water at Jericho to provide a way to sustain life. "But seek first His Kingdom and His righteousness, and all these things will be given to You as well." (Matthew 6:33)
5.

My prayer: Again I praise You for Your sustaining my life for the years I have had to serve You. You have been overwhelmingly gracious. Thank You for Your mercy and kindness.

Day 5: Elisha — God's Channel of Blessings

Read II KINGS Chapters 4-5

God chose to cooperate with Elisha to meet the needs of the people he came in contact with. One of Elisha's students died and left his wife destitute. She was left in poverty and was planning to sell her two boys into slavery. When Elisha learned of her condition he asked her two important questions. "How can I help you?" and "Tell me, what do you have in Your house" (4:2)? She needed money and she had a little oil in her house. Elisha went to the source of money and the One who made oil. He called on God to give her oil so she could get the money. God gave it but she had to work to pour the oil. There was cooperation between her and God.

When God supplies, He gives us more than we can ask or think. The jars represented people being filled with the Holy Spirit. God will continue adding to His Kingdom and filling believers with the Holy Spirit as long as we keep bringing them. Elisha raised a boy from the dead and healed Namaan of leprosy. He did not see impossible situations. He saw God bigger than any problem.

My prayer: Lord, help keep my eyes on You and not my circumstances. "Those who trust in the Lord are like Mt. Zion, which cannot be shaken but endures forever." (Psalms 125:1)

Day 4: God Vision

Read II KINGS Chapters 6-8

One man anointed of God was able to minister to peasants and kings. Elisha believed and lived as though God could resolve any problem. Like the angel told Mary he believed "...with God nothing shall be impossible" (Luke 1:37). Elisha kept his sight on God instead of life's difficulties.

The prophet that lost the ax head saw his future in jeopardy because at that time an iron implement was very costly and would be too much for a prophet to replace. The man possibly would have been forced to work as a bondservant to pay for the ax head. Elisha saw God overcoming nature by making iron float. Elisha's servant saw "...An army with horses and chariots..." surrounding the city (6:15). Elisha saw "...horses and chariots of fire..." sent from God to surround Elisha (6:17). The king of Israel saw Samaria starving to death. Elisha saw God making food plentiful the very next day. Hazael saw King Ben-hadad sick. Elisha saw Hazael murdering Ben-hadad of Aram and becoming King. We need to be like Elisha and see God working behind all the incidents in our life believing good will come from Him in spite of problems.

My prayer: Lord, give me Your vision so I can see Your hand in everything that comes into my life. Thank You for making good out of all of life's experiences.

Day 5: God Has a Time Limit

Read II KINGS Chapters 9-10

Many sports have time limits to complete the game. God has a time limit also. God told Noah, "My Spirit will not contend with man forever, for he is mortal, his days will be a hundred twenty years" (Genesis 6:30). God gave the Canaanites four hundred years to get right. God said to Abraham, "In the fourth generation your descendants will come back here, for the sin of the Amorites has not yet reached its full measure" (Genesis 15:16). Jonah told Nineveh it had forty days to get right. Jesus told the Jews they would be persecuted for a certain period of time. He said, "Jerusalem will be trampled only by the Gentiles until the times of the Gentiles are fulfilled" (Luke 21:24).

Ahab had been dead at least eleven years and Jezebel was still alive. God ordered Jehu to execute her. Her day of judgment came just as God said. Ahab's body had been dumped on Naboth's property. The dogs ate Jezebel as had been prophesied. God's time limit on these wicked people ran out. The Psalmist warned us that, "the length of our days is seventy-years-or eighty, if we have strength...Teach us to number our days aright..." (Psalms 90:10, 12).

My prayer: I am so grateful You are in charge of my life and know my time limit. Thank You for the wonderful life You have given me these over seventy years.

Day 6: A Residual Life

Read II KINGS Chapters 11-13

Residual has to do with "what is left behind" according to the dictionary. An entrepreneur's goal is to receive residual payments. A company that sells franchises receives a percentage from the profits of each franchise. They receive residual payments on a regular basis without having to do the work. Two men whose lives had residual effects on their nation were Jeroboam and Elisha.

Jeroboam was the King of the ten Northern tribes when they separated from David's son Rehoboam. He instituted the idolatress worship of the golden calf. Jehu the tenth King of the Northern Kingdom followed Jeroboam's influence. "He did evil in the eyes of the Lord by following the sins of Jeroboam..." (13:2). Jeroboam's life brought idolatry and degradation years after his death.

Elisha left a residual of the power of a holy God. That power continued in his dead body. Some men were burying a man and came under attack by their enemy "so they threw the man's body into Elisha's tomb. When the body touched

Elisha's bones, the man came to life and stood up on his feet" (13:21).

My prayer: *Dear Lord, may my life have a residual effect to bring people to the Lord. Keep my steps on Your path and my journey in Your direction.*

Day 7: Violence Follows False Worship

Read II KINGS Chapters 14-16

The Northern Kingdom of Israel was established as a nation that worshipped a golden calf. A nation or a person becomes like what they worship. The old saying is still true, "If you remove the blood of Christ from the preaching in Americas there will be blood in the streets of America." Men and nations cannot live together in peace without a commitment to a holy God. There must be a conviction that everyone is accountable to a holy God on judgment day.

Israel turned its back on Jehovah God and violence followed. When Zachariah became King "He did evil in the eyes of the Lord, as his father had done" (15:9). He was assassinated after six months by Shallum. Shallum was assassinated after one month as King. There were many wars and much bloodshed.

A nation will behave like the god it worships whether it's a golden calf or power, or pleasure, or money. America cannot continue to replace Christianity with secularism and escape being a nation filled with violence. Only Christ and His shed blood can bring peace to a nation.

My prayer: *Thank You Lord for shedding Your blood to cover my sin. I lift up America to You and ask that America would turn again to Jesus and His shed blood as the only means of saving souls and a nation.*

Yearly Devotions – Week 18

Day 1: One Person Can Make a Difference

Read II KINGS Chapters 17-18

The Northern Kingdom of Israel "worshipped other gods and followed the practices of the nations the Lord had driven out before them..." (17:7-8). "They bowed down to all the starry hosts, and they worshipped Baal. They sacrificed their sons and daughters in the fire. They practiced divination and sorcery and sold themselves to do evil in the eyes of the Lord, provoking Him to anger" (17:16-17). They went along with the pagan world. "So the people of Israel were taken from their homeland into exile in Assyria..." (17:23).

Then the Assyrians attacked the Southern Kingdom of Israel. One man made a difference and faced Assyria with God's protection. Hezekiah "did what was right in the eyes of the Lord, just as his father David" (18:3). Even though Hezekiah followed the Lord he still had to face an enemy. Godliness does not protect a person from being attacked. What is important is the response of a Godly person to an attack. God allows His follower's faith to be tested. "In fact, everyone who wants to live a godly life in Christ Jesus will be persecuted..." (II Timothy 3:12).

My prayer: Thank You Lord that I don't have to face the burdens of life alone. "Even though I walk through the valley of the shadow of death, I will fear no evil, for You are with me..." (Psalms 23:4).

Day 2: God's Comforting Words

Read II KINGS Chapters 19-21

Hezekiah is diligently following the Lord when Sennacherib attacks Jerusalem. He heard discouraging words from Sennacherib's commander. The commander declares Egypt can't protect him. He says, "The Lord Himself told me to march against this country and destroy it" (18:25). The commander gave Hezekiah a list of nations he had already conquered and asked him, "Did the gods of the nations that were destroyed by my forefathers deliver them? ..." (19:12).

Hezekiah turned to the only hope he had--God. Hezekiah sent word to Isaiah and pled for God's help. Hezekiah and Jerusalem were in danger of being destroyed. He told Isaiah that Sennacharib had ridiculed their God. He said, "it may be that the Lord will hear all the words of the field commander ...sent to ridicule the living God..." (19:4).

God's comforting words were heard when Isaiah said, "Tell your master, this is what the Lord says: Do not be afraid of what you have heard...I have heard your prayer concerning Sennacherib King of Assyria" (19:5, 20). "...if we ask anything according to His will, He hears us" (I John 5:14).

My prayer: Lord, it is amazing how You keep up with all the needs of Your people and provide exactly that which fits each situation. I praise You and honor You and depend on You to meet my needs.

Day 3: God's Word Brings Change

Read II KINGS Chapters 22-23

While repairing the temple, the high priest found God's Word. He had it taken to the King who was overwhelmed at learning of God's judgment on Israel for its idolatry. The King responded immediately with a vigorous campaign to rid Israel of idolatry.

This campaign did not prevent God's judgment of Israel. It did delay the judgment because of Josiah's response to God's Word. Josiah rid Israel of "...mediums and spiritists, the household gods, the idols and all other detestable things...this he did to fulfill the requirements of the Law written in the book...with all his soul and with all his strength..." (23:24-25).

This reform changed the lives of children who would have been sacrificed to pagan gods. God's Word brought reform that changed the timing of God's judgment. God told Josiah that "...because you tore Your robes and wept in my presence, I have heard You, declares the Lord...therefore...Your eyes will not see all the disaster I am going to bring on this place" (23:19-20). "Blessed are they whose ways are blameless, who walk according to the Law of the Lord" (Psalms 119:1).

My prayer: Help my life change to fit Your word and Your truth. Give me grace upon grace to serve according to Your word.

Day 4: Nebuchadnezzar – God's Tool

Read II KINGS Chapters 24-25

Nebuchadnezzar became God's tool which made him Israel's enemy. Israel opposed God and continued to worship false gods. God sent Nebuchadnezzar "...to destroy Judah, in accordance with the word of the Lord proclaimed by his servants the prophets. Surely these things happened to Judah according to the Lord's command, in order to remove them from His presence because...Manasseh...had filled Jerusalem with innocent blood, and the Lord was not willing to forgive" (24:2-4).

On April 2, 2012, the T.V. news reported a man was arrested for publicly reading the Bible in a legally accepted place. It appears that America has become an enemy of God among its leadership. The two things that caused God to bring judgment on Israel were idolatry and violence. When any nation rejects God and worships false gods it will become violent. Noah's flood came because of violence. "Now the earth was corrupt in God's sight and was full of violence" (Genesis 6:11). America must return to Jehovah-God or have God as an enemy.

My prayer: Lord bring conviction and a renewal to the churches of America so that a revival can bring it back to serving You.

Day 5: Christ's Father Was Not Human

Read I CHRONICLES Chapters 1-3

I Chronicles is a good example of God's bookkeeping. The Chronicles are almost exclusively concerned with the Kings of Judah and skips over many Kings of the Northern Kingdom. Chronicles is concerned more with the Temple in Jerusalem and its priesthood. This is the place where God's Son will arrive.

In I Chronicles 2:3 and following, the lineage of Judah is the main emphasis. David and Jesus are from the tribe of Judah. God made sure man can trace Christ's human heritage so no fake Messiah could confuse mankind. The Holy Spirit did not hide the truth about Christ's ancestors. They were ordinary men with sinful natures. "Er, Judah's firstborn, was wicked in the Lord's sight; so the Lord put him to death" (2:3). Judah himself was immoral. Judah fathered two sons by his daughter-in-law.

Jesus was the perfect man because He was born of a virgin and had no human father. He did not and could not inherit Adam's sinful nature.

My prayer: I praise You Lord for sending Your Son to be perfect so He could restore me to have fellowship with You. Help me share the good news.

Day 6: Pain Changed to Gain

Read I CHRONICLES Chapters 4-6

The name "Jabez" sounds like the Hebrew word for "pain" or "to grieve." It appears that Jabez had a difficult start in life. He may have had a difficult birth with all sorts of side effects. He may have been a child that didn't have much promise in life, either because of physical problems or just a very slow start. But without question there was more to him than meets the eye. "Jabez was more honorable than his brothers...Jabez cried out to the God of Israel, 'Oh, that You would bless me and enlarge my territory! Let Your hand be with me, and keep me from harm so that I will be free from pain.' And God granted his request" (4:9-10).

Jabez learned the source of all blessings--God. He not only learned the source of all blessings but he trusted and believed enough to seek those blessings from him by faith. God responded to his faith and his lifestyle and gave him his request. It is not wrong to ask for God's blessings.

My prayer: Thank You for answering prayer and providing grace to meet our needs. Thank You for being a prayer answering God.

Day 7: Gatekeepers

Read I CHRONICLES Chapters 7-9

The Temple was filled with valuable objects. The utensils used in worship were made of gold and bronze. The shields hanging on the walls were gold. The tables and much of the walls were covered in gold. The bread, the Ark and the Holy of Holies were sacred and were not to be touched or entered except by the priests who had been anointed and cleansed. To protect the Temple from being robbed or defiled God established gatekeepers to guard the entrances into the Temple. "They would spend the night stationed around the house of God, because they had to guard it; and they had charge of the key for opening it each morning" (9:27).

Christians are the gatekeeper to keep their temple from being defiled and their joy from being robbed. "Do you not know that Your body is a temple of the Holy Spirit, who is in You, whom You have received from God? …therefore, honor God with Your body" (I Corinthians 6:19-20). A believer's temple houses the most sacred and valuable object in creation – his Holy Spirit filled soul.

My prayer: Give me strength, wisdom and knowledge to know what to keep out of my life that robs me of joy and steals the power of a pure heart. I praise You for Your Word to guide me in the direction that brings me to Your riches.

Yearly Devotions – Week 19

Day 1: God's Security Program

Read I CHRONICLES Chapters 10-12

We know of two reasons God established Israel. He used Israel to bring mankind the Bible and the Lord Jesus. Israel's existence indicates the timing of Christ's second coming also. As soon as God formed Israel through Abraham Satan attempted to destroy and defile its lineage. God's protection is seen at every turn. God intervened and sent Ishmael away. He kept Sarah from marrying Pharaoh. He provided a ram and preserved Isaac. Over and over God protected Abraham and the nation of Israel.

God provided David with a powerful army to establish Israel as a nation. God sent mighty warriors to strengthen and empower David to lead Israel to greatness. For Israel to need an army created by God shows there are satanic forces in the world. Every person needs God's protection. "Day after day men came to help David, until he had a great army, like the army of God" (12:22). Every believer today has the strength and power of the Holy Spirit as his army. "…the one who is in you is greater than the one who is in the world" (I John 4:4).

My prayer: Thank You Lord for not only saving me but living through me in the person of the Holy Spirit. I yield to His control and rely on Him to keep me secure for eternity and in this world.

Day 2: Worship Exposes the Heart

Read I CHRONICLES Chapters 13-16

David was overjoyed after God established him as King and led Israel to defeat its enemies. After defeating his enemies he concentrated on spiritual matters. "So David did as God commanded him, and they struck down the Philistine army...and the Lord made all the nations fear him" (14:16-17). He learned how to worship in a way that pleased the Lord.

His worship consisted of humility by acknowledging that God was the reason he had defeated his enemies and became King of a peaceful nation. He abandoned any pretense of dignity and lost himself in worship. He became uninhibited in his praise of God.

The flesh does not like God getting all the attention and praise. The flesh resents being humbled before a Holy God. This became obvious when Michal, David's wife, was embarrassed by David's worship. "And when she saw King David dancing and celebrating, she despised him in her heart" (15:29).

My prayer: Lord, help me worship You in humility and seek to honor and glorify You. Teach me to worship like David in my heart and actions.

Day 3: The Source of Success

Read I CHRONICLES Chapters 17-19

Twice in these three chapters the Bible states "the Lord gave David victory everywhere he went" (18:6, 13). David wanted to honor God by building a temple to worship Him in. He broke out into praise when he heard God tell him that "I will also subdue all your enemies...I will raise up your offspring to succeed you...his throne will be established forever" (17:10, 11, 14).

It took two things for success to take place. It took an obedient servant of God and God who works through a person committed to Him. David's commitment to please and honor God is seen by what he did with his success. When he brought the articles of gold and silver home from defeating his enemies "…King David dedicated these articles to the Lord, as he had done with the silver and gold he had taken from all these nations…" (18:11) "Every good gift and every perfect gift is from above, and cometh down from the Father of lights…" (James 1:17).

My prayer: My desire is to be open and obedient to You Lord so You can cause me to experience Your success. Teach me to be a yielded servant seeking Your blessings.

Day 4: Leave More than Money

Read I CHRONICLES Chapters 20-23

It's good to leave a good amount of money for Your family when You die. David left more than money. He left an example of faith and zeal to trust God. He did this by killing the giant Goliath. His nephew followed his example when he faced a ferocious giant. When Israel first arrived in Canaan they were afraid of the giants. They said, "…all the people whom we saw in it are men of great stature…we were like grasshoppers…in their sight" (Numbers 13:31, 33). After David killed Goliath giants were no longer feared. "When he taunted Israel, Jonathan son of Shimea, David's brother, killed him" (20:7).

David left material to build a Temple so people could worship. David said, "Therefore I will make preparations for it. So David made extensive preparations before his death" (22:5).

David left a place for his people to worship. He personally paid for Mount Moriah where the Temple was built and where Christ ministered. What better inheritance could a person leave than an example of faith and a true way to worship?

My prayer: I pray that I will leave that which causes my family to have faith and want to worship our Lord and Savior.

Day 5: Godly Order

I CHRONICLES Chapters 24-26

God designed the world to be an orderly place. Paul told the church in Corinth in that "...everything should be done in a fitting and orderly way" (I Corinthians 14:40). God's orderliness is seen as He leads David to organize the priests and Levites for worship. The form of worship reflected the person of God. Confusion and chaos in worship does not reflect the God of the Bible. "...David separated them into divisions for their appointed order of ministering" (24:3).

David organized the musicians, gatekeepers and the ones in charge of the treasury. Music was used to prophesy. David "...set apart some of the sons of Asaph...for the ministry of prophesying, accompanied by harps, lyres and cymbals" (25:1). They "...prophesied, using the harp in thanking and praising the Lord" (25:3). Music is a powerful form of preaching, so "...King David put them in charge...for every matter pertaining to God and for the affairs of the King" (26:32). God designed earth and all living creatures to be organized and productive. There was order and stability until sin entered through Adam and Eve.

My prayer: Lord, provide our nation with Your righteousness so we can have a stable and orderly atmosphere to worship, work, and witness Your greatness.

Day 6: Follow With Diligence

Read I CHRONICLES Chapters 27-29

Diligent means (1.) "hard working" (2.) "showing care and effort" according to the Oxford New Essential Dictionary. David's message to his son Israel was to be diligent in following God. Why? The nation's tenure on the land was dependent on their diligence. David warns Israel to "Be careful to follow all the commands of the Lord Your God, that You may possess this good land and pass it on as an inheritance to Your descendants forever" (28:8).

David warns Solomon that God knows when he is not diligent in his heart to serve Him. David said to Solomon to "…serve Him with whole hearted devotion and with a willing mind, for the Lord searches every heart and understands every motive behind the thoughts…if you forsake Him, He will reject You forever" (28:9).

David encouraged diligence in their giving to finance the construction of the Temple. He reminds Israel it all belongs to God anyway. David prayed, "O Lord our God, as for all this abundance that we have provided for building You a Temple for Your holy name, it comes from Your hand, and all of it belongs to You" (29:16).

My prayer: Dear Lord cleanse my heart and fill it with a love and devotion that creates in me a devotion and dedication to serve You.

Day 7: A Carte Blanche Prayer

Read II CHRONICLES Chapters 1-4

"Carte Blanche" means "unlimited power to decide" or "full discretionary power given to a person." "God offered

Solomon the grand prize of all the spiritual lotteries of all time when He said, "Ask for whatever you want Me to give You" (1:7). Solomon's choice of the prizes was one that opened the door to many more prizes. He asked God to "Give me wisdom and knowledge..." (1:10). God told him he had hit the jackpot of all answered prayers. God said to Solomon, "since this is your heart's desire and you have not asked for wealth, riches, or honor...therefore, wisdom and knowledge will be given to You. And I will also give you wealth, riches and honor..." (1:11, 12).

God still offers to us believers a Carte Blanche prayer when He says that He is "...able to do exceeding abundantly above all that we ask or think, according to the power that worketh in us..." (Ephesians 3:20 KVJ). "If any of you lack wisdom, let him ask of God, that giveth to all men liberally and up-braideth not, and it shall be given him" (James 1:5 KJV).

My prayer: Thank You Lord for answering sincere and Biblical prayer. I ask from the depth of my heart for Your wisdom and guidance in all that I attempt to do. Thank You for giving it to me as You said, "If we ask anything according to His will, He heareth us..." (I John 5:14 KJV)

Yearly Devotions – Week 20

Day 1: Can God Live On Earth

Read II CHRONICLES Chapters 5-6

Solomon asked the question that all men ask in different ways. He prayed, "But will God really dwell on earth with men? The heavens, even the highest heavens, cannot contain You" (6:18). The Ark was the sacred object that symbolized God's presence in Israel. The Ten Commandments within it represented the Law of God and His demand for holiness.

When God did show up in all His glory it overwhelmed the priests and all of the people. "...they raised their voices in praise to the Lord and sang: 'He is good; His love endures forever. Then the Temple of the Lord was filled with a cloud, and the priests could not perform their service because of the cloud, for the glory of the Lord filled the Temple of God" (5:13). God's glory and presence stopped the worship service.

God returned years later in a different way. Can God really dwell on earth? Yes! "The Word became flesh and made His dwelling among us" (John 1:14). "He was in the world, and though the world was made through Him, the world did not recognize Him" (John 1:10).

My prayer: Lord, I praise You for not only creating us but living in us through the Holy Spirit. Thank You for being on earth now in my life and all who have Christ.

Day 2: All Believers in Heaven Will Be Richer Than Solomon

Read II CHRONICLES Chapters 7-10

"The book of Revelation says, "...To Him who loved us and washed us from our sins in His own blood, and has made us kings and priests to His God and Father, to Him be glory and dominion forever and ever. Amen" (Revelation 1:6).

The Apostle John's description of heaven states that "...the city was pure gold, like clear glass...And the street of the city was pure gold, like transparent glass" (Revelation 21:18, 21).

Believers in heaven will be wiser than Solomon. That is something that would impress the queen of Sheba. If she was impressed with Solomon she will be overwhelmed in eternity. Listen as she boasts of Solomon. She said, "...not even half the greatness of Your wisdom was told to me...how happy Your officials, who continually stand before You and hear Your wisdom" (9:6, 7)!

Solomon's acquisition of gold will be nothing compared to what believers will have in heaven. "The weight of the gold that Solomon received yearly was 666 talents (25 tons)..." (9:13). Gold is something You walk on in heaven. The greatest treasure in heaven is the nail-scared hands, however.

My prayer: I praise You and worship You in anticipation of the riches in heaven and the blessings on earth. Thank You for leaving a description of the joy to come and the contentment I have now. Help me share the riches of heaven with the poverty of this world.

Day 3: Thrive in Obedience and Strive in Disobedience

Read II CHRONICLES Chapters 11-13

Rehoboam behaved badly at the beginning of his reign. He corrected himself and gained power and prestige. Many Israelites from the northern tribes came to Judah to worship. "They strengthened the kingdom of Judah and supported Rehoboam, son of Solomon three years, working in the ways of David and Solomon during this time" (11:17).

Terrible and disappointing words follow his three years of obedience. "After Rehoboam's position as King was established and he became strong, he and all Israel with him abandoned the Law of the Lord" (12:1). Then Shishak, King of Egypt, attacked Jerusalem. Shemaiah brought God's word to Rehoboam stating that, "This is what the Lord says, 'You have abandoned Me; therefore, I now abandoned You to Sheshak" (12:5). When Rehoboam repented God blessed him and said, "My wrath will not be poured out on Jerusalem through Shishak" (12:7). Obedience always causes the faithful follower to thrive.

My prayer: I seek Your blessing by walking in Your will. Help me to seek You Lord and Your righteousness and accept the addition of supplies You provide.

Day 4: Keeping the Peace

Read II CHRONICLES Chapters 14-18

Peace comes from God in the hearts and lives of people. King Asa led Israel to worship Jehovah-God alone. "They sought God eagerly, and He was found by them. So the Lord gave them rest on every side" (15:15). "There was no more war until the thirty-fifth year of Asa's reign" (15:19). As long as Asa relied on the Lord for his supplies and protection his people live in peace. Later in his life he sought human help instead of God's. When he did that, his people no longer lived in peace. Believers must trust God for all their needs. "For the eyes of the Lord range throughout the earth to strengthen those whose hearts are fully committed to Him" (16:9).

Asa forgot that it was God who made his kingdom powerful and peaceful. He still worshipped the Lord but became arrogant and prideful. He lost his enthusiasm for the Lord. God said to him, "You have done a foolish thing, and from now on You will be at war" (16:9). "Do not be anxious about anything, but in everything, by prayer and petition, with thanksgiving, present Your requests to God...And the peace of God...will guard Your hearts and Your minds in Christ Jesus" (Philippians 4:6-7).

My prayer: Lord, again, I claim Matthew 6:33 and rely on what You chose to provide for my family. Thank You for always taking care of us.

Day 5: God's Courtroom is Fair

Read II CHRONICLES Chapters 19-22

The American courts were established with Biblical principles of fairness. Every person has a right in America to face their accuser and defend themselves. No matter what a person has done he is to be treated humanely and with dignity. Judges are to be neutral and fair in their interpretation of the Law. These principles are found only in the Word of God.

The Old Testament promotes fairness when we read of Jehoshaphat appointing judges. He said they were to remember to, "...consider carefully what You do, because You are not judging for man but for the Lord, who is with You whenever You give a verdict. Now let the fear of the Lord be upon You. Judge carefully, for with the Lord our God there is no injustice or partiality or bribery" (19:6-7).

God's courtroom in eternity will be fair because, "...the Lord Jesus Christ...will judge the living and the dead at His appearing..." (II Timothy 4:1). "...in that day when God will judge the secrets of men by Jesus Christ..." (Romans 2:16).

My prayer: Thank You Lord for being my judge and advocate. I praise You from knowing that You are fair and merciful. Thank You for paying for my sin with Your shed blood.

Day 6: One Person Can Make a Difference

Read II CHRONICLES Chapters 23-25

One person can make a difference for good or bad. Athaliah brought evil to Judah. She was the only woman who ever reigned over Judah. After the death of her son, King Ahaziah, she ruled Judah for six years. She killed all her grandsons except Joash who was hidden as a baby by her daughter, Jehosheba, who was the wife of Jehoiada the priest. Athaliah led Judah to worship Baal. One person can make a difference and her difference was an evil one.

Jehoiada the priest made a difference for good. "Joash did what was right in the eyes of the Lord all the years of Jehoiada the priest." (24:2) "As long as Jehoiada lived, burnt offerings were presented continually in the Temple of the Lord..." (24:14). This priest was buried with the kings "...because of the good he had done in Israel for God and His Temple" (24:16).

Joash started well but ended badly, leading Judah to idolatry. The whole nation suffered because of him. "Because of their guilt, God's anger came upon Judah and Jerusalem" (24:18).

My prayer: Lead me in Your paths so I can be a person who makes a difference. Thank You for heavens power and presence in my life so I can make a difference. Lead our churches to make a difference in the world. "With God nothing is impossible."

Day 7: Pride's Precipice
Read II CHRONICLES Chapters 26-28

A precipice is a "vertical or steep face of a rock, cliff, mountain etc." or a "dangerous situation" according to the dictionary. Biblical wisdom points to a spiritual principle in Proverbs. The warning reads, "Pride goeth before destruction, and a haughty spirit before a fall" (Proverbs 16:18). Pride is described as a "high or overbearing opinion of one's worth or importance." Pride can also be identified as having an attitude or arrogance. Pride can place a person in a position of believing that they can do without God or His help.

Uzziah did well as long as he remained humble and "As long as he sought the Lord, God gave him success" (26:5). "His fame spread far and wide, for he was greatly helped until he became powerful" (26:15).

Uzziah fell off the precipice of pride and paid a high price. "But after Uzziah became powerful, his pride led to his downfall" (26:16). He ignored God's order of worship and "...while he was raging at the priests...leprosy broke out on his forehead" (26:19). Without humility before the Lord the leprosy of pride will hinder God's work in people's lives.

My prayer: Lord, lead me to be Your humble servant at all times.

Yearly Devotions – Week 21

Day 1: Heaps of Response

Read II CHRONICLES Chapters 29-31

One meaning of "heap" is a large amount or quantity of something. When a person truly believes in the Lord he must turn away from something else. He will then turn to the Lord with all his heart. There will be a love for the Lord built on the foundation of faith in Christ. To have faith in the Lord means the absolute transference of trust from one's self to the Lord. When that transference takes place there will be a large amount of response as seen in Judah.

The first response when turning to Jesus will be what Judah did when they returned to God. "They brought out to the court yard of the Lord's temple everything unclean that they found in the temple of the Lord" (29:16). When our bodies become the temple of the Holy Spirit there will be a removal of that which defiles.

The second response of Judah was to be generous in tithing. "The men of Israel and Judah...brought a tithe...to the Lord...and they piled them in heaps" (31:6). Real faith always responds with action. Faith that doesn't produce works is not real faith and is a dead faith.

My prayer: Lord keep my heart focused on You so that my faith will grow and I will have heaps of works.

Day 2: God Will Not Be Mocked

Read II CHRONICLES Chapters 32-33

Paul's statement in the past is still true today. He said, "Do not be deceived: God cannot be mocked. A man reaps what he sows. The one who sows to please his sinful nature, from that nature will reap destruction; the one who sows to please the Spirit, from the Spirit will reap eternal life" (Galatians 6:7-8). This is true of an individual or a nation. America is in grave danger by those attempting to remove God from the market place and the governing process. America is in danger because of the secular movement to deny and mock our Christian heritage.

Sennacherib did not get by with mocking God. He said, "...no god of any nation or kingdom has been able to deliver his people from my hand..." (32:15). "They spoke about the God of Jerusalem as they did about the gods of the other peoples of the world..." (32:19). Hezekiah's response is what we need today. He said, "Be strong and courageous. Do not be afraid or discouraged...for there is a greater power with us than with him" (32:7). God was not mocked. He "...sent an angel, who annihilated all the fighting men...of the Assyrian King" (32:21).

My prayer: *Thank You Lord for allowing me to know the truth and receive salvation and an eternal existence that is beyond any experience here on earth. I do pray that Your Spirit would be drawing our nation back to humbly following Your righteousness.*

Day 3: Words That Terrify

Read II CHRONICLES Chapters 34-36

The words, "we've done all we can do," can be terrifying when they come for a doctor who has just treated a loved one. Usually those words imply death is imminent and a person should prepare to meet God. The nation of Israel had a spiritual sickness. They couldn't resist worshipping idols.

They would repent and worship right for a while and then return to idols. "The Lord, the God of their Fathers, sent word to them through His messengers again and again, because He had pity on His people and on His dwelling place. But they mocked God's messengers, despised His words and scoffed at His prophets until the wrath of the Lord was aroused against His people and there was no remedy" (36:15-16). "No remedy" are terrifying words.

Jesus' most terrifying words were in response to religious leaders determined denial of the truth. This was like Israel of old. Jesus said, "I tell You the truth, all the sins and blasphemies of men will be forgiven them. But whoever blasphemes against the Holy Spirit will never be forgiven, he is guilty of an eternal sin" (Mark 3:28-29). "...Now is the time of God's favor, now is the day of salvation" (II Corinthians 6:20).

My prayer: I can only praise You for providing a way of escape for all men so they don't have to hear those terrifying words. Give me a spirit to be a faithful messenger in spite of what people say or do.

Day 4: Who is Keeping Record?
Read EZRA Chapters 1-3

To serve as a priest or participate in Temple worship, a person had to prove they were an Israelite. They had to prove they were born of a priestly family to serve in the Temple. Once a person proved he was born into the proper priestly family his station in life became clear and had purpose. Someone had to keep the records of those who were born into the priesthood. If a person had no record of his birth, he lost the privilege of participating or serving in Temple worship. Such a loss would be devastating. These were awful words, "....they could not show that their families were descended from Israel...and from among the priests..." (2:59, 61). "These searched for their family records, but they could not find them and so were excluded from the priesthood as unclean" (2:62).

A correct record must be kept to enter heaven and New Jerusalem. A person's name must be written in the Lamb's book of life through the "New birth." "Nothing impure will ever enter it, nor will anyone who does what is shameful or deceitful, but only those whose names are written in the Lamb's book of life" (Revelation 21:27). God keeps record of those who are born-again.

My prayer: Lord, I truly rejoice that my name is written down in heaven as You said in (Luke 10:20). Thank You for saving me and giving me a heavenly home in the future and a fulfilling life now.

Day 5: Perseverance Pays Off in God's Time

Read EZRA Chapters 4-8

"The Cyrus Cylinder, an inscription on a clay barrel discovered in Babylon in 1879, documents Cyrus's policy of religious tolerance and liberation...Cyrus was determined to be a benevolent, rather than a heavy-handed ruler...in his own words, 'gathered all their inhabitants and returned (to them) their dwellings.'" (Arch. Bible)

The Jews began rebuilding the Temple in 536 B.C. under King Cyrus. They stopped construction when faced with strong opposition. Sixteen years later, Darius I allowed them to resume rebuilding the Temple. They restored the Temple but the city walls were still in ruins until 445 B.C. when Artaxerxes commissioned Nehemiah to rebuild them.

The Jews struggled to maintain their rebuilding of Jerusalem. It took years to complete their goals of restoring the Temple and building the walls. Ezra gave God the glory for his success. He said, "Praise be to the Lord, the God of our fathers...who has extended His good favor..." (7:27, 28). The work was done in God's time with God's men in God's way. It is still true today.

My prayer: It is a joy to serve You Lord to see how You get things done in spite of Satan's opposition and our weakness. Give me the faith to trust You to get Your work done in Your way and in Your time.

Day 6: Repentance Results in Rectification

Read EZRA Chapters 9-10

To rectify something means to make right what was wrong. The Israelites had disobeyed God and married pagan women. God had commanded them to destroy these nations who had become so perverse that they killed their own children as acts of worship. God said, "...thou shalt smite them, and utterly destroy them...nor show mercy unto them...neither shalt thou make marriages with them..." (Deuteronomy 7:2, 3). "And thou take of their daughters unto thy sons, and their daughters go a-whoring after their gods, and make thy sons go a-whoring after their gods" (Exodus 34:16). "For thou shalt worship no other god: For the Lord, whose name is jealous, is a jealous God" (Exodus 34:14).

When Ezra reminded them of being a conquered nation because of the sin of idolatry, they repented and then corrected their behavior. Ezra told them to "...separate yourselves from the peoples around you and from your foreign wives" (10:11). The people replied, "You are right! We must do as you say" (10:12). True repentance will always cause a person to rectify the wrong done by him or her.

My prayer: Teach me to know when I am marrying my thoughts to the world and help me to separate myself from pagan thoughts and idols. Thank You for Your mercy when I do fail You. I claim (I John 1:9) where You said, "If we confess our sins, He is faithful and just to forgive us our sins, and to cleanse us from all unrighteousness."

Day 7: Gates Are Where You Enter

Read NEHMIAH Chapters 1-3

Gates were very important in Biblical times because a walled city had to have an entrance way. Walls protected the city. The gates let the citizens in but kept the enemy out. Chapters one through three suggest that most of the rebuilding was concentrated on the gates, as enemy assaults would have focused on these structures. There are ten gates listed in chapter three. The families living around those gates worked diligently to restore them. Each gate was named because of different activities around them or because of their location.

Jesus said the gate You go through is very important. He said there were two gates to go through to enter an eternal abode. He said there was a narrow gate and a wide gate. "Enter through the narrow gate. For wide is the gate and broad is the road that leads to destruction, and many enter through it. But small is the gate and narrow the road that leads to life and only a few find it" (Matthew 7:13). The right road leads to the twelve gates that "were twelve pearls, each gate made of a single pearl" (Revelation 21:21).

My prayer: Thank You Lord for providing light through Your word so I could go through the right gate. Thank You that You have such a safe place to live.

Yearly Devotions – Week 22

Day 1: Opposition's Motive

Read NEHEMIAH Chapters 4-7

Why would anyone oppose someone doing a good work? Why would Tobiah, Sanballat and Geshem oppose the rebuilding of Jerusalem? Their opposition was not religious. It was possibly political and economical. The Arabs, led by Geshem, were probably afraid that a strong Jewish city would cut into their trade enterprise. Tobiah and Sanballat, who were governors of their cities, were afraid of losing political clout with the Persians.

When Judas opposed Mary anointing Jesus with a pound of ointment of spikenard he had an evil motive. She was doing a great work. Jesus defended her. He said, "...let her alone: against the day of My burying hath she kept this" (John 12:7). John explained Judas' motive. He said, "...not that he cared for the poor; but because he was a thief, and had the bag, and bare (stole) what was put therein" (John 12:6).

Jesus is the only person who ever lived who always had a pure motive. "For the Son of Man is come to seek and to save that which was lost" (Luke 19:10).

My prayer: I praise You for always having my best interest at heart. I ask that You cleanse my heart to keep my motives pure and serve to honor You.

Day 2: Strength's Source

Read NEHEMIAH Chapters 8-9

We are told to "take one day at a time." There are times in life when people say, "I need strength to go on." Where did the Israelites go for their strength to continue as God's people? They were a subjugated people by a powerful pagan nation. Where did they go for their strength? "The Levites...instructed the people in the Law while the people were standing there" (8:7). How did that affect them? "For all the people had been weeping as they listened to the words of the Law" (8:9). They were convicted of their sin.

Strength comes from knowing the truth. To learn the truth of God is a sacred thing. The Israelites were told, "this day is sacred to the Lord Your God. Do not mourn or weep...Do not grieve, for the joy of the Lord is your strength" (8:9, 1). "Then all the people went away...to celebrate with great joy, because they now understood the words that had been made known to them" (8:12). Jesus said, "Do not think that I have come to abolish the Law or the prophets, I have not come to abolish them but to fulfill them" (Matthew 5:17).

My prayer: Thank You for Your word which is truth and gives meaning to why I am alive. Fill me with Your Holy Spirit and joy.

Day 3: Music Matters

Read NEHEMIAH Chapters 10-12

After Israel committed to serving the Lord again and repented of their waywardness, they were ready to sing. Sin and sadness are not conducive to singing and rejoicing in the Lord.

Music was a big part in every aspect of Israel's life. Music effects the emotions and reflects a person's spiritual condition. It reflects a person's concept of God and life. Music can be uplifting or destructive. God used music to tear down the walls of Jericho. David used music to help King Saul. David used music to bring the Ark to Jerusalem.

A number of scholars believe Satan had the lead role of music in heaven. It says of him that "...thy tabrets (tambourines) and of thy pipes (organs) was prepared in thee in the day that thou wast created" (Ezekiel 28:13 KJV). It indicates music flowed from his body as he moved about. It was not unusual for Nehemiah to assign "...two large choirs to give thanks...one was to proceed on top of the wall to the right...the second proceeded in the opposite direction" (12:31, 38). Music either leads to worship the Lord or away from Him.

My prayer: Thank You for giving me the desire to sing praises to You because of Your grace and mercy. I praise You because of Your care and kindness.

Day 4: Marriages That Shaped Nations

Read NEHEMIAH Chapter 13 and ESTHER Chapter 1

It is interesting to note that the book of Nehemiah closes with marriages that impacted Israel. Esther opens with a marriage that created a national crisis because of a drunken husband and a defiant wife.

Nehemiah reported that the priests and men of Israel married pagan wives who influenced Israel to worship idols. Nehemiah rebuked the priests and men. "He (Solomon) was loved by His God, and God made him King over all Israel, but even he was led into sin by foreign women. Must we hear now that You to are doing all this terrible wickedness and are being unfaithful to our God by marrying foreign women (13:26, 27)?

When queen Vashti disobeyed King Xerxes Memucan said, "Queen Vashti has done wrong, not only against the King but also against all nobles and the peoples of all the provinces..." (1:6). Marriages do affect nations and that is why Paul said, "Do not be yoked together with unbelievers. For what do righteousness and wickedness have in common" (II Corinthians 6:14)?

My prayer: Thank You for making marriage a blessed thing through Jesus. His sacrifice for His bride models for every husband his relationship to his wife.

Day 5: No Need to Panic

Read ESTHER Chapters 2-4

Israel's death sentence had been announced and a date set for their execution. They wanted a remedy and were helpless to protect themselves. Unknown to them God was at work to rescue them. The banquet where queen Vashti refused to obey king Xerxes caused Esther to become queen. Mordecai's instruction to conceal her nationality was important. Mordecai's informing the king of a death plot against him was significant. It would have been difficult to see how all these incidents were connected at the time. Another significant sign of God's watch care was the date of the edict to kill them. The edict went out on the thirteenth day of the first month which was the eve of the Passover. This should have reminded them of God's watch care even though He is not mentioned.

Every person born on this planet has an edict of their death sentence. "And as it is appointed unto men once to die, but after this the judgment" (Hebrews 9:27). No need to panic because "...Christ was once offered to bear the sins of many..." (Hebrews 9:28). "For whosoever shall call upon the name of the Lord shall be saved" (Romans 10:13).

My prayer: I ask for Your protection while on earth and Your reception when I leave this earth. Thank You for Your promise of eternal life in Christ.

Day 6: Hatred Hurts the Hater

Read ESTHER Chapters 5-8

There are hate crime laws today that are supposed to keep acts of hatred down. A criminal that steals hates the fact someone owns something he wants and doesn't have. Haman hated the fact that he didn't have the adoration and respect of Mordecai. That hatred led to his demise.

Haman's hatred was the driving force in his life. His hatred led him to try to destroy Mordecai and his people. Mordecai's refusal to bow reminded him he was not to be worshiped or revered. What Haman did not know was that his hatred was really towards God who was the reason Mordecai did not bow down in his presence. Haman didn't realize that Mordecai was special to God and that his plotting against Mordecai was taking action against God through God's people. We see this in the Apostle Paul's life when Jesus said to him, "Saul, Saul, why do You persecute Me" (Acts 9:4)?

This hatred consumed Haman and caused him to try to destroy Mordecai. The problem with hatred is that it can never be satisfied. "Hatred stirreth up strife's: but love covereth all sins" (Proverbs 10:12).

My prayer: Lord, please fill me with Your love and remove any hate I might have hidden in my heart. Help me share Your love of all mankind.

Day 7: The Unseen Power

Read ESTHER Chapters 9-10

God's name is not mentioned in Esther but He was there. Esther shows God's faithfulness and watch care over His people. "From beginning to end the reader understands God's hand to be at work to deliver His people from threats of foreign enemies. The events are not 'miraculous' in a supernatural sense, but they suggest divine intervention." (Arch. Study Bible) The events pointing to God's hand are: 1) Vashti refusing to appear before the King, 2) Esther becoming queen and concealing her Jewish heritage, 3) Mordecai reporting a plot to kill the King, and 4) the Kings sleeplessness and having his records read to him, etc. We see God's humor as Haman leads Mordecai through the city praising him for saving the King. God is not mentioned but He is present in the preservation of the Jews.

"But when the plot came to the King's attention, he issued orders that the evil scheme Haman had devised against the Jews should come back on his own head..." (9:25). God is still in control of the world. He is the unseen power in His follower's lives.

My prayer: I praise You for ruling over all authorities and powers. I rejoice that You have provided a way of escape from this presence of the evil-one.

Yearly Devotions – Week 23

Day 1: God is the Subject

Read JOB Chapters 1-4

Paul Johnson states that "The Bible is not a work of reason; it is a work of history, dealing with what are to us mysterious and even inexplicable events. It is concerned with the momentous choices which it pleased God to make." It is essential to understand "...the importance the Jews have always attached to God's unrestricted ownership of creation."[4] The book of Job illustrates and emphasizes the sovereignty of God. His ways are beyond any human reasoning or comprehension. The only way we can understand wisdom is to fear God and obey His commands.

In Job, we see God allowing bad things to happen to a good person. Bad things can happen to good people sometimes because they made bad choices but there are times when only God knows why bad things happen. "...it is important to balance our honest questions with humility and reverence for God...God expects us to be faithful and to trust Him despite our suffering."[5]

My prayer: Teach me to trust You more and to anticipate Your blessings in spite of what the circumstances appear to be. I praise You for Your wisdom and sovereign rule of the world.

---

[4] http://www.goodreads.com/work/quotes/455718-a-history-of-the-jews

[5] NIV Archaeological Study Bible: An Illustrated Walk Through Biblical History and Culture, 2005, Zondervan Corporation.

Day 2: Finding Answers

Read JOB Chapters 5-8

Life is uncertain and there are many questions to be answered when bad things happen. Job and his friends attempted to figure out by reason as to the plight of Job. The use of reason is good, but there are times in life when reason doesn't answer the "Why" of certain events.

Job is convinced his suffering is not the result of his sin. His friend's premise of life is that bad things happen to people because of their sin. Job and his friends debate whether Job's sin caused his suffering. They had some truth but did not have "the" answer to the question they sought. The question they are trying to answer is, "Was Job's suffering from sin?"

Eliphaz was correct when he said, "Blessed is the man whom God corrects; so do not despise the discipline of the Almighty" (5:17). Bildad was correct when he said; "Surely God does not reject a blameless man or strengthen the hands of evil doers" (8:20). These two men found some answers to life but not to Job's suffering. Finding answers to life can only come from the One who created life.

My prayer: Your word is my only hope to discover Your answers to my life. I praise You that You did not leave us without the truth and the hope we have in Christ.

Day 3: The Right Question

Read JOB Chapters 9-12

Job was a man God declared to all of heaven that he was "...blameless and upright, a man who fears God and shuns evil..." (1:8). Job questioned why he was suffering. He suffered emotionally, all his children were killed; physically, he had sores over all of his body; and mentally, as he tried to understand why he suffered so. In the depth of that suffering a question erupted from his soul. It is a question every man should ask. "But how can a mortal be righteous before God" (9:2)?

By asking this question Job acknowledged that God was righteous and that man is not. He believed that God could do no wrong and that man would do evil. The New Testament verifies that truth. "For all have sinned, and come short of the glory of God" (Romans 3:23). Job made a plea for help when he said, "If only there were someone to arbitrate between us..." (9:33). God answered that request with His Son. "For there is one God and one mediator between God and man, the man Christ Jesus, who gave Himself as a ransom for all men..." (I Timothy 2:5).

My prayer: Help me share the "Good News" that a man can be righteous before God through Jesus. Thank You for providing a way to be cleansed from my sin and all of my unrighteousness. Thank You Jesus for paying for my sin with Your blood.

Day 4: Lessons Learned From Languishing

Read JOB Chapters 13-16

Suffering caused Job to see life from a different perspective. He lost everything but his life and his wife. To languish is to "go into decline, waste away, become ill, take sick, go downhill, etc." according to a dictionary. This accurately described Job's experience. He learned how to comfort others. He told his friends to shut-up. "If only You would be altogether silent! For You that would be wisdom" (13:5). He then instructs them to help him by listening to him. "Hear now my argument; listen to the plea of my lips" (13:6). The best thing a person can do for those suffering are to listen to them tell their story.

Job learned to trust God from his suffering. "Though He slays me, yet will I hope in him; ..." (13:15). He came to accept that life was filled with suffering. "Man born of woman is of few days and full of trouble" (14:1). He began to contemplate eternity when he asked, "If a man dies, will he live again" (14:14)? Later, he answers his own question. "And after my skin has been destroyed, yet in my flesh I will see God; ..." (19:26). Job learned what was important in life.

My prayer: Keep my mind fixed on the Lord who is the "author and finisher of my faith." Help me to see what is really important and to discard the distractions of this world. I praise You for the truth found in Your word.

Day 5: A Puzzle of Life

Read JOB Chapters 17-21

The question asked by many is "Why do 'good people' suffer and even die when worthless, evil people seem to flourish and live a long time?" As some scholars have stated, the pagan answered that question in a way that made their gods correctly appear inferior and cheapened human lives. The pagan's approach to solving this puzzle was to attempt to manipulate their deities through ritual and incantations. They relied on magic and ceremonies, not justice and divine purpose.

Job blamed the wrong person for his suffering. He cried out, "Have pity on me, my friends, have pity, for the hand of God has struck me...I know that my Redeemer lives ..." (19:21, 25). Job couldn't figure what was going on but he trusted that God did. He did, however, blame the wrong person for his suffering. He said God's hand struck him when it was Satan's. Satan always attacks those who serve the Lord. "In fact, everyone who wants to live a godly life in Christ Jesus will be persecuted..." (II Timothy 3:12).

My prayer: Lord, I plead with You to keep the evil-one away from me and my family. Block any effort on his part to deceive me into temptations that dishonor You and hurt me. I praise You that You are stronger than the god of this world.

Day 6: Biblical Accuracy

Read JOB Chapters 22-27

The Bible is always accurate when stating earth science. Even Bildad, who understood what was happening to Job, got it right when he talked about the earth. Bildad said, "He spreads out the northern skies, over empty space; He suspends the earth over nothing" (26:7). There is an empty space in the North.

Bildad stated that God put the earth in space and keeps it fixed in its orbit. The world is sustained and kept by God. There is no other explanation. Mark Cahill reminds us that "The earth is located the right distance from the sun...if the earth were any further away from the sun, we would all freeze. Any closer and we would burn up. Even a fractional variance in the earth's position to the sun would make life on earth impossible." "For by Him were all things created..." (Colossians 1:16 KJV). "And He Himself existed before all things and in Him all things consist – cohere, are held together" (Colossians 1:17 Amplified Version). "All things were made by Him; and without Him was not anything made that was made" (John 1:3 KJV).

My prayer: I praise You Lord for Your watch-care over all of earth. I praise You that You will set everything right in Your time.

Day 7: Something Money Can't Buy

Read JOB Chapters 28-31

There are expensive shops where if a person has to ask the price of an item he can't afford it. There is something in life so valuable and its depth so great that it is beyond the purchasing price of anyone. If a person could acquire it he would be able to answer Job's question of why the righteous suffer. Job said, "It cannot be bought with the finest gold, nor can its price be weighed in silver" (28:15).

This valuable treasure can be found in only one place. "God understands the way to it and He alone knows where it dwells" (28:23). Job's suffering caused him to seek God and His answer to why the righteous suffer. He discovered philosophy, education or debating weren't the answer. Job's conclusion was that wisdom was the most valuable thing a person could possess if it could be found. God "...looked at wisdom and appraised it; He confirmed it and tested it. And He said to man, 'the fear of the Lord – that is wisdom, and to shun evil is understanding" (28:27-28).

My prayer: No matter what is happening, Lord, I will cling to You and reverence Your person and rely on Your understanding of my situation. Thank You for the truth of Your holiness, love and forgiveness.

Yearly Devotions – Week 24

Day 1: Don't Blame God

Read JOB Chapters 32-34

Don't blame God for everything you say. People should be very cautious when they say, "God told me to tell you..." that is what Elihu said to Job. But when God finally spoke to Job and his friends they learned they were wrong about Job.

Elihu spoke as though he knew what God thought about Job's condition. Elihu was convinced Job suffered because of sin in his life. When you come to the end of Job, you discover Elihu was wrong. What we learned is that God put Job on display in heaven as a righteous man. That act initiated a contest between Satan and God. Elihu could not comprehend the possibility that Job could suffer without having sinned in some way. Elihu said to Job, "But I tell you, in this you are not right..." (33:12). He continued by saying, God "...repays a man for what he has done; he brings upon him what his conduct deserves" (34:11).

People have wrongly believed God was punishing them for a particular sin when a tragic event happened in their life. A tragedy sometimes has no explanation until we get on the other side.

My prayer: Help me not to judge people who have heartaches that I don't know anything about. Give me compassion and love for those who suffer. Thank You for Your mercy and longsuffering in my life.

Day 2: Trust the Bible

Read JOB Chapters 35-38

A Christian's authority for his doctrine and behavior comes from the Bible. It is reliable and always reveals God as holy, righteous and almighty. Can the Bible be trusted? It must be accurate in every category. It must be correct scientifically, historically and theologically. An example of this accuracy is seen in these passages of Scripture.

"This passage reveals a sophisticated observation of atmospheric conditions and their effects: the evaporation and distillation of water for rain, the clouds as holders of moisture and the cyclonic behavior of clouds." (Arch. Study Bible) "He draws up the drops of water, which distill as rain to the streams, the clouds pour down their moisture and abundant showers fall on mankind" (Job 36:27-28). "He loads the clouds with moisture; He scatters His lightening through them" (37:11). Moisture is drawn up into clouds until the right condition and then rain falls. The pagan gods cannot control the weather alone according to pagan myths. God alone created the earth. He asks, "Where were you when I laid the earth's foundation" (38:4)?

My prayer: Thank You for giving us an authoritative account to guide and give us light. Give me wisdom to understand it and faith to believe it and follow its instruction.

Day 3: The Creator Knows His Creation

Read JOB Chapters 39-42

Those who believe in evolution or that God is not interested in what goes on in His created world are wrong. When God finally revealed Himself to Job and his friends, He let them know they didn't understand the events in Job's life. God let them know it was impossible to compare themselves with Him. He said, "Do you know the laws of the heavens" (38:33)? God knew their answer would be "No".

God let them know He designed and maintained life on this planet. He gave details of the created creatures and how He cared for them. He listed the lion and it's stalking to get food. He described goats that lived on mountains. He reminded them that the donkey lived in barren areas. God listed the wild ox, ostrich, stork, horse and the hawk. He detailed the intimate activity of survival for each one. He described what is probably the hippopotamus in a way that revealed again that He knows all of His creation. Job and his friends could not answer God nor deny His authority to do with His creation whatever He wanted to do.

My prayer: It is a blessing to have You Lord in charge of the world and my life. Thank You for letting us know You are overseeing our lives and that You are interested in personally taking care of us.

Day 4: Man's Value

Read PSALMS Chapters 1-9

If a person's body could have all the chemicals extracted from it the value of the chemicals would not be worth the effort. Men's bodies that have performed great deeds in history had no more value than any other man. Where does a man's value come from?

The Psalmist answers that question with another question and answer. "What is man that You are mindful of him, the son of man that You care for him." His answer is that, "You (God) made him a little lower than the heavenly beings (Angels) and crowned him with glory and honor" (8:4-5). Man's value comes from being created in God's image. "God said, 'Let us make man in our image,' in our likeness…" (Genesis 1:26).

Man gets his value from being created in God's image and from his purpose in life. "You made him ruler over the works of Your hands; You put everything under his feet..." (8:6). Man's value is seen in the fact that God holds him accountable." He (God) will judge the world in righteousness" (9:8).

My prayer: You are worthy to be praised and worshipped for Your holy purpose for all mankind. I plead with You to reveal to all men their sacredness in Your plan to bless Your creation. Thank You for the privilege of being one of Your creations.

Day 5: The Gospel According to Psalms

Read PSALMS Chapters 10-18

In Psalms man is seen as a sinner. "The Lord looks down from heaven on the sons of men to see if there is any who understand, any who seek God" (14:2). What God sees describes man accurately. "All have turned aside, they have together become corrupt; there is no one who does good, not even one" (14:3).

The Psalmist declares that there is only one place to overcome sin. "Keep me safe, O God, for in You I take refuge. I said to the Lord, You are My Lord; apart from You I have no good thing" (16:1-2). The Psalmist is correct to turn to Jehovah-God because He is perfect as seen in Jesus. "As for God, His way is perfect; the Word of the Lord is flawless" (18:30).

God's perfection is established because of the Resurrection. The Psalmist celebrated "because You will not abandon me to the grave..." (16:10). He foretells the Resurrection of Jesus when he said, "...nor will You let Your Holy One see decay" (16:10). He then saw his Resurrection. "...when I awake, I will be satisfied with seeing Your likeness" (17:15).

My prayer: Thank You for loving us for becoming the cure for our sin through Jesus' death and Resurrection. I ask for boldness to share this good news so that many can be saved.

Day 6: The Cross Found in Psalms

Read PSALMS Chapters 19-25

When Jesus met the two people on the Road to Emmaus He rebuked them for not believing the Bible. "And beginning with Moses and all the prophets, He explained to them what was said in all the Scriptures concerning Himself" (Luke 24:27). Psalms 22 gives a vivid picture of Christ on the Cross.

- He died alone for man's sin. "My God, My God, why have You forsaken Me?" (22:1) Many scholars believe Jesus quoted all of Psalm 22 as He hung on the Cross.
- Psalms portrays what the world thought of Christ on the Cross. "But I am a worm and not a man, scorned by men and despised by the people. All who see Me mock Me; they hurl insults…" (22:6-7).
- When men were nailed to the Cross their arms were pulled out of their sockets. "…All My bones are out of joint" (22:14).
- Jesus cried, "I thirst." "…My tongue sticks to the roof of My mouth" (22:15).
- His hands and feet were nailed to the Cross." They have pierced My hands and My feet" (22:16).

My prayer: Lord, there are no words adequate enough to praise You and thank You for dying on the Cross for my sins. It is the greatest gift a God like You could give Your creation. Help me tell others of Your great sacrifice.

Day 7: Secure in God's Presence

Read PSALMS Chapters 26-32

The Psalmist told why he was unafraid and why he could become afraid. He was unafraid when he walked in God's light and salvation. "The Lord is my light and my salvation-whom shall I fear" (27:1)? His question was asked with the expectation of "None" as an answer. He was not afraid of his enemies as long as God was at his side. "...My heart will not fear" (27:3).

There was something that could cause him to lose his courage. If sin came between him and God, he no longer felt secure. Sin separated him from God's fellowship. Adam and Eve experienced that separation. "So He drove out the man: and He placed at the east of the garden of Eden Cherubim, and a flaming sword which turned every way to keep the way of the tree of life" (Genesis 3:24). That is why David said, "...but when You hid Your face, I was dismayed" (30:7).

Courage can be restored. "Then I acknowledged my sin to You...I said I will confess my transgressions to the Lord and You forgave the guilt of my sin" (32:5). "...the Lord's unfailing love surrounds the man who trusts in him."

My prayer: Thank You for being a loving God who forgives my sin. I praise You for being a merciful God who watches out for me.

Yearly Devotions – Week 25

Day 1: God's Conditional Promises

Read PSALMS Chapters 33-37

When God makes a promise He will keep it. As the saying goes, "you can put it in the bank." He usually has some conditions to go with His promises. Why would He do that? He cannot and will not give His blessings to sin and ungodly behavior. "If the Lord delights in a man's way, He makes his steps firm; though he stumbles he will not fall, for the Lord upholds him with His hand" (37:23-24).

What are some of the conditions to receive God's promises? First, a person must seek the Lord. "...those who seek the Lord lack no good thing" (34:10). "Blessed is the nation whose God is the Lord" (33:12). Secondly, a person must trust the Lord. "Trust in the Lord and do good; dwell in the land and enjoy safe pasture" (37:3). Thirdly, "Delight Yourself in the Lord and He will give You the desires of Your heart" (37:4). Fourthly, "Be still before the Lord and wait patiently for Him..." (37:7). When these conditions are met we will see what David saw, "I was Young and now I am old, yet I have never seen the righteous forsaken or their children begging bread" (37:25).

My prayer: I ask for Your strength to fulfill my part in order to receive Your blessings. I know my salvation is Your gift but help me treat Your gift in a way that honors You.

Day 2: God's Got More

Read PSALMS Chapters 38-42

A person gets all of God when they receive Jesus as Lord and Savior. The real challenge is to let Him get all of You. "Do not get drunk on wine, which leads to debauchery. Instead, be filled with the Spirit" (Ephesians 5:18). The Holy Spirit's goal is to control every believer.

A Christian is to strive for perfection. He has a specific time period to strive for it. That is why the Psalmist said, "Show me, O Lord, my life's end and the number of my days; let me know how fleeting is my life" (39:4). When opposing teams compete they have a specific time period to finish the contest. Many times teams lose a game because they run out of time.

Like a team that reminisces about what they should have or could have done to win a game the Psalmist states there could have been more to his life. He said, "Many, O Lord, My God, are the wonders You have done. The things You planned for us no one can recount to You; were I to speak and tell of them, they would be too many to declare" (40:5).

My prayer: _Teach me to number each day to be controlled by the Holy Spirit and fulfill Your plans rather than mine. Thank You for the time You have given me._

Day 3: Victories Come From God

Read PSALMS Chapters 43-49

The fact that God is sovereign and man is frail and finite reveals that any victory in life comes from God. That is true for an individual or nation. The Psalmist acknowledges that by saying that his forefathers victories came from God. "We have heard with our ears, O God; our Fathers have told us what You did in their days, in days long ago. With Your hand You drove out the nations and planted our Fathers; You crushed the peoples and made our Fathers flourish" (44:1-2).

America cannot defeat the terrorist nor solve its economic problems without God. America must remain strong militarily but that alone will not bring victory. The Psalmist knew that to be true of Israel and it is still true for America. He said, "I do not trust in my bow, my sword does not bring me victory; but You give us victory over our enemies" (44:6). The answer to any national crisis is to "Be still, and know that I am God..." (46:10).

My prayer: Help me to turn to You, Lord, first and not "lean unto my own understanding." Give me strength to wait on You to see what You can do.

Day 4: God Stores Our Tears

Read PSALMS Chapters 50-56

God knows our every heartache. He cares about people's suffering. Jesus said to Saul who became Paul who was persecuting Christians, "Saul, Saul, why are You persecuting me" (Acts 9:4)? We see from that that Jesus feels and experiences persecution along with His followers. In fact, He stores our tears when we weep from suffering and pain. The Psalmist referred to the ancient custom of actually storing tears at funerals. He let us know God collects our tears. "You number my wanderings; put my tears into Your bottle, are they not in Your book" (56:8)?

The Zondervan Pictorial Bible Dictionary describes how these tears were stored during the Psalmist's time. "Beautifully designed glass bottles, often found in Egyptian tombs, were used originally for burying some of the tears of the mourners with the deceased" (page 130). It was normal to hire professional mourners that were very dramatic in their expression of grief for a family. The tears saved however, did not come from the professional performers but from the genuine tears of the loved ones. "Cast Your cares on the Lord and He will sustain You..." (55:22).

My prayer: You are a wonderful, personal, holy God that I can have a personal relationship with for which I praise and thank You. Thank You for not leaving me alone on this earth even though I'm now an orphan. Thank You for going with me through the trials of this life.

Day 5: God Strengthens Us Through Trials
Read PSALMS Chapters 57-66

God tests us and then teaches us to strengthen us. We gain confidence in the Lord when we see Him carry us through our trials. Joseph was hated, sold into slavery, put in prison before he became prime minister of Egypt. David was hated and had to flee from King Saul and hide in caves before he became king. Jacob fled from Esau and worked for nothing for twenty years before God made him rich. Moses escaped the wrath of Pharaoh and watched over sheep for forty years before becoming the great law-giver. The Psalmist expresses this truth by saying, "...He has preserved our lives and kept our feet from slipping" (66:9).

The Apostle Peter reminds us that though we go through trials and testing's we will be rewarded and learn more about God's grace. "In this You greatly rejoice, though now for a little while You may have had to suffer grief in all kinds of trials. These have come so that Your faith...may be proved genuine and may result in praise, glory and honor when Jesus Christ is revealed" (I Peter 1:6-7).

My prayer: Lord, increase my faith so I will learn what You have for me as I go through the trials of faith. Open my eyes that I might see Your powerful hand as greater than any burden or circumstance.

Day 6: Goodness is God's Glory

Read PSALMS Chapters 67-71

Whatever God does is right and acceptable and beneficial. When the Psalmist prays for God's judgment on evil people he is asking God to rectify what is wrong. He wants people to see that righteousness will inevitably overcome evil. God's unchanging principle is the Law of sowing and reaping and it will be accomplished. "Do not be deceived: God cannot be mocked. A man reaps what he sows. The one who sows to please his sinful nature, from that nature will reap destruction…" (Galatians 6:7-8).

The Psalmist has given a prayer of imprecation when he says, "…May their eyes be darkened so they cannot see, and their backs be bent forever" (69:23). To pray for someone's destruction is to make an imprecation. These prayers in Psalms were not prayed for vengeance but are "…full of longing for the vindication of the Lord's good name. over and over the psalmist's desire was not personal relief but that the Lord should be seen in His goodness and holiness…there is such a thing as righteous indignation, an attitude which at the least is morally preferable to indifference about evil and human suffering." (Archeological Study Bible) For example: A man who rapes and kills a child should be executed.

My prayer: Dear Lord, I thank You and praise You for teaching me through Your word what is right and wrong. Thank You for always doing the right thing all the time.

Day 7: The Work of Worship

Read PSALMS Chapters 72-77

The Psalmist repeatedly questioned why non-believers did so well. "For I envied the arrogant when I saw the prosperity of the wicked. They have no struggles; their bodies are healthy and strong..." (73:3-4). He did find an answer when he worshiped. "When I tried to understand all this; it was oppressive to me till I entered the sanctuary of God; then I understood their final destiny" (73:16-17).

He reminds God how He was mocked by the wicked. "Rise up, O God, and defend Your cause; remember how fools mock You all day long. Do not ignore the clamor of Your adversaries, the uproar of Your enemies, which rises continually" (74:22-23).

While in deep depression the Psalmist cried out that, "...At night I stretched out untiring hands and my soul refused to be comforted" (77:2). Worship worked for him when he remembered God working in his life. "Then I thought...I will remember the deeds of the Lord...I will meditate on all Your works..." And then he could say, "What God is so great as our God" (77:10, 11, 12, 13).

My prayer: I seek Your presence in worship at home and at church. Help me to remember all of the wondrous things You've done in my life and my families. I praise You because there is no God but You.

Yearly Devotions – Week 26

Day 1: God's Face

Read PSALMS Chapters 78-80

John writes that "No man hath seen God at any time…" (John 1:18). The Apostle Paul describes God as the King of Kings "Who only hath immortality, dwelling in the light which no man can approach unto; whom no man hath seen, nor can see, to whom is honor and power everlasting. Amen (I Timothy 6:16). Humans cannot see God which is alright as long as He can see us. To get a glimpse of God in all His glory would be like looking in the brightest spotlight ever invented. It could cause a person to lose their sight. God's glory is greater than that.

Why does the Psalmist keep repeating the refrain "Restore us, O God; make Your face shine upon us, that we may be saved." (80:3, 7, 19)? We can't see God but He can see us. When His face is shining on a person or nation He is protecting them. Like the sun shining on the earth and giving it life even so God's presence shines and allows men to thrive rather than just survive. His protection and blessings come when His face shines on us. "Then we Your people, the sheep of Your pasture, will praise You forever…" (79:13).

My prayer: The earth needs Your face shining on us again. We do not deserve Your glorious light and Your attention but You have promised to give it when we obey You and live according to Your Holy Spirit's direction.

Day 2: Born Trouble

Read PSALMS Chapters 81-88

An infamous criminal had a tattoo that became famous – "Born to Kill." Without Jesus that is always a possibility for every person. Man's Adamic nature is never far from Cain and his defiance of God. God warned Cain, "If You do what is right will You not be accepted? But if You do not do what is right, sin is crouching at Your door; it desires to have You, but You must master it" (Genesis 4:7). Every person must decide whether to open the door to the "sin crouching at" their door. We are born in trouble because every person is born with an open door to sin. Man is born with an attraction to rebellion and sin. Bonnie and Clyde are more interesting than the quiet couple who spend a life time serving the Lord.

The Psalmist talked about enemies from the outside of one's life but the real trouble is on the inside of one's life. Good News! "In the day of my trouble I will call to You, for You will answer me" (86:7). Good News! God is gracious. "You are forgiving and good, O Lord, abounding in love to all who call to You" (86:5).

My prayer: Lord, I open my door to the Holy Spirit to take control of my life so that You will protect me from the evil-one. "And lead us not into temptation, but deliver us from the evil one." (Matthew 6:13).

Day 3: One Difference Between God and Man

Read PSALMS Chapters 89-93

One difference is that God has always existed and man has a beginning. The Psalmist said, "Your throne was established long ago; You are from all eternity" (93:2). "In the beginning God..." (Genesis 1:1) declares God's pre-existence. In the beginning of what, in the beginning of the creation of life on earth and the universe. The Apostle Paul bears this out. He declares that Jesus created the heavens and the earth. "Who is the image of the invisible God, the firstborn of every creature..." (Colossians 1:15). "Firstborn" is Prototokos in Greek. "The Greek word implied two things, priority to all creation and sovereignty over all creation. Thus he declares that Christ is the sphere in which creation took place or its source; He is the intermediate agent in the creative act...since our Lord existed before all created things, He must be uncreated. Since He is uncreated, He is eternal. Since He is eternal, He is God...[6]"

The Psalmist declares that one difference is that man must die. He asked, "What man can live and not see death (89:48)?" "The length of our days is seventy years – or eighty..." (90:10). "Just as man is destined to die once, and after that to face judgment, so Christ was sacrificed once to take away the sins of many people..." (Hebrews 9:27-28).

My prayer: O Lord, how can I not praise You for dying for me and giving me salvation by Your grace. I am overawed by the thought of spending an eternity with such an awesome God who has always existed.

Day 4: The Two Things That Last Forever
Read PSALMS Chapters 94-102

The Psalmist acknowledges God's eternal existence and that all created things will disappear. "In the beginning You laid the foundations of the earth, and the heavens are the work of Your hands. They will perish, but You remain; they will wear

---

[6] Wuest, Kenneth S., *Wuest's Word Studies from the Greek New Testament, Volume 1*, 1973, 1989, Wm. B. Eerdman's Pub Co., Grand Rapids Michigan 49502, Pg 183

out like a garment" (102:25-26). The Psalmist was scientifically correct! The universe is winding down. The theory of evolution cannot explain the loss of information in a species. There is "a contraction of gene pools, whereas evolution requires a massive expansion of them" (R. Grigg). The Apostle Peter predicted the earth would be diminished. "That day will bring about the destruction of the heavens by fire, and the elements will melt in the heat" (II Peter 3:12).

What two things last forever? God and His Word. The Psalmist declared God's eternal existence in Psalm 102:25-26. Jesus repeats the truth of the Word's indestructibility. He said, "Heaven and earth will pass away, but My words will never pass away" (Matthew 24:35). Jesus also said, "...the heavenly bodies will be shaken...and...when these things begin to take place, stand up and lift up Your heads, because Your redemption is drawing near" (Luke 21:26, 28).

My prayer: Even so come Lord Jesus. It is my heart's desire for You to return to earth and set up Your righteous kingdom. Lord let people see Your glory and Your sovereignty. Thank You for Your Word and Your forgiveness.

Day 5: Children on the Altar

Read PSALMS Chapters 103-106

The most important responsibility a person will ever have is to raise a child to serve the Lord. Their soul will exist eternally somewhere. What a parent teaches a child gives them their value system. Their training will either place them on the altar of humanism or the altar of God. If they are placed on the altar of humanism they are on the altar that worships Satan and his demons.

The Psalmist gave a vivid picture of children placed on Satan's altar. "They sacrificed their sons and their daughters to demons..." (106:37). Parents don't place their children on altars and literally sacrifice them today. If they fail to carry out God's plan to train their children the children end up on pagan altars. Parents are commanded to teach their children about God and His commandments. "Impress them on Your children. Talk about them when You sit at home and when You walk along the road, when You lie down and when You get up" (Deuteronomy 6:7).

My prayer: Thank You for giving me parents who strove to serve You and teach us. I pray for parents as they attempt to teach their children about You. Give them strength, wisdom and Your love so they can impart it to their children.

Day 6: Grateful Hearts Praise God

Read PSALMS Chapters 107-112

Storms of life come unexpectedly and can be overwhelming. God allowed us to have two wonderful girls. They had many emotional storms as teenagers that appeared to be the end of the world. However, the next day the storm was over and everything was calm and normal again.

The Psalmist could not keep from praising God for rescuing him from a storm. He talks about the monstrous waves that appeared to sink the boat. "They mounted up to the heavens and went down to the depths; in their peril their courage melted away. They reeled and staggered like drunken men; they were at their wits end. Then they cried out to the Lord in their trouble...He stilled the storm to a whisper; the waves of the sea were hushed" (107:26-29). That is what Jesus does with our storms of life. When Jesus is in our boat of life He is in the storm with us. Jesus was in the disciples' boat when a storm came. "He got up, rebuked the wind and said to the waves, 'Quiet! Be still!' Then the wind died down and it was completely calm" (Mark 4:39). "Let them sacrifice thank offerings and tell of His works with songs of joy" (107:22).

My prayer: I can only praise You and thank You for the times without number that You brought calm to my life and experience. You truly are the great storm chaser.

Day 7: Scripture In – Holy Life Out
Read PSALMS Chapters 113-119:40

Computers have brought in a new language. They have changed the lifestyles of citizens in every modern country. The terms "Data in – Data out" or "garbage in – garbage out" are now old computer language. These terms illustrate a scriptural truth God spoke of centuries ago. God taught that what a person puts into his mind and heart will eventually come out in his behavior. What a person believes determines his behavior. Normally what a person reads or listens to will shape his thinking.

The Psalmist was aware of this principle when he asked the question "How can a Young man keep his way pure? By living according to Your word...I have hidden Your word in my heart that I might not sin against You" (119:9, 11). He continues, "I will not neglect Your word" (119:16). The Psalmist sees the benefit of being saturated with God's word. "Turn my eyes away from worthless things: preserve my life according to Your word" (119:37). To stay close to the Lord, a person has to stay close to His word.

My prayer: Lord, guide my thoughts to receive what Your word says and then give me the ability to obey Your word. I truly desire to live out Your word and testify to Your grace.

Yearly Devotions – Week 27

Day 1: Troubled But Blessed

Read PSALMS Chapters 119:41-176

Heart-ache, illness and tragedy can come into a person's life in an instant. It may come from a doctor's diagnosis, a telephone call or a policeman knocking on Your door. It is always a shock and disorienting followed by many questions. God's will is not always seen when trouble comes but He gets our attention. The psalmist indicated that when he said, "Before I was afflicted I went astray, but now I obey Your Word" (119:67). He knew God would not let anything come into a person's life that would not be a benefit. He said, "You are good, and what You do is good..." (119:68).

God allows trouble to come to His followers to bring them back to a blessed relationship with Himself. God knows how to rearrange a person's priorities and help people to have a correct perspective of life. God can use a tragedy or a burden to illuminate that which hinders a person's relationship with Him. Jesus used hyperbole to illustrate this principle when He said, "And if thy right hand offends thee, cut it off, and cast it from thee..." (Matthew 5:30).

My prayer: Lord, help me see Your blessings in every event in my life. I plead the blood of Christ as protection from myself and from the evil-one. Thank You for always being good and doing good.

Day 2: Spiritual Contractor

Read PSALMS Chapters 120-133

Contractors can be used to do many things. A spiritual contractor in Psalms 127 is the Lord Himself. He builds homes where people live in peace and harmony. No one can build a home like the Lord God. "Unless the Lord builds the house its builder's labor in vain" (127:1). Jesus said, therefore whosoever heareth these sayings of mine, and doeth them, I will liken him unto a wise man, which built his house upon a rock: And the rain descended, and the floods came, and the winds blew, and beat upon that house, and it fell not: for it was founded upon a rock" (Matthew 7:24-25).

A home is built upon a rock when the couple receives Christ as Lord and Savior. It is built upon a rock when parents pray for and with their children and each other. A home is built on a rock when the whole family worships together at church and at home. The home honors the Lord when it establishes a Godly lifestyle and expresses love in the home.

My prayer: Forgive me when I have failed to carry out Your sayings, Lord. Give me the wisdom and strength to be an encourager of my own children and those I minister to at church.

Day 3: God is Interested All the Time

Read PSALMS Chapters 134-141

God starts with us in life and stays with us through life. God was there when conception took place. King David said, "My frame was not hidden from You when I was made in the secret place. When I was woven together in the depths of the earth, Your eyes saw my unformed body" (139:15-16). Not only is God present at conception but He is present when the fertilized egg becomes an embryo in the womb.

Not only is God with the person in the womb but He knows how long a person's body has been loaned to him. "All the days ordained for me were written in Your book before one of them came to be," David said (139:16). God just leases our body to us for a specific time period that only He knows. God lets us have our body and holds everyone accountable for what we do to it and with it.

God not only starts with us in the womb but stays with us through life. David asks, "Where can I go from Your Spirit? Where can I flee from Your presence" (139:7)? The answer is nowhere!

My prayer: Lord, give Your word with understanding so I will know how to treat this body so it will honor You. Thank You for the privilege of life.

Day 4: What is God Like?
Read PSALMS Chapters 142-148

What is God Like?
- He cares about the helpless. "The Lord watches over the alien and sustains the fatherless and the widow..." (146:9) "The Lord upholds all those who fall and lifts up all who are bowed down." (145:14)
- He is a loving and kind God. "The Lord is gracious and compassionate; slow to anger and rich in love." (145:8) "He heals the broken hearted and binds their wounds." (147:3)
- He can be depended to and keep His word. "The Lord is faithful to all His promises and loving toward all He has made." (145:13)
- He can only do what is right. "The Lord is righteous in all His ways..." (145:17)
- He rewards those who reverence Him. "He fulfills the desires of those who fear Him; He hears their cry and saves them." (145:19) "The Lord delights in those who fear Him, who put their hope in His unfailing love." (147:11)

- He has the right to be feared and worshipped because He created us and is all powerful. "He determines the number of stars and calls them each by name." (147:4)

My prayer: Open my eyes so that I can see what You are really like and guide my mind and heart to know what You're really like. I praise You for being good and righteous and merciful and loving.

Day 5: Kindergarten Theology

Read PSALMS Chapter 149 – PROVERBS Chapter 4

The basic beginner theological truth that a person must learn and believe with a genuine belief is that "The fear of the Lord is the beginning of knowledge, but fools despise wisdom and discipline" (Proverbs 1:7). A person is vulnerable to the deceit of Satan and the temptations of the world if not grounded in God's wisdom and word.

People have the potential to become skeptical and cynical if they do not fear God and obtain His wisdom and knowledge. That is why the writer of Proverbs warned people to "Let love and faithfulness never leave you..." (3:3). If anyone had lost love and faithfulness it appears to be the woman at the well who had five husbands and now lived with a man and was unmarried. Jesus was there to restore her hope of true love and faithfulness. He said, "Indeed, the water I give him will become in him a spring of water welling up to eternal life" (John 4:14). Jesus will restore trust (3:5); humility (3:7); prosperity (3:10); and a sense of being loved (3:12).

My prayer: Lord, help me to listen and learn from Your word how to be what You designed me to be. I trust Your faithfulness and love to give my life meaning and purpose.

Day 6: Freedom's Danger

Read PROVERBS Chapters 5-9

There are signs in yellow and black warning people of "Danger – High powered electrical lines with high voltage" posted at electrical power plants. A person can ignore these signs and enter the plant at their own risk if they choose. That freedom could be deadly. God has posted warning signs telling of danger when people disobey Him. God has given people freedom to make wrong choices.

The writer of Proverbs warns everyone about the consequences of making wrong choices. He says, "At the end of Your life You will groan, when Your flesh and body are spent" (5:11). He describes the wrong attitude toward freedom. "You will say, 'How I hated discipline! How my heart spurned correction! I will not obey my teachers or listen to my instructors" (5:12-13). Paul warned everyone. He said, "…since they did not think it worthwhile to retain the knowledge of God, He gave them over to a depraved mind, to do what ought not to be done. They have become filled with every kind of wickedness, evil, greed and depravity" (Romans 1:28-29).

My prayer: Lord, I seek You to find real freedom. I ask for power not to do the things I want to do and power to do what I don't want to do. Thank You, Jesus, for continuing to the cross after Gethsemane.

Day 7: Fruitful Lips

Read PROVERBS Chapters 10-13

Words have meanings and impact a person's life. A Christian's goal is to bring truth and a blessing with words. Jesus was concerned with what people say. He said, "…the things that come out of the mouth come from the heart, and these make a man unclean. For out of the heart come evil thoughts, murder, adultery, sexual immorality, theft, false testimony, and slander" (Matthew 15:18-19). Proverbs 12:13 correlates with what Jesus said. "An evil man is trapped by his sinful talk..." lips can bring forth bad fruit but it is still a fruit of the lips.

The goal of a Christian is to have lips that bring forth good fruit. Good fruit blesses the lips it comes from and to the hearer. Proverbs says, "...but a righteous man escapes trouble" (12:13). "From the fruit of his lips a man is filled with good things as surely as the work of his hands rewards him" (15:14). "...the tongue of the wise brings healing" (15:8). James said, "Out of the same mouth come praise and cursing. My brothers, this should not be" (James 3:10).

My prayer: Lord, thank You for warning me about what I say. Help guide my mind and my lips to be coordinated and connected to Your will. Thank You for free speech in America.

Yearly Devotions – Week 28

Day 1: Five Benefits of Fearing God

Read PROVERBS Chapters 14-18

Godly leadership in the home should come from the parents, especially the father. Many times a child's first impression of the heavenly Father comes from the earthly father. The prerequisite for the parents to give Godly leadership is to fear God and realize they are accountable to Him.

- When a home fears God there will be a sense of security for the children. "He who fears the Lord has a secure fortress, and for his children it will be a refuge." (14:26)
- When a home fears God there will be a sense of vitality of life permeating it. "The fear of the Lord is a fountain of life, turning a man from the snares of death." (14:27)
- When a home fears God they will know what to do with knowledge. "The fear of the Lord teaches wisdom…" (15:33)
- When a home fears God there will be contentment. "Better a little fear of the Lord than great wealth with turmoil." (15:16)
- When a home fears God it will avoid much heartache. "…through the fear of the Lord a man avoids evil." (16:6)

My prayer: Teach me to fear You in a Biblical way that will let my family receive the benefits You promise. I praise You for guiding us with Your word and wisdom.

Day 2: Harmony in the Home

Read PROVERBS Chapters 19-22

A husband and wife that work together in harmony is a gift from God. The husband has the greatest responsibility to make the home God centered. God designed the husband to love the wife with actions of kindness and caring. He is loving her when he encourages her and makes life for her to be beneficial and a blessing. "Husbands, love Your wives, just as Christ loved the church and gave Himself up for her..." (Ephesians 5:25). The wife should become a better person because of her husband's behavior. He should treat his wife as a gift from God. "He who finds a wife finds what is good and receives favor from the Lord" (18:32).

It may be difficult at times for a wife to wait on her husband to do that which is beneficial to her and the home. She must be careful not to become a nagging wife according to Proverbs. "...a quarrelsome wife is like a constant dripping..." (19:13). "Better to live on a corner of the roof than share a house with a quarrelsome wife...better to live in a desert..." (19:9, 19).

My prayer: Lord, please forgive me where I have failed to be a blessing to my wife. Help me become what Christ would have me to be as a husband.

Day 3: The Name to be Avoided
Read PROVERBS Chapters 23-26

There is a name no one should want. It is someone who continues to do the same thing over and over and expects a different result. It is someone who thinks he is superior to everyone else. Proverbs calls that person a fool. "As a dog returns to its vomit, so a fool repeats his folly. Do you see a man wise in his own eyes? There is more hope for a fool than for him" (26:11-12). The dictionary says a fool is "a person with little or no judgment, common sense, wisdom, etc.; silly or stupid person; simpleton..."

A fool can be sent by Satan to waste a dedicated Christian's time. Proverbs encourages wise people to be careful getting involved with a time-waster. There are times you "Do not answer a fool according to his folly..." (26:4). At other times, it is appropriate to answer a fool, especially if it makes him look wise. "Answer a fool according to his folly, or he will be wise in his own eyes" (26:5). "The fool says in his own heart, 'there is no God" (Psalms 14:1).

My prayer: Lord, give me discernment to know when to speak and when to remain silent. Help me not to be foolish in Your eyes.

Day 4: Paddling Promotes Peace
Read PROVERBS Chapters 27-30

Parents that refuse to spank their children are doing them a great disservice. Spanking teaches a child they are accountable for their actions and that they must submit to authority. Their will must be broken but not their spirit. If a child is undisciplined he will grow up with a rebellious spirit that is like witchcraft. "For rebellion is like the sin of witchcraft, and arrogance like the evil of idolatry" (I Samuel 15:23).

Corporal punishment should be used as a last resort. It should not be used as a threat and then neglect to carry through with it. Threats that are not carried out teach a child that obedience is not important. Spanking should be used for education not for relieving a parent's frustration. "The rod of correction imparts wisdom, but a child left to himself disgraces his mother...discipline Your son, and he will give You peace; he will bring delight to Your soul" (29:15, 17).

My prayer: Lord, help our nation's parents prepare their children to be obedient to authority so they can be prepared to submit to You as our heavenly authority. Give parents the wisdom, strength, patience and love to raise a great army of Godly boys and girls.

Day 5: Everyone Enters Eternity

Read PROVERBS Chapter 31 – ECCLESIASTES Chapter 3

Every human being conceived in a womb is destined to live forever either in heaven or hell. We know that because God said so. Solomon said, "I know that everything God does will endure forever..." (3:14). Man cannot not exist once he is conceived. Why? Man is created in God's image and He is eternal.

Since man will live forever somewhere he will have to make everything right with God here on earth or in eternity. God wants us to make things right with Him while we are on earth. Once a person leaves earth it is too late to get Your spiritual life in order. In eternity the righteous will be rewarded and Christ rejecters will be judged. The writer of Ecclesiastes stated it this way, "God will bring to judgment both the righteous and the wicked..." (3:17). Jesus said the same thing. He said, "...for a time is coming when all who are in the graves will hear His voice and come out – those who have done good will rise to live, and those who have done evil will rise to be condemned" (John 5:28-29).

My prayer: Thank You for Your word that warns us about judgment and tells us how to avoid being judged. Thank You Jesus for being judged in my place by dying on the Cross for my wickedness. Thank You for saving me from being judged and sentenced for my sin.

Day 6: People Need People

Read ECCLESIASTES Chapters 4-8

The song "People Need People" is true. It is true because the Bible says so. Ecclesiastes expresses that truth in practical terms.

- SUCCESS can be achieved easier when two people work together in harmony. "Two are better than one, because they have a good return for their work." (4:9)
- SUPPORT of a companion can be the very thing that gets a task completed and failure avoided. "If one falls down, his friend can help him up! But pity the man who falls and has no one to help him up! (4:10)
- SURVIVAL can be possible when there is someone to help in time of trouble. "Also, if two lie down together, they will keep warm. But how can one keep warm alone? (4:11)
- STRENGTH can be increased to overcome an obstacle when people work together. "Though one may be overpowered two can defend themselves. A cord of three strands is not quickly broken." (4:12)

My prayer: _Lord, I cannot praise You enough for those in my life that have supported me and given me strength to experience success and thrive rather than just survive. Your grace is greater than all my sin and failures! Thank You for Your watch care._

Day 7: The Speed of Life

Read ECCLESIASTES Chapters 9-12

The speed of light is faster than anything man can devise. As a person gets older it seems the speed of life is faster than the speed of light. Because life seems to pass by so fast, Ecclesiastes urges the youth to enjoy their brief time of health and strength. "Be happy, young man, while you are young..." (11:9). A person should be prepared for the vigor of youth to fade. That is why Ecclesiastes says, "Remember your creator in the days of Your youth, before the days of trouble come..." (12:1).

The trouble referred to is the body's deterioration because of age. No matter how many vitamins or lotions a person uses, eventually the body is going to age and fail to function correctly. A person will become weak and shake if they live long enough. "...the keepers of the house tremble..." (12:3). An aged person will soon stoop, lose their teeth, develop bad eyesight, and become hard of hearing. The only thing that is lasting is to "...fear God and keep His commandments, for this is the whole duty of man" (12:13).

My prayer: I thank You Lord for all Your blessings poured out in my life. You have made life worth living and given meaning to my life. Thank You for giving me a purpose for living on earth. Please help me share who You are to those lost on life's journey.

Yearly Devotions – Week 29

Day 1: Longsuffering Love

Read SONG OF SOLOMON Chapters 1-8

Solomon reveals the physical relationship in marriage as a gift from God. God based marriage on a love that was to be enjoyed and brought pleasure. Song of Solomon is a beautiful picture of people who enjoyed their marriage. Marriage God designed is based on total commitment. The physical relationship is an expression of that love and commitment. The most important commitment and love is to God, then Your spouse, family and others. It is a love that, "...suffers long and is kind; love that does not envy; love does not parade itself, is not puffed up...bears all things...endures all things" (I Corinthians 13:4, 7).

Solomon warns married couples that they must be careful not to let the daily pressures of life erode their love and commitment. It is the little things that can cause coupled to drift apart. He compares the little things of life to foxes and warns couples to "...catch for us the foxes, the little foxes that ruin the vineyards, our vineyards that are in bloom" (2:15). "For God so loved the world that He gave..." (John 3:16).

My prayer: Thank You for the wonderful marriage and wife You gave me. Help me to keep the annoyances out of our lives and give me wisdom to know how to strengthen my marriage.

Day 2: Coming Out of the Closet

Read ISAIAH Chapters 1-3

The Southern Kingdom of Israel did not repent of their idolatry and immorality when the Northern Kingdom was taken into captivity. Isaiah warned Judah that if they did not repent they would go into captivity like the Northern Kingdom. They lasted one hundred fifty years longer than the Northern Kingdom. During that time they became so brazen in their immorality and idolatry that God determined to have them removed into captivity.

What was the major factor that brought God's judgment? Isaiah answers that question. He said, "The arrogance of man will be brought low and the pride of men humbled; the Lord alone will be exalted in that day, and the idols will totally disappear" (2:17).

People coming out of the closet today and demanding that churches and society accept their perversions and endorse their sin are arrogant and prideful. God said in the last days that "...evil men and seducers shall wax worse and worse, deceiving and being deceived" (II Timothy 3:13). Coming out of the closet will bring God's judgment as men have their "pride days."

My prayer: Lord, Help us! Our nation is flaunting its sin in Your face and rejecting You as Savior. Help us to repent and turn to You and away from our sin. Have Mercy!

Day 3: Upside Down Cake

Read ISAIAH Chapters 4-8

I enjoy a cake where pineapple slices and other tasty stuff are put in the bottom of a pan with batter poured over it and baked to a golden brown. When it has cooled it is turned upside down and placed on a serving plate.

Satan has baked an upside down cake of immorality for mankind. He twists man's thinking to seek gratification immediately with no thought of the consequences. He has led America to take prayer, Bibles, the Ten Commandments and all references to a holy God out of the public schools. The anti-Christian crowd says it might warp the children to think about God. Yet, they proclaim it will develop students to hand out condoms, provide contraceptives, and place Planned Parenthood offices in the schools. God predicted and warned about this perversion of the truth. He said, "Woe to those who call evil good and good evil, who put darkness for light and light for darkness, who put bitter for sweet and sweet for bitter. Woe to those who are wise in their own eyes and clever in their own sight" (5:20-21).

My prayer: Dear Father, send Your power in an overwhelming, convicting and holy revival to America. Lord, lead our nation to repent of its wickedness and rebellion against Your word. We are a vile and violent people. Have mercy on us and rescue us from ourselves.

Day 4: Heaven on Earth

Read ISAIAH Chapters 9-12

To have heaven on earth there must be a heavenly person present. Without the right person to rule there can be no righteous civilization. God did send a heavenly person to earth to lead the world in righteousness rooted in Godliness. His righteousness was a brilliant light that revealed the unrighteous darkness of unbelief in the world. That darkness has kept mankind from living the life God had planned for man originally. When Jesus, the one God sent, appeared He lived a life that was different from any man that had ever lived. That is why Isaiah said, "The people walking in darkness have seen a great light; on those living in the land of the shadow of death, a light has dawned" (9:2).

Jesus was crucified the first time He came but He is not through bringing heaven to earth! He is coming again and will make everything right. "He will strike the earth with the rod of His mouth; with the breath of His lips He will slay the wicked" (11:4).

My prayer: Even so come, Lord Jesus. What a wonderful day Lord when You bring history to a close and begin Your rule on earth! Thank You for saving me by Your grace and allowing me to be a part of Your rule on earth. Help me prepare to meet You and to serve You throughout eternity.

Day 5: Bad News — Good News

Read ISAIAH Chapters 13-17

God's Word usually states the bad news first. The bad news is that there is evil in the world and God is going to judge it. He is going to judge sinners and remove them from the earth at His second coming. His first appearance revealed how evil man is. Jesus was crucified by evil men. Paul was accurate when he wrote, "There is none righteous, no, not one…for all have sinned and come short of the glory of God" (Romans 3:10, 23). Isaiah warned of God's judgment. "See, the day of the Lord is coming – a cruel day, with wrath and fierce anger – to make the land desolate and destroy the sinners within it" (13:9). John warned of His second coming. "And I saw heaven opened, and beheld a white horse; and He that sat upon him was called faithful and true, and in righteousness He doth judge and make war" (Revelation 19:11). The dread of judgment can bring Holy Spirit led conviction which leads to salvation.

The good news is when Jesus rules the world and men's hearts there will be peace. Isaiah predicts that peace. "In love a throne will be established; in faithfulness a man will sit on it –

One from the house of David – One who in judging seeks justice and speeds the cause of righteousness" (16:5).

My prayer: I praise You for giving us the truth about ourselves and the solution to deal with our sin. Help me to get the bad news out so I can tell the good news. Guide my speech to lead others to receive Jesus as Lord and Savior.

Day 6: The Ostrich Club

Read ISAIAH Chapters 18-22

Those who ignore the reality of a situation and stick their head in the sand belong to that club. Isaiah tried to wake up Jerusalem about the danger of their destruction. He said, "...You saw that the City of David had many breaches in its defenses..." (22:9). The city responded by repairing the walls, storing up water for a siege and preparing for battle with its enemies. They ignored the only defense that could save them when attacked. He said, "You counted the buildings in Jerusalem and tore down houses to strengthen the wall. You built a reservoir between the two walls for the water of the Old Pool, but You did not look to the One who made it, or have regard for the One who planned it long ago" (22:10-11). They ignored God! What an insult!

They not only ignored God and left Him out of the equation they also acted in a foolish manner. They said, "Let us eat and drink...for tomorrow we die" (22:13). The person who ignores the fact that God will judge all men is foolish and belongs to the Ostrich Club.

My prayer: Lord, help me live for eternity and keep me from ignoring Your plan for my life. Direct me to those You want me to minister to so I can help prepare them for eternity.

Day 7: All Bodies Will Be Recovered

Read ISAIAH Chapters 23-27

After a flood, fire or any disaster many bodies are unrecoverable. There is a life time of suffering when a missing child is never found. There are people still searching for soldiers' bodies in Vietnam. There is coming a day when every person's body will be recovered. It won't make any difference if they were buried on land or in the sea. Isaiah reveals that every murdered victim or warrior will one day stand up again. He said, "But Your dead will live; their bodies will rise. You who dwell in the dust, wake up and shout for joy...the earth will give birth to her dead" (26:19). "The earth will disclose the bloodshed upon her; she will conceal her slain no longer" (26:21).

Jesus referred to this time when He said, "Marvel not at this: For the hour is coming, in the which all that are in the graves shall hear His voice, and shall come forth..." (John 5:28-29). After Christ's Resurrection "...the graves were opened; and many bodies of the saints which slept [in death] arose, and came out of the graves..." (Matthew 27:52-53). Everyone's body will be operational again.

My prayer: Thank You! Thank You and thank You again for making everything right at the proper time. I praise You for being righteous and just and good.

Yearly Devotions – Week 30

Day 1: Discipline Hurts Then Helps

Read ISAIAH Chapters 28-30

No one likes to be disciplined. It hurts and humbles a person. When it is over a person will either be better or bitter. Discipline helps a nation or individual to be a blessing to others. This is especially true when disciplining a child. "Discipline your son, and he will give you peace he will bring delight to your soul...punish him with the rod and save his soul from death" (Proverbs 29:17; 23:14). God disciplines nations and individuals.

Israel was continually being disciplined by God for their idolatry. God said to them, "Woe to the obstinate children, declares the Lord, to those who carry out plans that are not mine, forming an alliance, but not by My Spirit, heaping sin upon sin..." (30:1). "These are rebellious people, deceitful children, and children unwilling to listen to the Lord's instruction" (30:9). God sent nations to attack them and then He would restore them after they repented. "...the Lord binds up the bruises of His people and heals the wounds He inflicted" (30:26). "...the Lord disciplines those He loves, and He punishes everyone He accepts as a son" (Hebrews 12:6). Discipline "...produces a harvest of righteousness and peace who have been trained by it" (Hebrews 12:11).

My prayer: Thank You for loving me enough to discipline me so I will learn to follow Your instructions and have a richer life. You have truly made life worth living. I praise You for that!

Day 2: A Better Day

Read ISAIAH Chapters 31-35

Politicians are not trusted. The government is broke and unable to find a solution to the nation's problems. The educational system is in turmoil. The medical field is in crisis. The military is not able to meet all the needs of troubled nations and has its own inner struggles with terrorism. The economy of the world is on the verge of collapse. What in the world is going on? Is there a better day coming?

YES! YES! And YES! And Isaiah saw that better day. He shouted, "strengthen the feeble hands, steady the knees that give way; say to those with fearful hearts, "Be strong, do not fear, Your God will come...He will come to save You" (35:3-4). Isaiah was saying that to Israel and to us today.

When Jesus comes there will be a new interstate highway to bring everyone together. "And a highway will be there; it will be called the Way of Holiness...only the redeemed will walk there...they will enter Zion with singing; everlasting joy will crown their heads" (35:8, 9, 10).

My prayer: Even so come, Lord Jesus. Help me know how to prepare for Your coming and tell others of Your return. Thank You for the bright future for all believers.

Day 3: One Angel is Enough

Read ISAIAH Chapters 36-39

Hezekiah faced an overwhelming army that could easily conquer him. He faced a hopeless situation. He did what all men must do to get real help – he prayed. God was not overwhelmed or upset. Sennacherib's boast of all the nations he had conquered did not impress God. All God had to do was call up one angel to take care of Sennacherib's army. "Then the angel of the Lord went out and put to death a hundred and eighty-five thousand men in the Assyrian camp" (37:36).

For one angel to be able to destroy such a large army without any effort demonstrates how powerful God is. If an angel has so much power it must be astounding to know how powerful God is. It is beyond man's comprehension. This demonstration of God's power reveals the fact that Jesus set aside His power and voluntarily died on the cross to pay for man's sin. Jesus said, "Do You think I cannot call on My Father, and He will at once put at My disposal more than twelve legions of angels? But how then would the Scriptures be fulfilled that say it must happen in this way" (Matthew 26:53-54)?

My prayer: Again, Lord we see how much You loved us and we praise You for providing a way to escape Satan and sin and judgment. Lord, I plead with You to help me share the good news.

Day 4: Time Traveler

Read ISAIAH Chapters 40-42

There is a continuing and bitter debate today about the age of the earth and how it came into being. The secularist and evolutionist reject any concept of an intelligent design of life and material objects. They insist that all of life came into existence in a random manner. I will believe that philosophy when they can answer the Biblical questions in Isaiah.

There was a T.V. program about a time traveler called Dr. Who. He supposedly would go into a phone booth that was a gateway to time travel. The only way anyone could scientifically prove that our universe came into existence randomly would be to travel back in time and observe the beginning of all life. Isaiah 40 has its own Dr. Who. He asks,

Spoonful

"Who saw God make water?" "Who saw God make dirt?" "Who could tell the weight of the dirt?" "Who taught God to do all of this?" "Who instructed God?" "Who showed Him the path of understanding" (40:12-14)? The greatest question asked was, "To whom, then, will You compare Him to? ...Before Him all nations are as nothing...and less than nothing" (40:18, 17).

My prayer: Help us to see how mighty and awesome You are. You are our creator and are the only One that has the right to control us and have us worship You. Lord, You made me and have the power and right to demand I submit to You. Thank You for revealing who You are through Your word.

Day 5: Made in Heaven

Read ISAIAH Chapters 43-45

The items a person purchases today always have a tag showing where it was manufactured. Atheist and agnostic's believe God was made up in the minds of men on earth. They believe only what their senses can experience. Yet, they believe in evolution which cannot be proven. There is not one piece of evidence that any living or dead creature has changed into a different species. It takes a lot of faith to believe in atheism.

The ancient nations didn't have a problem with atheism. Their problem was having too many false gods. Those who worshipped idols had closed minds about who God is. He said they prayed to something they made with their own hands. Isaiah said, "they know nothing, they understand nothing; their eyes are plastered over so they cannot see, and their minds closed so they cannot understand" (44:18). That describes people who believe in evolution and atheism.

194

Creation of man and the earth were in the mind of God in heaven when He spoke them into existence. We were made in heaven. God said, "I have made You..." (44:21). God said, "It is I who made the earth and created mankind upon it..." (45:12).

My prayer: It is my prayer that You would open the eyes of non-believers so they could see how glorious and powerful You are. Help me declare the truth that You are in charge of Your creation and that You have provided salvation for all peoples.

Day 6: Bronze Head

Read ISAIAH Chapters 46-49

As a child, my father would tell me "to get the lead out of my pants" when he wanted me to hurry. God wasn't worried about the lead in Israel's pants. He was concerned about their bronze headed stubbornness. He said, "For I know how stubborn you were; the sinews of your neck were iron, your forehead was bronze" (48:4). Why does God want us to be sensitive and alert to His commands? He is concerned because He knows we will miss His blessings when we are stubborn and refuse to obey Him.

God told Israel what they would miss if they disobeyed Him. He said, "...I am the Lord Your God, who teaches you what is best for you, who directs you in the way you should go" (48:17). What do stubborn people miss? "If only you had paid attention to My commands, your peace would have been like a river, your righteousness like the waves of the sea...your children like its [sand] numberless grains..." (48:18, 19).

My prayer: Thank You Lord for showing that You are faithful by giving the peace that surpasses all understanding. Thank You that I can lay down at night and not worry about tomorrow. Keep me yielded to Your will and help me not to be hard-headed.

Day 7: An Early Portrait of a Crucified Christ

Read ISAIAH Chapters 50-54

God designed a process of salvation that no human would ever desire. He chose to leave the supernatural realm to become a part of His own natural creation. He yielded to being executed by His creation to pay for mankind's sin. God gave a preview in Isaiah as to what His execution would be like. His suffering was described in detail seven hundred years before it happened. We see a picture of Jesus being whipped when we read, "I offered my back to those who beat me..." (50:6). The soldier's and Pharisees cruelty is seen in these words..."I offered...My cheeks to those who pulled out My beard" (50:6). The words that best describe His crucifixion are, "...His appearance was so disfigured beyond that of any man and His form marred beyond human likeness" (52:14). "...But He was pierced for our transgressions..." (53:5).

How do we know these passages refer to Jesus? Jesus said so on the Road to Emmaus. "And beginning with Moses and all the prophets, He explained to them what was said in ALL the scriptures concerning Himself" (Luke 24:21) (Luke 24:27).

My prayer: Thank You Lord for loving me and caring enough to send Your Son. I must say like the Psalmist, "Great is the Lord, and most worthy of praise, in the city of our God, His Holy Mountain." (Psalms 48:1)

Yearly Devotions – Week 31

Day 1: God's Deafness Can Be Cured

Read ISAIAH Chapters 55-59

God cannot be manipulated by ritualistic shenanigans and false adoration. He recognizes genuine worship. "Yet on the day of your fasting, you do as you please and exploit all your workers. Your fasting ends in quarreling and strife, and in striking each other with wicked fists. You cannot fast as you do today and expect your voice TO BE HEARD on high" (58:3-4, emphasis added). "Surely the arm of the Lord is not too short to save, nor His ear too dull to hear. But your iniquities have separated you from your God; your sins have hidden His face from you, SO THAT HE WILL NOT HEAR" (59:1-2, emphasis added).

How can God's deafness be cured? "Seek the Lord while He may be found; call on Him while He is near. Let the wicked forsake His way and the evil man his thoughts. Let him turn to the Lord, and He will have mercy on him, and to our God, for He will freely pardon" (55:6-7). God said, "I live in a high and holy place, but also with him who is contrite and lowly in Spirit…and to revive the heart of the contrite" (57:15).

My prayer: Please hear my prayer through Jesus and His shed blood. Thank You for answering prayer in the past and thank You for prayers answered in the future. Please forgive me of my sin and my nation for turning its back on You.

Day 2: Divine Amnesia

Read ISAIAH Chapters 60-66

Memory can be good or bad. It depends on what the memory is. It could be a memory of a missed opportunity or a tragic experience. One torture of hell will be the memory of those things. Abraham reminded the rich man in hell about his life on earth. He said, "Son, remember that in your lifetime you received your good things while Lazarus received bad things..." (Luke 16:25). The rich man remembered his family. He asked Abraham to "...send Lazarus to my father's house. For I have five brothers. Let him warn them, so that they will not come to this place of torment" (Luke 16:27).

There will be a time in eternity when Christians will judge the world with Jesus." Paul said, "Do You not know that the saints will judge the world" (I Corinthians 6:2)? What a sad job. Praise the Lord! Isaiah says all our bad experiences will be removed from our memories. He said, "The former things will not be remembered, nor will they come to mind" (65:17). Why? Because God said, "...I will create new heavens and a new earth...be glad and rejoice forever..." (65:17-18).

My prayer: Help me remember all of the blessings You have placed in my life. Thank You for all of the wonderful experiences You allowed me to have. Thank You for the memories of how You sustained me in times of sorrow and sickness. I praise You for Your mercy.

Day 3: Wrong Worship Leads to Wrong Living

Read JEREMIAH Chapters 1-3

Wrong worship leads to losing the dignity and value of life. "Has a nation ever changed its gods? (Yet they are not gods at all.) But My people have exchanged their glory for worthless idols" (2:11).

Wrong worship leads to becoming useless. "They followed worthless idols and became worthless themselves" (2:5).

Wrong worship leads to filthy communication and living. "Although You wash Yourself with soda and use an abundance of soap, the stain of Your guilt is still before Me" (2:22). God cannot fellowship with an unrepentant person.

Wrong worship will not lead to repentance of sin. God told Judah He saw innocent blood on their clothes. But "…You say, 'I am innocent'…but I will pass judgment on You because You say, 'I have not sinned…You refuse to blush with shame" (2:35) (3:3).

How do we correct wrong worship? "If we confess our sins, He is faithful and just and will forgive us our sins and purify us from all unrighteousness." (I John 1:9) "…everyone who calls on the name of the Lord will be saved" (Romans 10:13).

My prayer: Thank You Lord for revealing how we can be cleansed and forgiven of our sin. Thank You for bringing me to a time of repentance and surrender to Jesus.

Day 4: Blessings From Fully Following the Father

Read JEREMIAH Chapters 4-5

Jeremiah reveals the heart of God and His longing to have faithful followers. All He wants to do is bless obedient children. He cannot bless when sin is present. God said to Israel, "How gladly would I treat you like sons and give you a desirable land, the most beautiful inheritance of any nation. I thought you would call Me Father and not turn away from following Me" (3:19). God wants to give His children the best that life has to offer.

What does His children need to do to receive the best life?
1.   "...do not sow among thorns" (4:3).
2.   "...circumcise Your hearts..." (4:4). "...wash the evil from Your heart and be saved. How long will You harbor wicked thoughts..." (4:14)?
3.   God demands honesty in all of life. He said to Israel, "If You can find but one person who deals honestly and seeks the truth, I will forgive this city" (5:1).
4.   Preachers are required to preach the truth. God said to the prophets, "A horrible and shocking thing has happened in the land; the prophets prophesy lies...and My people love it this way" (5:30-31).

My prayer: Thank You for giving me a life better than I could have planned or strived for. I praise You for all of Your abundant blessings.

Day 5: Brazen, Backward and No Balm

Read JEREMIAH Chapters 6-8

Israel was sick spiritually and did not seek the right cure. They had adjusted to the pagan lifestyle in a way that caused them to become brazen in their sins. Twice in these three chapters Jeremiah tries to get Israel to see how far they had fallen morally. He said, "Are they ashamed of their loathsome conduct? No, they have no shame at all; they do not even know how to blush. So they will fall among the fallen; they will be brought down when they are punished" (6:15). Our so-called "sophisticated society" today has come out of the "closet" with all sorts of perversions. Morally and spiritually God said, "They went backward not forward" (7:24). What the world calls sophistication is just old fashioned sin.

What is the cure of a dying and degraded society? Jeremiah asked, "Is there no balm in Gilead? Is there no physician there" (8:21-22)? The balm in Gilead was a famous healing ointment. What ointment do we need today? "Stand at the crossroads and look; ask for the ancient paths, ask where the good way is, and walk in it, and you will find rest for your souls" (6:16). The Old time Religion!

My prayer: Wash me and I will be whiter than snow. Keep the truth before me and help me to walk on the narrow road. I lift up America to You to bring about repentance and revival. Thank You for answered prayer.

Day 6: There is Something to Brag About

Read JEREMIAH Chapters 9-11

As I write this devotion, firecrackers are going off with loud booms and many pops. America is celebrating another Independence Day. America has a lot of things to be proud of. It has been a world power for many years. It has been a world leader in every area of life. It seems to be losing that place of leadership now. America may have been proud of the wrong things. What should we as Americans brag about?

Jeremiah addressed that question when he reminded Israel they should only brag about one thing. He relayed God's message to Israel. "…let not the wise man boast of his wisdom or the strong man boast of his strength or the rich man boast of his riches, but let him who boasts boast about this: that he understand and knows Me, that I am the Lord, who exercises kindness, justice and righteousness on earth. For in these I delight" (9:23-24). "Righteousness exalts a nation, but sin is a disgrace to any people" (Proverbs 14:34).

My prayer: Help me speak in a way that You are honored, Lord. May I brag on You from the heart and give You credit for all the good in my life, family, church and nation. Thank You for Your word.

Day 7: Slim to None Without Repentance

Read JEREMIAH Chapters 12-15

Without God's power in a person's life it is impossible to change their sinful nature. A person's chance of honoring God are slim to none. The prophet makes that plain when he said, "Can the Ethiopian change his skin or the leopard its spots? Neither can You do good who are accustomed to doing evil" (13:23).

The only hope a person has to change and have the ability to be a blessing is to repent and turn to God. To repent means acknowledging one's sinfulness and then change the direction of their life. It is to seek God's will and His purpose for one's life. God said to Israel, "If you repent, I will restore you that you may serve Me; if you utter worthy not worthless words, you will be My spokesman" (15:19). God demands repentance to serve Him. Isaiah had to experience repentance and cleansing before he could say, "Here am I. send me!" (Isaiah 6:8). David confessed, "Against You, You only, have I sinned..." (Psalms 51:4). And then he could say, "...I will teach transgressors Your ways..." (Psalms 51:13).

My prayer: Thank You for making it plain that we must turn to You to be a blessing and get blessed at the same time. Cleanse me and give Your strength to me so I can remain useful and teach Your word. Give me a caring heart and a clear conscience.

Yearly Devotions – Week 32

Day 1: Man Repents and God Relents

Read JEREMIAH Chapters 16-18

As this devotion is being written, the United States has a president who got elected by using the theme of "Hope and Change". He didn't bring hope or change as he promised. Why did he use that theme? He implied that America was in such bad shape and that he was needed to make things right. He did not bring hope and he did not change America for the better.

God said to Israel that they had no hope if they didn't change. They worshipped idols and lived immorally. They had turned their back on a holy God who never changed. What does it mean to say God never changes? It means that His character and will never changes. He is holy, righteous, loving, just, pure, hates sin, and is good eternally. He does change His actions when men change their actions. God said to Israel, "if at any time I announce that a nation or kingdom is to be uprooted, torn down and destroyed, and if that nation I warned REPENTS of it evil, then I will RELENT and not inflict on it the disaster I had planned" (18:7, emphasis added).

My prayer: Teach me to know when to change my actions to receive Your mercy and blessing. I seek Your peace to rule and regulate my actions. I praise You for Your love and kindness.

Day 2: Kingly Traits

Read JEREMIAH Chapters 19-22

A position of power can be used for self-interest or it can be used for selfless purposes. There is a tendency in everyone to desire what Eve wanted. She wanted to be a goddess instead of a gardener's wife. A child left to its self will not be selfless but will become selfish quickly. Jeremiah gives some traits that make a person like a Godly King.

Jeremiah said having an ostentatious lifestyle did not make a person Kingly. He asked, "Does it make You a King to have more and more cedar" (22:15)? Cedar at that time was a visible sign of wealth and power. A person can have all the amenities of wealth and still be poor in what is important. What makes a person wealthy is to be loved by friends, family and one's peers. Jeremiah listed a few traits that revealed what a Godly King was like. The good king he said "...did what was right and just...He defended the cause of the poor and needy, and so all went well" (22:15-16). Jesus is the maker of good kings. He is the one "...who loved us and washed us from our sins in His own blood, and has made us kings and priests to His God and Father..." (Revelation 1:5-6).

My prayer: It is my plea to You O Lord to have the Kingly traits Jeremiah mentioned. It is my earnest plea to be filled with the mind of Christ and His fullness. Thank You for Your word that feeds my soul.

Day 3: Preaching to Pieces

Read JEREMIAH Chapters 23-25

Preaching and teaching are two different things. Preaching is proclaiming the truth seeking a response from the listeners. It is proclaiming the truth of God and His Word. Biblical teaching is to inform, educate and edify a believer. Sometimes preaching and teaching overlap during a session.

Jeremiah shared God's message to Israel about what preaching should be about. God said, "But if they had stood in

My council, they would have proclaimed My words to My people and would have turned them from their evil ways and from their evil deeds" (23:22). A person who thinks Pastoring and preaching is a profession a person chooses and doesn't understand it as a calling of God should do something else. When a person is called of God he will know that what he does is supernatural and can change people. "Is not My Word like fire; declares the Lord, 'And like a hammer that breaks a rock in pieces?" (23:29). Jeremiah expressed God's call in a man's life. He said, "...His Word is in my heart like a fire, a fire shut up in my bones. I am weary of holding it in..." (20:9).

My prayer: Your call is the greatest event in my life other than salvation and I thank You for it. I praise You for allowing me to share Your word and minister to Your people. I plead with You to call many more preachers and teachers to witness to others about Your grace.

Day 4: Perilous Preaching

Read JEREMIAH Chapters 26-29

Preaching the truth is a great responsibility. True Biblical preaching involves telling people they are sinners in need of a Savior. Everyone must hear that "bad news" before they can respond to the "good news." People must know they are a sinner before they see a need for a Savior. Just preaching the love of God without the judgment of God is perilous preaching. It is perilous to the one who doesn't see a need for a Savior.

God told Jeremiah to "Tell them everything I command you; do not omit a word. Perhaps they will listen and each will turn from his evil way. Then I will relent and not bring on them the disaster I was planning because of the evil they have done" (26:2, 3).

Preaching that doesn't disturb a person first won't bring the peace of repentance. God warns Israel, "do not let the prophet and diviners among You deceive You...they are prophesying lies to You in My name. I have not sent them..." (29:8, 9). Peace comes after repentance. God said, "For I know the plans I have for You...plans to prosper You and not to harm You, plans to give You hope and a future" (29:11).

My prayer: Use me to bring the bad news so I can share the good news. Thank You for the hope and security I have in Christ.

Day 5: Multiple Messages of Punishment and Promises

Read JEREMIAH Chapters 30-32

God does not accept ignorance as an excuse to escape judgment. He warns of judgment over and over. Jeremiah emphasized at least thirty seven times in these three chapters that it was God who gave him these messages of judgment and hope. God is more interested in people repenting than punishing them. Jeremiah reflected God's heart by wanting Israel to change so God's judgment would not be implemented.

Each message from God had a terrifying portion and an encouraging portion. God said, "The fierce anger of the Lord will not turn back until He fully accomplishes the purpose of His heart. In days to come you will understand this" (30:24). "Because of Your great guilt and many sins...I have struck you as an enemy would and punished you as would the cruel..." (30:15, 14).

God promised not to desert them after punishing them. He promised to restore them. He said, "For I will forgive their wickedness and will remember their sins no more" (31:34). That is what God does for everyone who asks for forgiveness of their sin and receives Jesus as Savior and Lord.

My prayer: Thank You for being a God of forgiveness and for being Holy and righteous in the process. Thank You for punishing my sin through Jesus so I can enjoy the blessings of being forgiven and spending eternity in heaven.

Day 6: What Will Be is God's Will

Read JEREMIAH Chapter 33-35

Jeremiah confronted Israel with their inevitable defeat and capture by Babylon. God did give them hope of a better future. Even though their defeat and captivity was a result of their disobedience God promised that there was a time coming when a perfect man would be their king and priest.

God's timing of that fulfillment of His promise was to be kept by heaven's timetable. God stated emphatically that "David will never fail to have a man to sit on the throne of the house of Israel, nor will the priests, who are Levites, ever fail to have a man to stand before Me continually to offer burnt offerings..." (33:17-18). Notice it is to be a man standing before God and sitting on a throne. "For there is one God and one mediator between God and men, the man Christ Jesus..." (I Timothy 2:5). Jesus had to become a man to fulfill God's will. "...Jesus lives forever, He has a permanent priesthood. Therefore He is able to save completely those who come to God through Him..." (Hebrews 7:24-25). The Apostle Peter said of David "that God had sworn with an oath to him, that of the fruit of his loins, according to the flesh, He would raise up Christ to sit on the throne..." (Acts 2:30). In God's time, His will be done and Christ will rule from Jerusalem.

My prayer: Thank You for the comfort I receive from knowing that Your righteousness will overcome all evil and satanic forces. Help keep before me that You are in charge and that Your will, will be done in spite of all opposition to it.

Day 7: No Repentance Means No Relief

Read JEREMIAH Chapters 36-38

Jeremiah had a message that brought bad news and good news. The bad news was Jerusalem would be destroyed if they did not repent. The good news was that if they repented of their sin God would protect them from destruction. The king did not like the message so he punished the messenger. Jeremiah was faithful to tell the truth because he wanted Jerusalem and its people to be spared. "Perhaps when the people of Judah hear about every disaster I plan to inflict on them, each of them will turn from his wicked way; then I will forgive their wickedness and their sin," God said (36:3).

Preachers are to preach the truth whether it offends people or not. His heart should be broken when he preaches about sin, hell and judgment. His goal is for people to repent so they can avoid judgment and then live to glorify God. Paul warned about a time when preaching the truth would not be popular again. "For the time will come when they will not endure sound doctrine; but after their own lusts shall they heap to themselves teachers, having itching ears; and they shall turn away their ears from the truth, and shall be turned to fables" (II Timothy 4:3-4).

My prayer: *Open my spiritual ears so I will hear and repent when You correct me. I pray for my nation that it will repent of its pride, rebellion and Godless living. Have mercy O Lord.*

Yearly Devotions – Week 33

Day 1: Hearing is Not Listening

Read JEREMIAH Chapters 39-41

A young pastor, who had very little experience with a multiple staff, kept having conflict with a number of church leaders. He sought council from experienced older pastors. Their council went unheeded even though he kept saying, "I hear you." He heard the older pastors, but he didn't listen to what they said.

Gedaliah heard the warnings of his supporters but he didn't listen to them and it cost him his life. Johanan said to Gedaliah, "Don't you know that Baalis King of the Ammonites has sent Ishmael...to take your life? But Gedaliah...did not believe them" (41:14).

The Israelites sought God's counsel through Jeremiah. God responded and said, "If you stay in this land, I will build You up and not tear You down..." (42:10). They heard what God said but they did not listen. Not listening cost them their lives. Jeremiah warned, "So now, be sure of this: You will die by the sword, famine and plague in the place where you want to go to settle" (42:22). You can hear, "Everyone who calls on the name of the Lord will be saved" (Romans 10:13). But you must listen to receive eternal life by calling on His name.

My prayer: Help keep my ears open to hear from You, Lord and keep my heart open to listen to what You have to say.

Day 2: It Matters Who You Trust

Read JEREMIAH Chapters 42-44

There is a growing so-called church movement that does not believe the Bible. They claim that Aliens planted humans on earth. They believe a human must clear his mind of all negativity to gain power over his own life. They believe that as you get rid of mental negativity you will be able to communicate with the Aliens. They base their beliefs on books written by a science-fiction writer. Many people, including many famous people, trust what this science-fiction writer wrote.

These people are trusting in one man's ideas that were voiced centuries ago. The Israelites worshipped a goddess called the Queen of Heaven. They informed Jeremiah that they, "...will not listen to the message you have spoken to us in the name of the Lord...We will burn incense to the Queen of Heaven and will pour out drink offerings to her..." (44:16-17). God's response was very threatening. He said, "Those who escape the sword and return to the land of Judah from Egypt will be very few. Then the whole remnant of Judah who came to live in Egypt will know whose word will stand-mine or theirs" (44:28). I trust God's Word rather than a science-fiction author.

My prayer: I praise You and honor You for the truth of God's Word. Thank You as an eternal, sovereign God for giving us our knowledge of how we got here and why You put us on earth. Thank You for sending Jesus to become one of us so He could pay for our sin.

Day 3: Israel's Enemies Are God's Enemies

Read JEREMIAH Chapters 45-48

God uses Israel's enemies to chastise Israel but then judges them by how harsh they treated Israel. God can and will use anybody or nation to discipline His children. "...the Lord disciplines those He loves..." (Hebrews 12:6). God said, "So

My heart laments for Moab like a flute..." (48:36). Flutes were instruments of mourning at funerals. God has no pleasure in the death of the wicked.

Egypt and Moab had seen God's power demonstrated in Israel and yet refused to worship Him. Egypt saw God's power through Moses and refused to acknowledge Jehovah as God alone. Moab had a long history with Israel. They were descendants of incest from Lot and his daughter. When Israel arrived in the Promised Land Moab sensed they could not save themselves from Israel by force of arms. Moab determined to seduce Israel into idolatry with Moabite girls. "...And the people began to commit harlotry with the women of Moab" (Numbers 25:1). God said of Moab, "Make her drunk, for she has defied the Lord" (48:26). The word "drunk" was a term used to express God's judgment. To be God's enemy means disaster.

My prayer: It is my plea that I remain an obedient child. Give me the strength, wisdom, and patience to wait on You to guide my life in such a way to bring honor to You. Help our nation to remain open to Jesus as Lord and Savior and Your Word as the truth.

Day 4: The Root Determines the Fruit

Read JEREMIAH Chapters 49-50

God predicted that He was going to punish Ammon, Edom, Elam, Kedar, Hazor and Babylon. All of these nations were antagonistically opposed to God. Their root was bad.

The nation of Ammon came from an incestuous relationship from Lot and his daughter. The Ammonites were baby killers by sacrificing their children to Molech.

The people of Edom were descendants of Esau who despised his birthright and sold it for a bowl of soup. He planned to kill his brother Jacob for stealing his blessing. Esau migrated to Mt. Seir and lived in the caves after defeating the Horites.

Kedar and Hazor were descendants of Ishmael who mocked Isaac and was driven into the desert. They became nomads living in Arabia.

Elam was one of the nations that attacked Sodom and took Lot and his family captives. Abraham rescued Lot from them.

Babylon was the place of God's judgment where He said, "...let us go down and confuse their language so they will not understand each other" (Genesis 11:7). For years these nations had opposed God and His people which caused God to punish them.

My prayer: Thank You for being a righteous and Holy God that brings justice to the world in Your time. Thank You that You can change a person to have good fruit by replacing the root with Your salvation through Jesus Christ.

Day 5: Barren Living

Read JEREMIAH Chapters 51-52

The dictionary states that barren means to be "unable to produce fruit or vegetation... unprofitable." That describes a life without the Lord Jesus. It is impossible to make sense out of life without God. Babylon had risen to glorious heights as a conquering, powerful nation. When God determined to remove them and their false gods they became helpless in His presence. The prophet warned them of their coming destruction. "The Lord will carry our His purpose, His decree against the people of Babylon" (51:12). What were Babylon's offenses?

They worshiped idols. "...every goldsmith is shamed by his idols" (51:17). "For the time will surely come when I will punish the idols of Babylon..." (51:47).

They slaughtered Israelites unmercifully and without compassion or considering God's will. "Babylon must fall because of Israel's slain, just as the slain in all the earth have fallen because of Babylon" (51:49).

Even though Babylon ruled the world at one time God still turned it into a barren, desolate place because they defied Him. God declared that "Her towns will be desolate, a dry and desert land, a land where no one lives..." (51:43). That is the picture of a lost man.

My prayer: I plead with You to move in America as a nation, state and city so we can be what You designed us to be. We need You now as a nation more than we've ever needed You. Please remove the gods of pleasure, perversion and money so we will turn back to You as our God individually as well as nationally.

Day 6: Warnings Reveal Danger

Read LAMENTATIONS Chapters 1-3

A good parent warns his children about the danger of being burned by a hot stove. A toddler has no concept of the danger of fire until it burns him. He might be burned a little bit and learn from the experience or he could lose his life. A good parent doesn't want to take any kind of chance. A good parent will even inflict pain on a child he loves by spanking him if the child insists on going toward a hot stove or fireplace.

God warned Israel over and over about idolatry through many Godly prophets. He finally had to inflict pain on Israel who kept listening to false prophets. The false prophets refused to warn Israel about God's judgment of sin. Jeremiah laments the tragedy of what the false prophets brought on Israel. "The visions of your prophets were false and worthless; they did not expose your sin to ward off your captivity. The oracles they gave you were false and misleading" (2:14). What we need today are preachers who will warn people of God's judgment.

My prayer: Thank You for the truth of Your word that warns us of the coming judgment and what we can do to escape it. Thank You for sending Your Son to die and shed his blood to pay for our sin. Give us the wisdom and anointing to know how to be heard in a noisy market place about Your judgment that is coming.

Day 7: Believe it or Not

Read LAMENTATIONS Chapters 4-5

As I write this in less than a month Pastor Terry Fox and I are scheduled to observe an execution in Oklahoma. We do not look forward to the experience. Each day seems to race by towards that date. It must be worse for the one to die. It must seem unbelievable. Whether we believe it or not the day of judgment is coming. That is what the Israelites finally realized when Babylon attacked Jerusalem. God's judgment had finally arrived because of their idolatry.

The author of Lamentations could hardly believe God's judgment had arrived. He cried out, "Our end was near; our days were numbered, for our end had come" (4:18). "The Kings of the earth did not believe, nor did any of the world's people, that enemies and foes could enter the gates of Jerusalem" (4:12). Lamentations declares God was righteous in His judgment. "But it happened because of the sins of her prophets and the iniquities of her priests, who shed within her the blood of the righteous" (4:13). Lamentations reveals that God has no joy in bringing judgment. "For He does not willingly bring affliction or grief to the children of men" (3:33).

My prayer: Help me to number my days and redeem the time to bring others to Christ and grow in grace. Teach me what Your priorities are for my life so I can be useful to You.

Spoonful

Yearly Devotions – Week 34

Day 1: God's Curriculum

Read EZEKIEL Chapters 1-3

God wanted Israel to know what their offense was and why they were being punished. That is still a good curriculum when chastising a child. God chose the prophet Ezekiel to teach the Israelites. God gave him the curriculum that would prepare him to teach Israel. God wanted Ezekiel to LOOK at His glory and power so that he could not be intimidated by men. So God gave him a vision that caused him to be in awe and worship. "...When I saw it I fell down..." (1:28).

After Ezekiel saw God's glory he listened to God and learned what his part was in God's plan. God commissioned him. "Son of man, I am sending You to the Israelites, to a rebellious nation that has rebelled against Me...You must speak My words to them, whether they listen or fail to listen, for they are rebellious" (2:3, 7). God then assigned him the task of being a watchman. "Son of man, I have made you a watchman for the house of Israel; so hear the word I speak and give them warning from Me" (3:17). Christians have the same curriculum today. We are to be watchmen in His service.

My prayer: Lord, help me to look for You in all things. Help me to listen to You and learn Your will for my life. Give me strength to labor in Your vineyard and harvest souls for Your kingdom.

Day 2: God's Favor

Read EZEKIEL Chapters 4-7

To have God's favor is to have the most important benefit a man can receive on earth. To have God's favor is to be blessed of God. That means to have His protection. It means to be given the ability to be effective and efficient in accomplishing God's plan and will for one's life. The by-product of having His favor means God provides whatever is needed to care for your family, community and nation.

To lose that favor is to be under His curse. A curse is to have God's protection and favor removed. A person or nation becomes vulnerable to attacks from the evil-one and his emissaries without God's shield of protection. That is why it was devastating news for Israel when God said, "...because you have defiled My sanctuary with all your vile images and detestable practices, I Myself will withdraw My favor; I will not look on you with pity or spare you" (5:11). A person without Christ is outside the sphere of His favor. The Apostle Peter had God's favor when the angel led him out of prison (Acts 12:7).

My prayer: Help me live a life that will allow You to let me have Your favor. I desire Your favor above anything the world has to offer. Thank You for the years of protecting my family and for caring for our needs.

Day 3: We Have an All-Seeing God

Read EZEKIEL Chapters 8-11

God doesn't need help to see sin. He sees it with His own eyes. Ezekiel experienced what Jesus referred to in John 3:19-20. Ezekiel was transported to Jerusalem by a spiritual being to observe idolatry. God said to Ezekiel, "Son of man, have you seen what the elders of the house of Israel are doing in the darkness, each at the shrine of his own idol? They say, 'The Lord does not see us...'" (8:12). Jesus tells us why these men worshipped in darkness. Jesus said, "...this is the condemnation, that the light has come into the world, and men loved darkness rather than light, because their deeds were evil. For everyone practicing evil hates the light, lest his deeds should be exposed" (John 3:19-20).

Evil deeds done in darkness usually lead to death. God said to Ezekiel, "the sin of the house of Israel and Judah is exceedingly great; the land is full of bloodshed and the city is full of injustice" (9:9). It started with Cain. God said to Cain, "Your brother's blood cries out to Me from the ground" (Genesis 4:10). Violence brought God's judgment and helped cause the flood. "Now the earth was corrupt in God's sight and was full of violence" (Genesis 6:11). Jesus was arrested in the dark and brutally crucified. Jesus brings light and life.

My prayer: Thank You for the light of God's Word that reveals the light of heaven. Help me to walk in that light until I'm in the very presence of light.

Day 4: Pastors You Can Trust

Read EZEKIEL Chapters 12-14

Ezekiel's messages came directly from the Lord. Twenty-nine times in these three chapters the phrases "declares the Lord" or "the Sovereign Lord says" are used. How do we know when a message is from the Lord? We can know it is true because what is said becomes true. God gave a test to know who preaches the truth. "When a prophet speaketh in the name of the Lord, if the thing follow not, nor come to pass, that is the thing which the Lord hath not spoken, but the prophet hath spoken it presumptuously..." (Deuteronomy 18:22 KJV).

A true prophet or preacher is committed to making sure God is honored in every aspect of life. Ezekiel warned the Israelites of imminent judgment. He instructed them as to the purpose of God's judgment. God said, "Yet there will be survivors...when you see their conduct and their actions, you will be consoled regarding the disaster I have brought upon Jerusalem...for you will know that I have done nothing in it without cause..." (14:22-23). You can trust a pastor when he preaches the truth to bring salvation to the people and glory to God.

My prayer: Teach me how to know Your message and share it with others so they will receive salvation and bring glory to You. Thank You for allowing me to preach and share Your message of hope and salvation.

Day 5: God's Trophy Wife
Read EZEKIEL Chapters 15-17

There have been men who have become successful and respected as professionals who left their wives for younger women. That younger woman is known as a trophy wife. God compared Israel to being a young beautiful wife to Him that became unfaithful by worshipping idols. God compared the worship of Himself to the intimacy of marriage.

When a spouse seeks an intimate relationship with someone other than their marriage partner, they are being unfaithful. Israel was to be a trophy wife that displayed God's glory and righteousness by how they worshipped and lived. All of their actions falsely reflected on who God is. He is the almighty, living God and no statue or idol could represent Him. So when Israel bowed down to an idol and felt they were in the presence of God they committed spiritual adultery. God charged them with spiritual adultery and announced to the world that Israel "...trusted in Your beauty and used Your fame to become a prostitute" (16:15).

If Christians seek to get their needs met from any other source than Jesus they commit spiritual adultery. Jesus said, "...seek first His Kingdom and righteousness." (Matthew 6:33).

My prayer: I pray that Your Word will keep me seeking You and that I do not bow down to the world's offer to meet my needs with carnal activities. Bring my church and nation to seek Your righteousness and kingdom. Thank You for making me a part of the bride of Christ.

Day 6: For God's Sake
Read EZEKIEL Chapters 18-20

Israel's deliberate, stubborn rebellious refusal to worship God hurt them more than it did Him. God removed His blessing and protection from them. When God did that they became vulnerable to being attacked and destroyed as a nation.

Like Israel every individual has the choice to reject God. Rejection of God always produces bondage. An addict never intended to be an addict. Addicts refused to believe the warnings of the dangers of addictive substances or perverted behavior. The rebel against God always ends up in bondage. Why?

God tells us the answer to the "why" question three times in this passage. God warned Israel that sin brings its own punishment. He said, "But they rebelled against Me and would not listen to Me...so I said I would pour out My wrath on them and spend My anger against them in Egypt...But for the sake of My name I did what would keep it from being profaned in the eyes of the Nations..." (20:8, 9). God's righteousness cannot let sin go unpunished if there is no repentance.

My prayer: It is my prayer that my life be used for Your sake O Lord! Guide me to know when I step off Your path and start going in the wrong direction. Thank You for warning us and loving us.

Day 7: It IS Everyone's Business

Read EZEKIEL Chapters 21-23

How many times have people said, "It's no one's business what I do?" That is a false statement that Satan likes to sell to a lot of people. What anyone person does always affects more people than oneself. Pastor Terry Fox and I are scheduled to go to McAlester, Oklahoma soon. We are scheduled to make two trips because one man killed a woman and her two small children. He not only caused her family great suffering but his family and two pastors he has never met are affected. Pastor Terry and I are scheduled to minister to him before his execution and minister to his family after his execution. Our church has been impacted by one man's action.

The innocent people are the ones hurt the most many times. Israel experienced the innocent people suffering along with the wicked. God said to Israel, "I will draw My sword from its scabbard and cut off from You both the righteous and the wicked...EVERY heart will melt and EVERY hand go limp; EVERY spirit will become faint and EVERY knee becomes as weak as water" (21:3, 7, emphasis added).

My prayer: I plead the blood of Jesus over many of my actions that God won't allow them to cause others to suffer. Thank You Lord that Your action on the Cross affected millions of people for good.

Yearly Devotions – Week 35

Day 1: Pride Does Go Before a Fall

Read EZEKIEL Chapters 24-26

Tyre was a mighty city in Lebannon. It thought it was invincible because of its location and because part of it was built on an island. It was rich and powerful because of its ability to trade with all the nations with its port.

It was a city that worshiped Baal and many other gods. It was a bustling port city filled with a raucous, crowded citizenry. They prided themselves in their success and wealth. It was the New York city of the ancient world. It was a city where Satan had a stronghold. It was a fountainhead of pure evil that flowed to Israel in the form of Baal worship. Baal worship was transported to Northern Israel through Jezebel who married Ahab, the King of Northern Israel. She persecuted God's prophets and promoted Baal worship. God warned Tyre that He was going to judge them and that His patience had run out.

God said to Tyre, "They (the Babylonians) will plunder Your wealth and loot Your merchandise..." (26:12). It took two great kings and a couple of a hundred years to conquer Tyre but it finally was completely captured by Alexander the Great in 332 B.C. America must humble itself before the Lord or it could fall.

My prayer: Lord, I lift up America to You and confess we are a wicked people who have turned our back on You. Please forgive us and send Your mighty Holy Spirit to revive us.

Day 2: Everyone Reflects Someone

Read EZEKIEL Chapters 27-29

A person can be distracted by the reflection of the sun off of a windshield of another car. Everyone's life reflects some facet of the person they admire.

This is vividly seen in Ezekiel 28 when God declared His judgment of Tyre and its king. The worship of idols is the worship of Satan. The king of Tyre became like what he worshiped. The king of Tyre was never in the Garden of Eden so God compared the king's actions with those of Satan. From that comparison God revealed Satan's beginning and fall. God said of Satan, "You were anointed as a guardian cherub...You were in Eden, the garden of God..." (28:14, 13). Jesus used this kind of comparison when He rebuked Peter and said, "Get behind Me, Satan" (Matthew 16:23).

Satan was God's most glorious creation who sought glory and praise because of pride. God said of Lucifer, "Your heart became proud on account of your beauty, and you corrupted Your wisdom because of Your splendor" (28:17). The wealth of the King of Tyre reflected the pride of Satan and his fall. God's goal for every person is to reflect the love of Christ.

My prayer: Thank You for Your revelation of where Satan and evil had their beginning. It is my prayer and goal to seek Your knowledge so I can reflect the person of Jesus.

Day 3: Every Nation Has Its Day

Read EZEKIEL Chapters 30-32

Nations exist only on earth and will be dealt with by God as a nation while here on earth. Nations develop their own personalities and character. That is developed by their leader's and follower's beliefs. God is concerned about every aspect of a nations actions and their theology.

Each nation rises to power and has its day of influence and glory. During Egypt's glory day God said, "You are like a lion among the nations, you are like a monster in the seas..." (31:2). At one time in history Egypt, Iraq, Iran, Greece, Rome and other nations were world powers that ruled the world. America is at present the world power. There is no guarantee it will remain so. America's greatness is dependent upon its character developed by a belief in God.

Each nation has had another day when God judged them. That terrible day of judgment is seen in the life of Egypt when God said to Egypt, "Wail and say, 'Alas for that day!" (30:2). "Dark will be the day at Tahpanhes when I break the yoke of Egypt" (30:18). God has given America its day of glory. Pray that the Day of Judgment on American can be avoided.

My prayer: First, Lord I want to praise You and thank You for allowing me to live in the greatest nation that has ever existed. Please forgive us as a nation for our immorality, abortions, foul language, and greed and for turning our back on You. Have mercy and send a spiritual awakening that will cause churches to preach Your word and bring the lost into salvation. Have mercy!

Day 4: Decisions Can Be Deadly or Divine

Read EZEKIEL Chapters 33-35

God assigned people to be watchmen to warn their city of an attack. If they warned the city and people died they were not held accountable. If they failed to warn people they were held liable. Why does God want people to be warned of judgment? Why does He want the wicked to repent? "...surely as I live, declares the Sovereign Lord, I take no pleasure in the death of the wicked, but rather that they turn from their ways and live..." (33:11). God warns people about death and hell because He cares about them.

An individual can decide to obey or disobey God either by responding to Him or by ignoring Him. God informed Ezekiel that his "countryman" were "Saying to each other, 'Come and hear the message...and listen to your words, but they do not put them into practice" (33:30, 31). God proclaimed that, "...if a wicked man turns away from his wickedness...he will live by doing so." (33:19). "When I say to the wicked, you shall surely die..." and he does not turn away from his wickedness..."he will die..." (33:8, 9). "Seek the Lord while He may be found..." (Isaiah 55:6).

My prayer: I LIFT UP my nation, my region, and my city to You Lord and plead with You to bring Your convicting power into the hearts of the people so we will decide to repent of our wickedness and determine to follow Jesus. Again, I cry out for Your mercy.

Day 5: Profanity

Read EZEKIEL Chapters 36-37

What is profanity? It is more than using curse words. According to the dictionary profanity is being "...irreverent toward God or holy things; speaking or spoken, acting or acted in contempt of sacred things or implying it; blasphemous; polluted..." God had created Israel to be the only nation to display who He is. They were to reflect His holiness, character and greatness. Instead of fulfilling their role God said, "...when the people of Israel were living in their own land, they defiled it by their conduct and their actions...so I poured out My wrath on them because they had shed blood in the land and because they had defiled it with their idols" (36:17, 18). "Wherever they went among the nations they profaned My holy name..." (36:20).

Profanity, according to God, is not only blasphemous words but living in a manner that indicates God condones evil conduct. What we do can be profanity as well as what words we use. Christians are chosen to reveal Jesus by their actions and words. "You are the Light of the World...let Your light shine before men, that they may see Your good deeds and praise You Father in Heaven" (Matthew 5:13, 16).

My prayer: Again, I ask for forgiveness and confess I have not been a good display of who Jesus is when I have been impatient and unkind in words and deed. Thank You for Your word that convicts and teaches what my behavior should be. Help me today to display Jesus in all my actions.

Day 6: Back to the Future

Read EZEKIEL Chapters 38-39

Ezekiel prophesied of the world attacking Israel in the future. God not only revealed that nations will attempt to destroy Israel in the final World War but He even revealed the thoughts of those who will try to destroy Israel. Ezekiel gave details as to the mind-set of the nations who hate Jehovah-God. He said of those pagan nations, "On that day thoughts will come into your mind and you will devise an evil scheme. You will say, 'I will invade a land of un-walled villages; I will attack a peaceful and unsuspecting people...'" (38:10-13).

God is a mind reader and sees what a person is going to think in the future. God doesn't need to go "Back to the Future" because He lives in the future. Isaiah declared that God said, "For I know their works and their thoughts..." (Isaiah 66:18). The Psalmist said, "The Lord knoweth the thoughts of man..."

(94:11). More importantly Jesus knows our thoughts. "And Jesus knowing their thoughts said, "Wherefore think ye evil in Your hearts?" (Matthew 9:4 KJV).

My prayer: Thank You for loving me even though You know my thoughts. Thank You for loving me while I was dead in my sins. I praise You and thank You for knowing the future and that You will be there for all who call on You.

Day 7: Today's Temple
Read EZEKIEL Chapters 40-42

An angel showed the Temple to Ezekiel in Jerusalem. God was emphasizing the Temple's place in Israel. The Temple must have had a great significance to God and man for Him to spend so much time on it.

The Temple was designed to be the center of all of Jewish life. The Temple was to display God's glory to Israel and the rest of the world. Its square shape was "...the 'shape' of perfection, or holiness. At its geometric center was the altar, the place of sacrifice.[7]" At the very center of the Temple was the altar where the main function of the Temple took place. Just to approach a holy God people had to cover their sins with the blood of animal sacrifices.

Today's Temple is not made of stone and wood. It is alive in the body of Christ's church and its believers. Christ's blood is at the center of this Temple. "Don't you know that you yourselves are God's temple and that God's Spirit lives in you?" (I Corinthians 3:16). Paul said, "...I urge you...to offer your bodies as living sacrifices..." (Romans 12:1).

---

[7] NIV Archaeological Study Bible: An Illustrated Walk Through Biblical History and Culture, 2005, Zondervan Corporation.

My prayer: It is my heart's desire to be continually filled with the Holy Spirit so that my temple will always honor You. Your presence gives purpose to my life. I praise You for the truth found in Your Word.

Spoonful

Yearly Devotions – Week 36

Day 1: Brighter Than the Sun

Read EZEKIEL Chapters 43-45

What is brighter than the sun? The Son of God is brighter. No human can be in the presence of Christ's heavenly glory and not be humbled and become prostrate. His disciple could not stand in the presence of His glory. The disciples reaction to His glory showed how magnificent is His glory. "His face shown like the sun, and His clothes became as white as the light...A bright cloud enveloped them..." And they heard a voice in the cloud. "When the disciples heard this, they fell face down on the ground terrified" (Matthew 17:2, 5, 6).

Not only is God brighter than the sun, He is greater than the sun. Ezekiel said, "...I saw the glory of the God of Israel coming from the east. His voice was like the roar of rushing waters, and the land was radiant with His glory...the glory of the Lord entered the Temple through the gate facing east." (43:2, 4) The sun rises in the east and was outshone by the presence of God. No one was to forget God's glory entering Jerusalem from the east so God said, "This gate is to remain shut. It must not be opened; no one may enter through it." (44:2) That gate will remain closed until Jesus returns and enters through it.

My prayer: Even so, come Lord Jesus. I truly want You Lord to return and display Your glory to the whole world again.

Day 2: The River of Life

Read EZEKIEL Chapters 46-48

An angel took Ezekiel inside the Temple and showed him a river flowing from its threshold. That river ran into the Dead Sea. The Dead Sea is the saltiest body of water in the world. Nothing can live in it because it is 25% salt. The only way water can escape from the Dead Sea is by evaporation because there are no outlets so that the stagnate water can flow out.

The angel revealed to Ezekiel that God was going to turn the Dead Sea into a live sea. Ezekiel reported that "the man brought me back to the entrance of the Temple, and I saw water coming out from under the threshold of the Temple toward the east..." That stream turned into... "A river that no one could cross..." and "...when it empties in the sea (Dead Sea), the water there becomes fresh. Swarms of living creatures will live wherever the river flows" (47:1,5,8,9). This river could be called the "River of Life." Lost people are like the Dead Sea. Jesus is the Temple from which the River of Life flows to bring life to the lost. "He who believes in Me, as the scripture has said, out of his heart will flow rivers of living water" (John 7:38).

My prayer: _Thank You for quenching my thirst with the truth of my sin and Your grace that gave me eternal life through Jesus shed blood._

Day 3: God Uses Commitment at Any Age

Read DANIEL Chapters 1-2

For a young Daniel to remain calm when his life was threatened showed his dependence on God. He believed his life rested in God's hands. Even though he was a captive and trophy of war he committed to trust God with his life. He refused to eat food that had been dedicated to pagan idols and the gods they stood for. "But Daniel resolved not to defile himself with the royal food and wine…" (1:8). His parents must have done a great job in raising him to trust the Lord.

Even though he trusted the Lord for his very life he still had a God-given drive to survive. He asked his companions to pray for God's protection. "He urged them to plead for mercy from the God of heaven…so that he and his friends might not be executed with the rest of the wise men of Babylon" (2:18). Daniel practiced what Jesus taught. Jesus said, "Do not be afraid of those who kill the body but cannot kill the soul. Rather be afraid of the One who can destroy both soul and body in hell" (Matthew 10:28).

My prayer: Thank You for the knowledge that life is precious and for teaching me to fear the right things. Help me share that You are the only source of survival.

Day 4: Commitment Can't Compromise

Read DANIEL Chapters 3-4

To be committed to something or some belief means to bind oneself to a certain behavior or action and refuse to change to accommodate others or to seek safety because of the consequences. Commitment is different than a preference. A preference is something a person would like to have or enjoy but would be willing to change or compromise if needed. A true commitment to something means a person could not and would not compromise.

Shadrach, Meshach and Abednego are vivid examples of what a commitment is and how it effects decisions and behavior. These three Israelites committed to worship only Jehovah-God even if it meant they had to forfeit their lives. Because of their commitment to God they refused to bow down to an idol even when they knew they would be thrown in fire. "If we are thrown into the blazing furnace, the God we serve is able to save us from it, and He will rescue us...But even if He does not, we want You to know, O King, that we will not serve Your gods or worship the image of gold You have set up" (3:17-18).

My prayer: Lord, I ask for Your gift of courage so that I will be committed to avoid the impurity of this world and walk in faithfulness to Christ's mission without compromise. Lead my church, city, state and nation to be committed to Christian values and Godly righteousness.

Day 5: Knees Will Knock

Read DANIEL Chapters 5-7

To face God without an advocate will be the most terrifying experience a person can have. God is holy, just, all powerful, all knowing and hates sin. He dispenses justice and no one can avoid facing Him. If a person does not have a mediator he will have to face Him all alone. Just the announcement of Belshazzar's judgment caused him to be overcome with fear.

It will be a sudden appearance of judgment to those who face God without a Savior. They will have Belshazzar's experience. "Suddenly the fingers of a human hand appeared and wrote on the plaster of the wall...the king watched as the hand wrote. His face turned pale and he was so frightened that his knees knocked together and his legs gave way" (5:5-6).

There was a secret analysis from the Lord of Belshazzar's spiritual condition. "Tekel: You have been weighed on the scales and found wanting" (5:27). No person's works can ever out-weigh their sin. "Salvation is found in no one else, for there is no other name under heaven given to men by which we must be saved" (Acts 4:12). Only Christ's shed blood outweighs our sin.

My prayer: I praise You for providing salvation as a gift. Thank You for allowing me to work with You to bring people to Your salvation. I pray for an opportunity to share Your salvation today. Give me the sensitivity to recognize that opportunity.

Day 6: The Glory Yet to Come

Read DANIEL Chapters 8-10

Our minds can hardly grasp the magnitude of the awesomeness of heavenly life. Just the messenger from heaven was an overwhelming sight to Daniel. We can only discover the glory yet to come in heaven through God's Word.

Paul testifies that human words are inadequate to describe the glory of our heavenly home. He said, he "…was caught up to paradise. He heard inexpressible things, things that man is not permitted to tell" (II Corinthians 12:4). The prophet Isaiah said, "For since the beginning of the world men have not heard, nor perceived by the ear, neither hath the eye seen, O God, beside thee, what He hath prepared for him that waiteth for Him" (Isaiah 64:4).

Daniel let us get a glimpse of that glorious place by describing what one of God's messengers looked like. He said, "I looked up and there before me was a man dressed in linen, with a belt of the finest gold around his waist. His body was like Chrysolite, his face like lightening, his eyes like flaming torches, his arms and legs like the gleam of burnished bronze, and his voice like the sound of a multitude" (10:15).

My prayer: Thank You for giving me Your salvation so I can be part of the glorious world to come. Help me bring people to You so they can have a glorious eternal future. Help me to fill up Your banquet room.

Day 7: History's Conclusion

Read DANIEL Chapters 11-12

God lives outside of time and has seen the conclusion of His creation. These two chapters reveal that governments, kings and armies come and go. Nations are continually in conflict with each other. There was one conclusion for all the men involved. They all died. The righteous have always suffered when nations fought. God has always made good out of the suffering of the righteous. "Some of the wise will stumble, so that they may be refined, purified and made spotless until the time of the end, for it will come at the appointed time" (11:35).

The righteous have always suffered from evil's presence. The Christian life is a series of tests called "crises." God warned of conflicts that come in life. "Dear friends, do not be surprised at the painful trial You are suffering, as though something strange were happening to You...if You are insulted because of the name of Christ, You are blessed" (I Peter 4:12, 14).

Daniel reminds us of the main event of history's conclusion. "Multitudes who sleep in the dust of the earth will awake: some to everlasting life, others to shame and everlasting contempt" (12:2). History concludes with all men standing before God and giving an account of their behavior.

My prayer: Dear Lord, Your control of history is an assurance to me and I thank You for the hope You give me that You will make everything right in Your time. Help give me Your vision of what is happening when I go through the trials of life. Thank You for going through every trial I have gone through so You can minister to my heart.

Yearly Devotions – Week 37

Day 1: Sustainable Civilization

Read HOSEA Chapters 1-6

In 1997, the United Nations developed a process they thought would preserve civilization. That process is called the "United Nations Agenda 21." Its purpose is to control the population of the world with regulations that are designed to rescue earth from man's industrialization and abuse of the natural resources. What the U.N., politicians and evolutionist don't understand is that to sustain life on earth spiritual means must be used. It has always been a spiritual matter.

God said, "...My people are destroyed from lack of knowledge" (4:5). What knowledge do people lack? They had plenty of human knowledge. God let them know what knowledge they lacked. He said, "...You have ignored the Law of Your God" (4:6).

Until America turns back to teaching the Ten Commandments and seeking God through prayer it will continue to experience what Israel went through. "There is no faithfulness, no love, and no acknowledgment of God in the land. There is only cursing, lying and murder, stealing and adultery, they break all bounds, and bloodshed follows bloodshed" (4:1-2). Only a return to worshiping Jesus will sustain civilization.

My prayer: Please give our pastors boldness to preach the truth so the people won't perish. I pray for our nation and ask that You send a spirit of conviction to our leaders that will cause them to repent of ignoring You.

Day 2: Truth's Reception

Read HOSEA Chapters 7-11

Tim Tebow, the NFL player that honors Christ on the football field, is mocked and ridiculed. Jesus warned that the world would resist the truth. He said, "Blessed are you when people insult you, persecute you and falsely say all kinds of evil against you because of me" (Matthew 5:19).

Hosea told why truth's reception is mocked and ridiculed. "Because your sins are so many and your hostility so great the prophet is considered a fool, the inspired man a maniac. The prophet along with my God is the watchman over Ephraim, yet snares await him on all his paths, and hostility in the house of God" (9:7-8).

Israel's rejection of the truth was reflected in their behavior. "They make many promises, take false oaths and make agreements; therefore lawsuits spring up like poisonous weeds in a plowed field" (10:4). The only antidote to Godless behavior is the truth. Jesus said, "IF you hold to My teaching...then you will know the truth, and the truth will set you free" (John 8:32, emphasis added). Jesus prayed to the Father, "Sanctify them by the truth; Your Word is truth" (John 17:17).

My prayer: Thank You again for Your word which is truth. Thank You that You told us we are sinners and that we must turn away from our sin and turn to You for all of life through Jesus. I am humbled to live in a free country where I can hear Your word. Thank You again for the truth.

Day 3: The Gift Giver Gets the Glory

Read HOSEA Chapters 12-14

Israel received God's blessings and then came to believe He was obligated to bless them no matter what they did. God reminded them, "But I am the Lord your God, who brought you out of Egypt. You shall acknowledge no God but Me, no Savior except Me...When I fed them, they were satisfied; when they were satisfied, they became proud; then they forgot Me" (13:4, 6). Israel fell in love with their wealth and fell out of love with God. "They offer human sacrifices and kiss the calf-idols" (13:2).

When God's judgment came it was swift and just. "The ways of the Lord are right; the righteous walk in them, but the rebellious stumble in them" (14:9). God said to Israel, "You are destroyed, O Israel, because you are against Me, against Your helper" (13:9). God's grace gave them a way of escape. They must repent and give God, the Gift-Giver, the glory. If they repented they would confess and seek God's forgiveness. God expected and demanded they say, "Forgive all our sins...we will never again say our gods..." (14:2, 3). Anything we receive above hell is a gift from God.

My prayer: I praise You for all the wonderful blessings You have poured out on me and my family. Your word has always been true and Your grace has always been present in my life. Thank You and I give You the glory for all the good in my life. You are truly worthy to be worshiped.

Day 4: The Age of God

Read JOEL Chapters 1-3

The title is not a reference about how old God is because He is ageless. The term "age" is being used to describe an era of God working through the Holy Spirit in a unique way. God had never dispensed the Holy Spirit to all of mankind until

Jesus sent Him as a gift from heaven. After the resurrection Jesus said, "I am going to send You what My Father has promised; but stay in the city until You have been clothed with power from on high" (Luke 24:49). During the church age the Holy Spirit has the church to live in and work through.

It is made evident that Joel is referring to the age or era of the Holy Spirit working through the church by the Apostle Peter. After the one hundred and twenty had prayed during Pentecost the Holy Spirit sent "...tongues of fire that separated and came to rest on each of them. All of them were filled with the Holy Spirit..." (Acts 2:3-4). The Apostle Peter said, "...this is what was spoken by the prophet Joel: in the last days, God says, I will pour My Spirit on all people" (Acts 2:16-17). We live in the Age of God not the Age of Aquarius.

My prayer: Thank You for the privilege to be living when the Resurrection of Jesus has taken place and the Holy Spirit is empowering the church. Please help us to release any control of our lives to the Holy Spirit so He can have the freedom to do whatever He chooses through me. I praise You that You did not leave us as orphans.

Day 5: Worship Rejected in Heaven

Read AMOS Chapters 1-5

The age old problem of Israel was idolatry and immorality. Israel became like what they worshiped. They became corrupt because they worshiped corrupt gods.

Worship refused in heaven is:
1) Worship that doesn't prepare to meet God. God said, "...prepare to meet Your God, O Israel" (4:12). What

preparation was needed? Repentance of sin was needed or judgment would come.

2) Worship that ignores sin. God said, "For I know how many are Your offenses and how great Your sins" (5:12).
3) Worship with wrong values. God said, "Seek good, not evil, that You may live...hate evil, love good..." (5:14-15).
4) Worship without a passion for the Lord. God said, "I hate, I despise Your religious feasts; I cannot stand Your assemblies...though You bring choice fellowship offerings, I will have no regard for them. Away with the noise of Your songs! I will not listen to the music of Your harps" (5:21-23).

What does God want in worship? He wants worshipers that live out their faith. "But let justice roll on like a river, righteousness like a never-failing stream" (5:24).

My prayer: Lord, help me to have a heart to please You daily as well as in worship services. May my life be an act of worship as I seek Your forgiveness and mercy. Lead our entire nation to worship and follow You.

Day 6: Genuine Preachers are Called

Read AMOS Chapters 6-9

Pastoring a church or preaching the gospel is not a profession. It is a calling of God. A pastor is not a hired hand that is the employee of the church. He is called of God to lead a church to reach the lost and edify believers. He has an awesome responsibility to please God by leading a church to obey God. His goal is to please God even if it offends the people. A genuine preacher is chosen by God rather than him choosing to preach. Amos let us know he didn't choose to be a prophet. He said, "I was neither a prophet nor a prophet's son, but I was a shepherd, and I also took care of sycamore trees. But the

Lord took me from tending the flock and said to me, 'Go prophecy to My people Israel" (7:14-15).

A genuinely called preacher of God will always be challenged about his message. The world never likes to hear God's message and attacks the messenger. Amaziah said to Amos, "Get out, You Seer! Go back to the land of Judah. Don't prophesy any more at Bethel..." (7:12-13). Even though the preacher is challenged he must continue to carry the message of God.

My prayer: I praise You and thank You for the Godly preachers I have heard who preached without fear or favor towards man. I pray for God called pastors to stay by the call and continue to preach the whole Word of God. Thank You for calling me to pastor.

Day 7: Behavior of Belief

Read OBADIAH – JONAH Chapters 1-4

It is rare for an entire city to repent of their evil behavior and admit to their sinfulness. Only belief in the prophet's message could change them. Whether Jonah's story of being thrown into the sea was known before he preached to Nineveh is not recorded in Scripture. It is possible that the incident had reached Nineveh by the sailors who threw him overboard. They could have believed he either drowned or was eaten by the big fish. Then when he appeared preaching of Nineveh's doom it would have seemed that a dead man from the grave was preaching. Nineveh's response showed the tremendous impact his sudden appearance and message had. Their behavior demonstrated their belief. "The Ninevites believed God. They declared a fast, and all of them, from the greatest to the least, put on sackcloth...When God saw what they did and how they turned from their evil ways He had compassion and did not bring upon them the destruction He had threatened"

(3:5, 10). This illustrates what Jesus said, "By their fruit you will recognize them" (Matthew 7:16).

My prayer: Your mercy and compassion are wonderful and I praise You for it. Fill me with Your Holy Spirit so my life will produce good fruit.

Yearly Devotions – Week 38

Day 1: Carrot and Stick

Read MICAH Chapters 1-5

God called, warned, and threatened Israel to stop worshiping idols or He would judge them. He said, "Those who live in Maroth writhe in pain waiting for relief, because disaster has come from the Lord, even to the gate of Jerusalem" (1:12). He promises to restore Israel after punishing it. The carrot is God's promise to restore Israel and the stick is the prediction of judgment if they refuse to obey. Godly prophets preached using the carrot and stick predictions. The false prophets only used the carrot incentive. History showed the Godly prophets had God's message.

God promised that all nations would one day worship Him. That time will be when Jesus returns to earth. God said, "I will take vengeance in anger and wrath upon the nations that have not obeyed Me" (5:15). He predicts where Jesus will land at His first coming. "But You, Bethlehem Epharathah, though You are small...out of You will come for Me one who will rule over Israel, whose origins are from old, from ancient times [He is eternal]...And He will be their peace" (5:2, 5). Jesus is the peace the world is looking for. "Consider therefore the kindness and sternness of God" (Romans 11:22).

My prayer: Please bring the message of hope to a desperate world that seems bent on destroying itself. Help us get Your message of salvation and judgment out in an effective way. I pray for Christ's second coming to be soon.

Day 2: Heavenly Indictment

Read MICAH Chapters 6-7 - Nahum Chapters 1-3

To be indicted on a criminal charge is very serious and costly. It involves the court, lawmen, lawyers, the victims and the accused. The legal process involves uncertainty, tensions, adversarial feelings, strategy and the confrontation of the accused and the accuser. There are debates about the circumstances. There are pleas of innocence and a challenge of guilt. The jury or judge must decide the truth. The process is of the utmost importance because of the seriousness of the outcome.

God's indictment has no uncertainty. He knows all the facts and circumstances. God indicted Israel and knew for certain they were guilty. God said, "Am I to forget, O wicked house, your ill-gotten treasures...dishonest scales...Her rich men are violent; her people are liars..." (Micah 6:10, 11, 12). Israel's "rap-sheet" was posted publicly by God Himself. Without Jesus as a lawyer and Savior every person's "rap-sheet" will be posted by God and judgment passed. "...the dead were judged out of those things which were written in the books, according to their works" (Revelation 20:12).

My prayer: I thank You for paying for my sin through the death of Jesus on the cross. I pray for those who have no advocate that they will repent of their sin and receive Jesus as Savior and Lord.

Day 3: God is Plain Spoken

Read HABAKKUK Chapters 1-3

Habakkuk questioned God why evil men had such power over Israel and other nations. Habakkuk acknowledged Israel's sins of idolatry and injustice. When God answered Habakkuk He gave a direct answer. God let him know that the evil treatment of Babylon and Assyria would not go unpunished. They would be treated the same way they treated others. The pagan prophets prophesied of future events also but were never specific.

Biblical prophet's messages were distinct from pagan prophets in at least three ways. First, all of God's dealings and prophecies were based and inferred on a covenant relationship with Israel. Second, biblical prophecy was generally clear and specific. Third, Israel's prophets based all their messages on a monotheistic theme and opposed all polytheistic idolatry. God's clarity is seen by his warning to Babylon and Assyria. "Woe to him who piles up stolen goods...Woe to him who builds his realm by unjust gain...Woe to him who builds a city with bloodshed...Woe to him who gives drink to his neighbors...Woe to him who says to wood, "come to life!" (2:6, 9, 12, 15, 19).

My prayer: Thank You for Your word that is specific and clear. Thank You for telling us plainly about sin, death and hell and a way of escape through Jesus' shed blood.

Day 4: Mixed Worship

Read ZEPHANIAH Chapters 1-3

India has thousands of gods over all their land. People worship gods of every kind. The most difficult concept for the Indians who worship many gods is to grasp the Biblical teaching that there is only one God and only one way to God. Missionaries emphasize to the people of India that they have to reject and repudiate all gods and worship only Jehovah-God of the Bible. Jesus as the only Savior and Lord caused Christians to be thrown to the lions when Romans ruled the world. Only the God of the Bible is worthy to be worshiped because He is the only creator and holy God. Because of Israel's idolatry God warned them that He would punish them for their mixed worship. He said, "...I will cut off from this place every remnant of Baal...those who bow down and swear by the Lord and also swear by Molech" (1:4, 5).

Christians today may not bow down to idols but they may let the possession of "things" or activities have priority over serving God and that is idolatry. Jesus said, "No one can serve two masters...You cannot serve God and money" (Matthew 6:24).

My prayer: *Keep my eyes on You and help me put You first in my life. Thank You for allowing me to possess the greatest gift in life – Jesus.*

Day 5: We Are On the Winning Side

Read HAGGAI Chapters 1-2

God is going to take the world back from Satan soon. Adam surrendered the control of the world to Satan when he disobeyed God and believed Satan's lies. Satan's biggest lie was that God was unjust and unfair. Israel had experienced captivity in Babylon because of their disobedience and then had been allowed to return to Palestine. They had lost their freedom by listening to Satan's prophets. God told them He was going to restore them. "Tell Zerubbabel governor of Judah that I will shake the heavens and the earth. I will overturn royal thrones and shatter the power of the foreign kingdoms..." (2:21, 22).

Israel and Zerubbabel had become discouraged in restoring the temple and their land. They were facing great opposition in doing God's work. God sent Haggai to encourage them by letting them know they would someday see God's victory over evil and wicked men. Paul encouraged the Galatians to be faithful because they were on the winning side. Paul said, "Let us not become weary in doing good, for at the proper time we will reap a harvest if we do not give up" (Galatians 6:9).

My prayer: I thank You Lord for Your faithfulness. I ask for Your strength to remain faithful in spite of opposition from Satan.

Day 6: Satan's Obsession

Read ZECHARIAH Chapters 1-6

Satan is a real person who has one burning passion. He hates God and man who was created in God's image. He continually attempts to destroy man by tempting him to sin. His goal is to bring God's judgment on man. Satan's goal is to fill hell with mankind. Jesus will say to the unbeliever, "...Depart from Me, You who are cursed, into eternal fire prepared for the devil and his angels" (Matthew 25:41).

Satan is the great accuser seeking God's judgment on sinful man. According to the Scriptures Satan still has access to heaven and God Himself. "One day the angels came to present themselves before the Lord, and Satan also came with them" (Job 1:6). Satan will eventually be banned from heaven. Before Christ returns to earth Satan will be ejected from heaven permanently. "Now have come the salvation and the power and the kingdom of our God, and the authority of His Christ. For the accuser of our brothers, who accuses them before God day and night, has been hurled down" (Revelation 12:10). Zechariah saw this phenomenon in his vision when he saw "...Joshua, the high priest, standing before the angel of the Lord, and Satan standing at his right side to accuse him" (3:1).

My prayer: "And lead us not into temptation, but deliver us from the evil one." (Matthew 6:13)

Day 7: The Prophet Without Profit

Read ZECHARIAH Chapters 7-11

Israel's prophets and leaders worshiped idols and practiced pagan rituals. God called them false shepherds. Zechariah announced that God's patience had run out and that they would be punished. They would be dispersed until the true shepherd arrived. Zechariah said, "The flock detested me, and I grew weary of them and said, 'I will not be Your shepherd...'" (11:8, 9).

He broke his staff to illustrate his covenant with Israel was ended. He told them to pay him what they thought he was worth. "I told them, 'If You think it best, give me my pay; but if not, keep it! So they paid me thirty pieces of silver" (11:12). That was the price of a useless slave that had been gored by a bull. The amount was an insult for a Godly prophet. "If the bull gores a male or female slave, the owner must pay thirty shekels of silver..." (Exodus 21:32).

Jesus said, "I am the good shepherd" (John 10:11). The world believes there is no profit in following Him. Judas said, "What are You willing to give me? ...So they counted out for him thirty silver coins..." (Matthew 26:15).

My prayer: Thank You for making life profitable and worth all the effort to follow You. I pray for a world that doesn't know the value of a Savior who gave His life for His sheep. Help me to get this truth out.

Yearly Devotions – Week 39

Day 1: An Earth-Shattering Appearance

Read ZECHARIAH Chapters 12-14

Jesus came humbly as a baby in very serene circumstances the first time. Angelic activity had to be incorporated to let a few shepherds know of His arrival. A star was lit by God to guide the wise men to Him.

It is going to be completely different the second time. Movies have been made about aliens landing on earth and creating panic and all sorts of havoc. Christ's second arrival on earth will be a shattering experience for believers and none believers. "On that day His feet will stand on the Mount of Olives, east of Jerusalem, and the Mount of Olives will be split in two from east to west...You will flee as You fled from the earthquake in the days of Uzziah...then the Lord my God will come, and all the holy ones with Him" (14:4-5).

The climate will be affected when He arrives the second time. "On that day there will be no light, no cold or frost. It will be a unique day, without day time or night time – a day known to the Lord. When evening comes, there will be light...the Lord will be King over the whole earth" (14:6-7).

My prayer: Even so come Lord, Jesus. My desire and prayer is that I could be alive when You rapture the church and experience that victory. Thank You for letting me know You have overcome sin and Satan.

Day 2: Honorable Mention

Read MALACHI Chapters 1-4

God stated His grievances against Israel through Malachi, especially toward the priests and prophets. He is specific when listing their acts of disloyalty and behavior. Their indifference seen in their dead orthodoxy and deadness in worship angered the Lord. They tried to get by with the minimum that their faith required. "When You bring injured, crippled or diseased animals and offer them as sacrifices, should I accept them from Your hands? Says the Lord" (1:13). "Because of You I will rebuke Your descendants..." (2:3).

The one bright spot is when God mentions Levi. What an honor to be mentioned by God for faithful behavior. Amid all the corruption in worship God names a man He is pleased with. God tells why He was pleased with Levi. "...he revered me and stood in awe of my name. True instruction was in his mouth and nothing false was found on his lips...he turned many from sin" (2:4-6). That should be the goal of every believer. We should long to hear Jesus say, "Well done, good and faithful servant" (Matthew 25:21).

My prayer: Lord, strengthen my resolve to remain faithful until I am in Your presence. Teach me to walk closer to You each day. Give me Your wisdom to turn many from sin.

Day 3: God's Defense Against Deception
Read MATTHEW Chapters 1-4

Deception comes from one place. Jesus revealed the source when He said of Satan, "He was a murderer from the beginning, not holding to the truth, for there is no truth in him. When he lies, he speaks his native language, for he is a liar and the Father of Lies" (John 8:44). He introduced lying into the world by creating doubt and lying to Adam and Eve. He implied God didn't mean what He said when he asked, "Did God really say 'You must not eat from any tree in the garden?" He then lied when he said, "You will not surely die...when you eat of it your eyes will be opened, and you will be like God..." (Genesis 3:1, 4). He told a half-truth. Their eyes were opened but they were not like God.

When the last Adam, Jesus, came Satan again tried to deceive Him to gain control of Him. He tried to tempt Jesus to meet His physical need, food, aside from God's will and then to display His deity in a spectacular way. He offered Jesus a short cut to ruling the world if He would worship him. Christ's only answer to this series of temptations was, "For it is written..." (4:4, 7, 10). The truth in God's Word is the only defense against Satan's deception.

My prayer: Thank You for Your word which is truth. Thank You for giving us the truth who is Jesus. I praise You for allowing the truth to be my Savior to guide me through the mine-field of Satan's deceptions.

Day 4: The Real Hope of Change

Read MATTHEW Chapters 5-7

President Obama campaigned on the theme of "Hope and Change." He ran on the idea that he was going to change America. Jesus warned His disciples about trying to change others. A spouse may have legitimate complaints against their partner. That doesn't mean that only one of them should change. Sometimes the best antidote to a stubborn spouse who insists on continuing offensive behavior is for the offended spouse to change some of their own behavior. Jesus said, "How can you say to your brother, 'Let me take the speck out of Your eye,' when all the time there is a plank in Your own eye? You hypocrite, first take the plank out of your own eye, and then You will see clearly to remove the speck from Your brother's eye" (7:4-5).

Only God can change a spouse, business partner or friend. If a person plans to change the person they are going to marry they are marrying the wrong person. Only God's grace brings hope and change.

My prayer: Lord, bring to my heart and mind where I need to change so others can see Your grace in my life. I pray for our nation that it will depend on God's grace for the right kind of change.

Day 5: Values Determine Priorities

Read MATTHEW Chapters 8-10

The Apostle Paul valued a knowledge of Jesus above anything in this world. Christ Jesus was like a treasure to him. He was willing to abandon all of his ambitions and goals in life just to know Jesus better. He said, "What is more, I consider everything a loss compared to the surpassing greatness of knowing Christ Jesus my Lord, for whose sake I have lost all things. I consider them rubbish that I may gain Christ and be found in Him...the righteousness that comes from God and is by faith" (Philippians 3:9-9).

Anyone who rejects Christ values this world and all that is in it. They have no love for Jesus nor things that are spiritually related to Jesus. They are focused on this world and what it has to offer unless they are deceived by a cult leader. They despise anything that relates to Jesus' blood being shed for mankind's sin. Jesus said, "All men hate you because of Me..." (10:22). He said we should not let that bother us. He said, "When you are persecuted in one place, flee to another" (10:23). We are to get over any mistreatment and move on with our life.

My prayer: Let me see Your hand working in my life when I am rejected by those who have no knowledge of Your salvation. May they be like Paul who hated Christians and come to know You as the risen Savior.

Day 6: Where is Heaven and Paradise?

Read MATTHEW Chapters 11-12

Jesus preached to Israel that they must "Repent for the Kingdom of heaven is near" (4:17). To have a kingdom there must be a King. If the kingdom was near as Jesus said, then the King must be near. The kingdom Jesus and John the Baptist talked about is in a place called heaven. It is a place that is completely different than an earthly kingdom. It is in a spiritual dimension that is unearthly. It is a dimension where time, space and earthly, physical materials do not exist. The earth reflects the spiritual dimension because God created it.

The King of that dimension, Jesus, left His spiritual realm and entered into this earthly dimension. It is evident that heavenly conditions do not exist on earth. There is murder, lying, stealing, hatred, and immorality on earth. None of these things exist in the presence of a holy, righteous God in heaven. So where is heaven? Heaven is wherever God is! "Jesus said, 'I praise You, Father, Lord of heaven and earth, because You have hidden these things from the wise and learned, and revealed them to little children" (11:25). Paradise is wherever Jesus is. Jesus said to the thief on the cross, "I tell you the truth, today You will be with me in paradise" (Luke 23:43). Paradise and heaven are places where God lives and operates.

My prayer: Thank You for preparing a place for us to spend eternity with You. Thank You for paying for our way there with Your life and shed blood.

Day 7: A Faith That Brings Results

Read MATTHEW Chapters 13-15

A faith that brings results is a desperate faith that is convinced that only Jesus can meet a desperate need. The mother of a demon-possessed girl abandoned all protocol between Jesus and Gentiles to have her daughter cured. She did not care that Jesus had come to save the Jewish nation. Jesus had come to be the King of Israel and to rule the world through them and they rejected Him. This woman who was not a part of the Jewish covenant or a part of the chosen people believed in Him and His sovereign power.

This woman had no idea of the theological implications of Christ's prescience or about the Jews place in history. She was driven by one motive. "Lord, Son of David, have mercy on me! My daughter is suffering from demon-possession...Lord, help me!" (15:22, 25). Opposition from Jesus and His disciples to do what she asked did not stop her. Her faith in Jesus compelled her to overcome every obstacle to voice her request. Jesus responded to her faith. He said, "Woman, You have great faith! Your request is granted" (15:28).

My prayer: Lord, help me to have this woman's kind of faith. You are the only source for salvation and meeting all my needs.

Yearly Devotions – Week 40

Day 1: Deadly Business

Read MATTHEW Chapters 16-19

Serving as a policeman can be a deadly business today. There is a business more dangerous than that. That is the business of living your life for the wrong purpose.

If you sell an item at a pawn shop, the price is negotiated. The item sold needs to bring a profit. A good negotiator will make a profit whereas a bad negotiator will lose money. The worst and most deadly transaction a person negotiates is when he exchanges his soul for material wealth. Jesus warned man about the seriousness of that transaction when He said, "What good will it be for a man if he gains the whole world, yet forfeits his soul? Or what can a man give in exchange for his soul?" (16:26).

What does a man lose if he forfeits his soul? The soul is the real person housed in a physical body. When the body dies, the soul continues to live for eternity. The soul will either go to exist in hell or live in heaven. If a person rejects Jesus as Lord and Savior he forfeits the gift of eternal life and exists forever eternally damned. That is a transaction that can be deadly.

My prayer: I bow before You, Lord, and rejoice that You sought me out and offered eternal life. Thank You for saving me and writing my name in the Lamb's Book of Life.

Day 2: God is Never Surprised

Read MATTHEW Chapters 20-21

Armies spy on each other to prevent a surprise attack. There are satellites, listening devices, surveillance cameras and other gadgets used by governments and businesses to learn what the enemy or competition is doing.

God can never be surprised! He knows what is going to happen before it takes place. Jesus tried to prepare His disciples for the future event of His arrest and crucifixion. Jesus said to the disciples, "We are going up to Jerusalem, and the Son of Man will be betrayed to the chief priests and the teachers of the Law. They will condemn Him to death and will turn Him over to the Gentiles to be mocked and flogged and crucified. On the third day He will be raised to life" (20:17-19).

He rode a donkey to show that He is the real King of Israel who came in peace the first time. Four hundred years before Christ was born God revealed through the prophet that Jesus would ride into Jerusalem on a donkey "See, your King comes to you...riding on a donkey, on a colt, foal of a donkey" (Zechariah 9:9).

My prayer: I praise You and honor You for loving us even when You see our behavior before we commit it. I plead for Your patience for America and the people who You see doing ungodly things beforehand.

Day 5: Jesus Lived in the Present While Seeing the Future

Read MATTHEW Chapters 22-24

Jesus was burdened with the knowledge of Israel's destruction. He made two things clear to them. First, the Temple and Israel would be destroyed and second, His followers would be persecuted and killed. Only Jesus could carry this burden.

Jesus saw Nero, Caligula, Titus, Domition and Saul who became Paul killing those He loved. Jesus said of the Temple, "...I tell you the truth, not one stone here will be left on another; everyone will be thrown down" (24:2). Forty-one years later the Jewish historian, Josephus, saw this prophecy come true. He described it thus: "No pity was shown on account of age or out of respect for anyone's dignity – children and elderly, lay people and priests alike were slain...those who begged for mercy and those who resisted...the whole city was aflame." (WARS 6.5.1)

Jesus saw the Pharisees persecuting Christians. He said to the Pharisees, "...others you will flog in Your synagogues and pursue them from town to town" (23:34). We next read of Saul/Paul, "...breathing out murderous threats against the Lord's disciples" (Acts 9:1). Every believer must live in the present while seeing the future. "...He who does not believe will be condemned" (Mark 16:16).

My prayer: It is my prayer Lord, that I keep the future of every soul I meet in mind so that I can share Your salvation with them. Thank You for letting me see the future as a time to anticipate.

Day 4: Unseen Acts

Read MATTHEW Chapters 25-26

Every believer in Christ will be rewarded for their faithfulness, their motives and their behavior while on earth. The Apostle Paul wrote, "For we must all appear before the judgment seat of Christ, that each one may receive what is due him for the things done while in the body, whether good or bad" (II Corinthians 5:10). Paul wrote this to believers. He warned them that their behavior effected their rewards in heaven. Every person will be held accountable for their behavior.

A person cannot lose his eternal life or it would not be eternal. He can lose his fellowship with the Lord and his rewards in heaven. Jesus gave a parable about God rewarding faithfulness when He said, "...Well done, good and faithful servant! You have been faithful with a few things; I will put you in charge of many things...take Your inheritance, the Kingdom prepared for You since the creation of the world" (25:21, 34).

My prayer: Have mercy on me and guide my behavior as I live each day. I invite the Holy Spirit to control my behavior, motives and actions. Forgive me for not surrendering to Him from time to time.

Day 5: Calm Arrival and an Earth-Shattering Departure Read

Read MATTHEW Chapters 27-28

Jesus arrived on earth during a star-studded night with the calm announcement of an Angel to Shepherds. "And there were shepherds living out in the fields nearby, keeping watch at night. An angel of the Lord appeared to them, and the glory of the Lord shone around them..." The angel said, "Today in the town of David a Savior has been born to you; He is Christ the Lord" (Luke 2:8, 11). God arrived on earth as a man like all men arrive – through the birth-canal of a mother. He humbled Himself so He could completely and forever pay the penalty for man's sin as a man.

When Christ died, like all of humanity must when their heart stops and their lungs empty all of nature, the spiritual world knew a supernatural event had taken place. "And when Jesus cried out again in a loud voice, He gave up His spirit. At that moment the curtain of the Temple was torn in two from top to bottom. The earth shook and the rocks split. The tombs broke open and the bodies of many holy people who had died were raised to life" (27:50-51). More powerful than a space shuttle's rockets blasting off from Florida was the Lord's departure as He paid for all men's sin.

My prayer: *I praise You for the power of Your death and resurrection.*

Day 6: The Unpardonable Sin

Read MARK Chapters 1-3

The most significant battles Jesus fought were with the spiritual world of darkness. He defeated demons and evil spirits in every encounter. "The people were so amazed that they asked each other, 'What is this? A new teaching-and with authority! He even gives orders to evil spirits and they obey Him" (1:27). "He appointed twelve-designating them Apostles-...that He might send them out to preach and to have authority to drive out demons" (3:14). "He also drove out many demons, but He would not let the demons speak because they knew who He was" (1:34). Jesus and the disciples cast out demons through the power of the Holy Spirit.

The Pharisees and Sadducees were jealous of the popularity and the Holy Spirit's power working through Jesus. They knowingly and deliberately rejected Jesus' Messiahship even after seeing His supernatural powers. They had been in the presence of God and refused to accept Him in the person of Christ. That is the unpardonable sin. Jesus said, "I tell you the truth, all the sins and blasphemies of men will be forgiven them. But whoever blasphemes against the Holy Spirit will never be forgiven; he is guilty of an eternal sin" (3:28). The Pharisees knowingly and falsely assigned the Holy Spirit's work to Satan.

My prayer: I pray that the Holy Spirit will have full sway in my life, home church and nation. Thank You for sending the Comforter.

Day 7: Faith Brings Life

Read MARK Chapters 4-5

The demon possessed man did not control his life because it was in the possession of demons. Jesus' response to this man's desperate condition was to heal him. This man's faith did not have anything to do with his miraculous deliverance. God can choose to work because of someone's faith or He can work without someone's faith.

Jesus at other times chose to respond to a person's faith. The woman who had been bleeding for twelve years was healed because of her faith. Jesus said to her, "Daughter, your faith has healed you. Go in peace and be freed from suffering" (5:34).

Jairus' daughter died and his faith in Christ caused him to seek Jesus' help. The dead daughter's faith was not a factor. Her father's faith was what Jesus responded to. Jesus said to Jairus, "Don't be afraid; just believe" (5:36). The father's faith brought life and joy when Jesus raised her from the dead. "Immediately the girl stood up and walked around (She was twelve years old). Faith in Christ brings life either here on earth or in eternity. "Before this faith came, we were held prisoners by the law, locked up until faith should be revealed" (Galatians 3:23).

My prayer: I believe Lord; help my unbelief that I may get a concept of how great You are and the divine power that belongs to Your children.

Yearly Devotions – Week 41

Day 1: Sustainability Comes From Jesus

Read MARK Chapters 6-8

The lost world is afraid our natural resources are going to be depleted and cause the extinction of man and all living creatures. They cannot comprehend that the sustaining of life comes from one source – God. Jesus demonstrated that when He fed 5000 men at one setting and 4000 at another. If Jesus can multiply the food source for multitudes at one time He can keep our world stocked with food. The earth will continue to exist as it is until God decides to replace it.

The disciples were like people today. They worried about where their groceries would come from. They experienced Jesus taking care of their supply of food. Listen to the despair of the disciples about their need to supply food to the people. When they needed to feed 5000 men they said, "That would take eight months of a man's wages! Are we to go and spend that much on bread and give it to them to eat?" (6:37) Jesus took five loaves and two fishes and prayed and then "they all ate and were satisfied, and the disciples picked up twelve basketfuls of broken pieces of bread and fish." (6:42)

My prayer: Thank You Lord, for sustaining my family in all things during our ministry to serve You.

Day 2: Faith is the Key to Victory

Read MARK Chapters 9-11

Salvation is a gift from God that comes by God's grace and is received by faith. "For by grace are ye saved through faith;

and that not of yourselves: it is the gift of God: And not of works lest any man should boast" (Ephesians 2:8-9). The Holy Spirit's presence activates a person's faith to cause people to believe God will save them if they ask Him. Faith is believing God will do what He says He will do. After a person's conversion victory over Satan, the world and the flesh comes by the believer's faith in God's ability and power to overcome sin, Satan and self. A victorious Christian has confidence in God's power to answer prayer. Every believer needs a child-like faith in Jesus to see God work supernaturally in their life.

Jesus was adamant that His followers believe in God's power. He said, "Have faith in God...I tell you the truth; if anyone says to this mountain 'Go,' throw yourself into the sea, and does not doubt in his heart but believes that what he says will happen, it will be done for him. Therefore I tell you, whatever you ask in prayer, believe that you have received it and it will be yours" (11:22-23). A Christian's faith must grow to experience victory.

My prayer: Help my unbelief to grow into a dynamic belief system that nothing is impossible with God.

Day 3: Results of the Church's Absence

Read MARK Chapters 12-13

Mark 13 gives a snapshot of the earth's condition after the church's removal. Satan will have his way on earth for seven years. The majority of the people will worship Satan which will result in chaos and devastation. "For the Lord Himself will come down from heaven, with a loud command, with the voice of the arch angel and with the trumpet of God, and the dead in Christ will rise first. After that, we who are alive and are left will be caught up together with them in the clouds to meet the Lord in the air" (I Thessalonians 4:16-17). "Blessed and holy are those who have part in the First Resurrection" (Revelation 20:6).

Jesus describes the chaos of the earth after the church is removed.
1) There will be "wars and rumors of wars…" (13:7)
2) "Nation against nation and kingdom against kingdom" (13:8)
3) "Earthquakes in various places" (13:8)
4) "Famines" (13:8)
5) Believers will be arrested, "You will stand before governors and kings" (13:9)
6) "The gospel must first be preached to all nations." (13:10)
7) Families will be divided. "Brother will betray brother to death and a father his child. Children will rebel against their parents and have them put to death." (13:12)
8) The world will hate all believers. Jesus said, "All men will hate you because of Me…" (13:13)

My prayer: I praise You for giving me Your salvation and saving me from Hell, death and the Great Tribulation described by Jesus. Give me the wisdom to know how to share the gospel so others can obtain eternal life and miss Your judgment.

Day 4: Jesus' Word is Always Accurate
Read MARK Chapters 14-15

Preachers can mistakenly give the wrong account of an event while preaching. People can give wrong directions to a person trying to locate an address. The electronic equipment on an airplane can become defective while in the air and give wrong indications of the engine's operation and wrong information can be more dangerous than at other times. Some bad indications can be deadly.

The Apostles discovered that when Jesus gave them information and instructions it was always accurate. His instructions were accurate in every detail when He sent them into Jerusalem to prepare for the Passover. "The disciples left went into the city and found things just as Jesus told them" (14:16). Eternity is going to be exactly as Jesus described. We can believe it when He said, "...In My Father's house are many rooms; if it were not so, I would have told you. I am going to prepare a place for you" (John 14:2, 3). It is accurate when Jesus says, "I am the way and the truth and the life. No one comes to the Father except through Me" (John 14:6).

My prayer: Thank You Lord that You are the truth and have given accurate information to live by.

Day 5: Believing is Seeing

Read MARK Chapters 16 - LUKE 1

Faith lets people see what God can do and allows Him to work through them. To have victory in the Christian walk a person must believe Gabriel's statement to Mary. "For nothing is impossible with God" (Luke 1:37). Unbelief limits God's work through people. Jesus was displeased when His disciples refused to believe the reports of His Resurrection. They didn't believe Mary Magdalene. "When they heard that Jesus was alive and that she had seen Him, they did not believe it" (Mark 16:11). They did not believe the two who saw Jesus on the Road to Emmaus. "...these returned and reported it to the rest; but they did not believe them either" (Mark 16:13). Later, Jesus "...rebuked them for their lack of faith and their stubborn refusal to believe those who had seen Him after He had risen" (Mark 16:14).

Mary's faith allowed God to use her. She believed God could perform the impossible even after asking, "How will this be since I am a virgin?" (Luke 1:34). She believed Gabriel when he said, "...the Holy Spirit will come upon you..." (Luke 1:35). Her belief allowed her to have a great part in God's redeeming work. Elizabeth was right when she said of Mary, "Blessed is she who has believed that what the Lord has said to her will be accomplished!" (Luke 1:45).

My prayer: I praise You for Your holy power to always work when we believe You and trust You. I praise You for Your faithfulness. I ask that Your grace be multiplied in my life, my family and my nation. Help us to believe so strongly that we can see by faith what a family and nation can be when they believe You.

Day 6: God's Spotlight

Read LUKE Chapters 2-3

During a theatrical performance, a spotlight is focused on the main actor or personality from time to time. The Holy Spirit is like a spotlight pointing out God's Son as the main character in all of human history. History could be spelled "His-story." Luke states that Simeon was anointed by the Holy Spirit. It says, "...the Holy Spirit was upon him" (2:25). What did the Holy Spirit have him do? He let Mary and the world know Jesus had arrived. Simeon told Mary, "This child is destined to cause the falling and rising of many in Israel...so that the thoughts of many hearts will be revealed" (2:34, 35).

John the Baptist was filled with the Spirit while still in his mother's womb. What did the Holy Spirit have him do? He had him point Jesus out to the world. John said, "I baptize You with water. But one more powerful than I will come...He will baptize You with the Holy Spirit and with fire" (3:16).

"When he saw Jesus passing by, he said, 'Look, the Lamb of God!" (John 1:36). Every Christian who is filled with the Holy Spirit will keep the spotlight on Jesus.

My prayer: I ask for a fresh filling and anointing so I can keep my life focused on Jesus and point others to Him.

Day 7: It Pays to Serve the Lord

Read LUKE Chapters 4-5

Jesus amazed the people of Israel as He preached and acted with authority. He healed people and preached powerfully because His authority came from God the Father. The religious leaders debated and questioned every issue before making a decision. They quoted other men and their thoughts before they could act on an issue. Jesus didn't rely on men's sayings and thoughts. He knew what heaven wanted. He spoke clearly and simply. He spoke with the authority of God.

We see Christ's authority and power when He commandeered a boat to use it as a platform to preach from. He knew to get into a boat to address a crowd without being overwhelmed by the multitude of people. Much to the surprise of the boat's owners, Jesus paid them for using their boat. Jesus told them to fish. Jesus' authority over all creation was seen when they did what He said. "When they had done so, they caught such a large number of fish that their nets began to break" (5:6). A person is always blessed when he turns his life over to God. "But seek first His Kingdom and His righteousness, and all these things will be given to You as well" (Matthew 6:33).

My prayer: Thank You for all the awesome blessings You have poured out on my life as I've attempted to yield my life to Your use. I trust You and You alone to meet my needs and all of my family. I *pray that America will seek to serve You so You can bless our nation again.*

Yearly Devotions – Week 42

Day 1: The Difference Between Sinners and Saints

Read LUKE Chapters 6-7

The difference between sinners and saints is in their reactions to mistreatment and bad relationships. Jesus said, "If you love those who love you, what credit is that to you? Even 'sinners' love those who love them" (6:32). He said saints are to "...love your enemies..." (6:27). Jesus said, "And if you do good to those who are good to you, what credit is that to you? Even 'sinners' do that" (6:33). He said to the saints who have been hit on the cheek that they are to "...turn to him the other also" (6:29). He said if you lend money and "...expect repayment, what credit is that..." to a saint. "Even sinners lent to 'sinners', expecting to be repaid in full" (6:34). He said the saint should "...Give to everyone who asks you, and if anyone takes what belongs to you, do not demand it back" (6:30).

Jesus was an example for all believers. "When He was accused by the chief priests and the elders, He gave no answer...Jesus made no reply, not even to a single charge-to the amazement of the governor" (Matthew 27:12, 14). The Roman soldiers "...spit on Him, and took the staff and struck Him on the head again and again" (Matthew 27:30). He said and did nothing when He could have called down "twelve legions of angels" (Matthew 26:53).

My prayer: Lord, help me live what You lived and taught. Please fill me with the Holy Spirit today.

Day 2: Decision Time is Now

Read LUKE Chapters 8-9

No human being can accurately know what the future holds without Divine help. The only day we can be sure of is the one we presently occupy. We cannot do anything about yesterday and we can't guarantee what will happen tomorrow. The only rock-solid time and opportunity we have is in the immediate present. That is why Jesus said, "Therefore do not worry about tomorrow, for tomorrow will worry about itself. Each day has enough trouble of its own" (Matthew 6:34). That is why Paul said, "I tell You, now is the time of God's favor, now is the day of salvation" (II Corinthians 6:2).

Jesus illustrates this urgency and commitment when a man said to Him, "I will follow You wherever You go" (9:57). Jesus told him he must abandon all plans for the future and change his lifestyle. He said, "Foxes have holes and birds of the air have nests, but the Son of man has no place to lay His head" (9:58). He asked another man to follow him whose father had died. He asked him to change the burial custom of the day and "Let the dead bury their own dead, but You go and proclaim the Kingdom of God" (9:60). Jesus is to be the priority of our life now.

My prayer: Lord guide my heart to be about Your business the way You designed my life to operate.

Day 3: All Joy Comes From Jesus

Read LUKE Chapters 10-11

The difference between being happy and having joy is that happiness is based on circumstances. Joy is a sense of fulfillment and the knowledge that what is being accomplished in life pleases the Lord and blesses others. Paul's circumstance of being in prison did not rob him of his joy. He said, "...I always pray with joy..." (Philippians 1:3).

Jesus possessed a joy no man could match. He had joy in His life even though He knew how long He had to live. He knew the exact day, hour and minute He would die. He knew the kind of horrible execution He would experience. How could He have that joy? "At that time Jesus, full of joy through the Holy Spirit said, I praise You, Father, Lord of heaven and earth..." (10:21). He was anointed with the Holy Spirit at His Baptism. "...He saw the Spirit of God descending like a dove and lighting on Him. A voice from heaven said, 'this is My Son, whom I love; with Him I am well pleased" (Matthew 3:16-17). There can be no joy in life without Jesus, the Holy Spirit and obedience to the Word of God. Jesus was beaten, spat upon and crucified and yet He never lost His joy.

My prayer: *Lord, may I be filled anew with the Holy Spirit and guide me in Your word and my obedience.*

Day 4: Worry Free

Read LUKE Chapters 12-14

In his biography "Life without limits," Nick Vujicic, who was born with no legs or arms, said, "Hope is His (God's) gift to us, a window to look through. We cannot know the future He has planned for us. Trust in Him, keep hope in your heart, and even when faced with the worst, do whatever you can to prepare yourself for the best!"[8] Where could he get such a positive attitude towards life when he had such a difficult beginning in life? He got it from the Lord and His promises.

---

[8] Vujicic, Nicholas, *Life Without Limits*, 2010, Waterbrook Press, Colorado Springs, CO 80921.

Jesus gave us the formula to be worry free. He said, "who of you by worrying can add a single hour to his life? Since you cannot do this very little thing, why do you worry about the rest? And do not set your heart on what you will eat or drink; do not worry about it" (12:25-26,29). The key to being worry free is to realize how God has provided for all His creation and to know you are fulfilling God's purpose for your life. The real key to being worry free is to "...seek His kingdom, and these things will be given to you as well" (12:31).

My prayer: Again, I praise You for giving me purpose and I ask that You help me be focused on Your kingdom.

Day 5: Faith Results in Action
Read LUKE Chapters 15-17

The Biblical definition of faith is "...the assurance (the confirmation, the title deed) of the things [we] hope for, being the proof of things [we] do not see and the conviction of their reality – faith perceiving as real fact what is not revealed to the senses" (Hebrews 11:1 AMP). Faith believes and then sees the reality and fruition of what it believed.

The size of faith does not affect the result of believing. The disciples asked Jesus to increase their faith and He said the size of faith doesn't matter. He said, "If you have faith as small as a mustard seed..." (17:6). You could do mighty things. Faith in Jesus means a person takes himself out of his own keeping and entrusts himself into the Lord's keeping. Then the Lord can work through him. Jesus works through the person who believes Him. Jesus doesn't act when there is unbelief. Faith continues serving even when the duty is difficult." Jesus said, "So you also, when you have done everything you were told to do should say, 'we are unworthy servants; we have only done our duty" (17:10). Faith allows Jesus to heal. He said to the leper, "…your faith has made you well" (17:19).

My prayer: _My prayer is the same as the disciples and that is to increase my faith in order that You can do more through me so that You are glorified._

Day 6: The Greatest Question Ever Asked

Read LUKE Chapters 18-20

The young ruler and the disciples asked the greatest question. The disciples asked the same question in a different way. The rich young ruler asked, "Good Teacher, what must I do to inherit eternal life?" (18:18). The disciples asked, "Who can be saved?" (18:26).

The ruler must have reasoned that death would separate him from his wealth. He sought eternal life to continue his life of luxury. His action showed he loved the kind of life he had experienced already. Jesus answered that he could have eternal life but it depended on what and who he worshipped. If he worshipped anything other than the Savior he would not inherit eternal life. It became apparent he loved wealth more than God. Jesus exposed what he worshipped when He asked him to give all his money away. His wealth would be lost to him when he died.

Both questions were based on the assumption that not everyone would inherit eternal life when they died. They were correct in their assumptions because God said, "Blessed and holy are those who have part in the First Resurrection. The second death has no power over them…" (Revelation 20:6).

My prayer: Thank You for Your gift of eternal life through Jesus. Thank You that my name is written down in the Lamb's Book of Life.

Day 7: Times That Tell the Future

Read LUKE Chapters 21-22

Jesus answered the disciples questions, "…when will these things happen? And what will be the sign that they are about to take place?" (21:7). What things were they talking about? Jesus had stated the Temple would be destroyed. He said, "As for what you see here, the time will come when not one stone will be left on another; every one of them will be thrown down" (21:6). He revealed Israel would be removed from the Holy Land. They would be scattered throughout the world. The Temple's destruction was a symbol of Israel's demise. Jesus gave them hope because of His return to Israel.

The world could know that His return was imminent when Israel became a nation again. He said, "Jerusalem will be trampled on by the Gentiles until the times of the Gentiles are fulfilled" (21:24). He compared the nation of Israel to a fig tree. "Look at the fig tree and all the trees. When they sprout leaves, you can see for yourselves and know summer is near. Even so, when you see these things happening…I tell you the truth, this generation will certainly not pass away until all these things have happened" (21:29-31). In 1948 Israel returned and the "fig tree" (Israel) sprouted leaves and now it appears Jesus' return is soon.

My prayer: Even so come Lord Jesus! Help me get the good news out to a lost world.

Yearly Devotions – Week 43

Day 1: Slow Learners

Read LUKE Chapters 23-24

Living in the physical realm of this world where there is time, space, and people living in fleshly bodies makes it difficult to understand and believe supernatural events can really happen. It is hard to grasp that there is a spiritual world that is not limited to physical bodies and earthly dimensions.

Jesus had plainly told His disciples He would be crucified and resurrected after three days. The disciples could not comprehend that happening. Jesus described in detail days before His crucifixion that He would raise from the dead. "Jesus took the twelve aside and told them, 'we are going to Jerusalem, and everything that is written by the prophets about the Son of Man will be fulfilled. He will be handed over to the Gentiles. They will mock Him, spit on Him, flog Him and kill Him. On the third day He will rise again" (Luke 18:31-33).

These slow learners did not believe the resurrection was possible when the women reported that angels told them that Jesus had risen." But they did not believe the women, because their words seemed to them like nonsense (24:11). Jesus said, "Yes, I am coming soon" (Revelation 22:20). Let's not be slow learners. Let's believe it.

My prayer: I believe, help though my unbelief. Give me the faith and insight to see the truth of Scripture that is taking place in my life time. I praise You for Your Word that gives me insight on current events.

Day 2: The Last Will Be the Best

Read JOHN Chapters 1-3

The first sign that Jesus is God in the flesh came at Cana when He turned water into wine. One reason John wrote his gospel was to combat the Greek philosophies claiming that Jesus was divine but not truly human. John wrote, "Jesus did many other miraculous signs in the presence of His disciples, which are not revealed in this book. But these are written that You may believe that Jesus is the Christ, the Son of God, and that by believing You may have life in His name" (20:31). "This, the first of His miraculous signs, Jesus performed at Cana in Galilee. He thus revealed His glory, and His disciples put their faith in Him" (2:11).

The lack of wine is a picture of a person, church or nation without the presence of the Holy Spirit in them. A life has no purpose or meaning and is empty without Jehovah-God to serve and live for. Only Jesus' righteous presence in a person's soul can cause a life to be the best it can be. Like the host at the wedding who tasted the wine from the Lord's hand said, "...You have saved the best till now" (2:10). Believers have a good life with the Lord but the last part of life in eternity will be the best.

My prayer: Thank You for the certainty of Your gracious goodness being conferred on me in Eternity through Jesus.

Day 3: The Jew's Accusers

Read JOHN Chapters 4-5

A Gentile with a dying son believed Jesus and took Him at His word that his son was healed. He believed Jesus when He said, "You may go, your son will live. The man took Jesus at

His Word and departed" (4:50). The man was so relieved and relaxed he waited until the next day to start home. His servants verified his faith and his son's healing.

Jesus pointed out that the Jews were going to miss all God had for them because they refused to believe God. Jesus warned them that they were going to be judged by the Word of God given to Moses who gave it to them. Jesus said, "Your accuser is Moses, on whom your hopes are set. If you believed Moses, you would believe Me, for he wrote about Me. But since you do not believe what he wrote, how are you going to believe what I say?" (5:45-47). The rich man in hell wanted dead people to be raised to go warn his brothers about hell. "Abraham replied, 'they have Moses and the prophets let them listen to them...if they do not listen to Moses and the prophets, they will not be convinced even if someone rises from the dead" (Luke 16:29, 31). All lost people will be judged by what is in God's written Word. "And I saw the dead, great and small, standing before the throne, and books were opened" (Revelation 20:12). One of those books will be the Bible.

My prayer: Thank You Lord that You did not leave us in the dark. Thank You that we have the light of Your Word.

Day 4: Christian Drinkers

Read JOHN Chapters 6-7

Jesus said things that puzzled the people. He said things that seemed repulsive and irrational when taken literally. Jesus being a master teacher knew how to get the people's attention so they wouldn't forget what He said.

Good water was a very valuable commodity. They had no filtration system or distilled water. Animals, bugs, and all sorts of parasites could contaminate their drinking water. When Jesus used an object lesson like water they could relate to how important it was. When He told the people to eat His flesh and drink His blood He made them aware of a greater hunger and thirst that could only be met by the One who sent Him – God the Father. He said, "If anyone is thirsty, let him come to Me and drink" (7:37). "Whoever eats My flesh and drinks My blood remains in Me, and I in him" (6:56). John explains the meaning of what He said, "By this He meant the Spirit, whom those who believed in Him were later to receive. Up to that time the Spirit had not been given, since Jesus had not yet been glorified" (7:39). Every believer drinks from the Holy Spirit and eats the Word of God.

My prayer: Lord, may I surrender anew to the control of the Holy Spirit and be directed by Your Word in situations.

Day 5: It Takes More Than Truth to Set You Free

Read JOHN Chapters 8-9

"The truth will set you free" is quoted by every level of society at some time during a conversation. That phrase is correct but people forget what Jesus said right before that statement. Jesus said, "If you hold to My teaching you are really My disciples. Then you will know the truth and the truth will set you free" (8:31). The truth did not set the Pharisees free.

Jesus told the Pharisees the truth repeatedly. He said to them, "You do not know Me or My Father" (8:19). "You are from below; I am from above" (8:23). "I tell you the truth, everyone who sins is a slave to sin" (8:34). "You belong to your Father, the devil, and you want to carry out your father's desire" (8:44). They refused to accept Christ's truth. Jesus exposed the truth when He said, "As it is, you are determined to kill Me, a man who has told you the truth that I heard from God" (8:40). "Yet because I tell the truth, you do not believe Me!" (8:45). James said, "You believe that there is one God. Good! Even the demons believe that – and shudder" (James 2:19). A person must incorporate truth into his life as a principle to live by to gain freedom.

My prayer: it is my prayer that I not only know the truth but I stake my future and my life on it by believing and living the truth.

Day 6: Life is the Monopoly of God

Read JOHN Chapters 10-12

All life comes from God! "…the Lord God formed the man from the dust of the ground and breathed into his nostrils the breath of life, and the man became a living being" (Genesis 2:7). Man has not, cannot and will not ever be able to create life from nothing like God. Man can destroy life but he cannot create life other than through God's ordained method of procreation. When a baby is born it came from two living beings. Physical life must come from existing life. That is why Jesus said, "I am the way and the truth and the life" (14:6). Jesus doesn't possess life, He is life. It is what and who He is.

Jesus not only created physical life. He provided spiritual life that results in eternal life. Jesus said, "I have come that they may have life and have it to the full" (10:10). To give man eternal life He had to give up His physical life. He said, "The reason My Father loves Me is that I lay down My life – only to take it up again" (10:17). To believe in and receive Jesus means a person receives Christ's Resurrected life.

My prayer: I praise You and am amazed that You offered me eternal life and just gave it to me through Jesus Christ. Thank You for giving the truth of life through Your Son and Your Word.

Day 7: The Test of Love

Read JOHN Chapters 13-15

When used lightly the word "love" can lose its significance. Jesus said, "If you love Me, you will obey what I command" (14:15). Real love is not a feeling but is what a person does. The Greek word Jesus used in this statement is AGAPAO. The Greek professor Dr. Wuest says, "Agapao speaks of love which is awakened by a sense of value in an object which causes one to prize it."

Jesus also said, "If you belonged to the world, it would love you as its own" (15:19). The word "love" Jesus uses here is Phileo, "...A love which is the response of the human spirit to what appeals to it as pleasurable..."[9] God cannot have a Phileo kind of love for a lost person. God's holiness rebels against unforgiven sin in a sinner. Real love for God is seen when a person so values the Lord that one's life is centered on Him and is focused on pleasing Him. God's Agapao love for mankind was due to man being created in His image and because through redemption man could be conformed to Christ's image. Love is what you do! "For God so loved the world that He gave..." (John 3:16).

My prayer: Lord, I need Your Spirit to focus my life on the person of the Lord Jesus.

---

[9] Wuest, Kenneth S., *Wuest's Word Studies from the Greek New Testament, Volume 3*, 1973, 1989, Wm. B. Eerdman's Pub Co., Grand Rapids Michigan 49502, Pg 183

Yearly Devotions – Week 44

Day 1: The Holy Spirit's Assignment

Read JOHN Chapters 16-18

God loves mankind and has always worked to bless them and give them what would benefit them. A problem arose after man sinned. That severed their relationship with God. He had to address the sin problem before that relationship could be restored. So God sent directions for the restoration of His relationship with man. He sent His directions through angels, prophets and the written word. He eventually sent His Son who man rejected and crucified. Christ's death and Resurrection meant Jesus would return to heaven and send the Holy Spirit in His place. God is a giving God. He gave His Son and His Son gave the Holy Spirit.

The gift of the Holy Spirit was designed to perform a specific task. There would be no conviction of sin without His presence. Jesus said when He came "...He will convict the world of guilt in regard to sin, righteousness and judgment in regard to sin..." (16:8-9). Jesus said sin was when "...men do not believe in Me..." (16:9). His righteousness meant He was going back to be with the Father and "...You can see me no longer" (16:10). In regard to judgment, His crucifixion and resurrection meant "...the prince of this world (Satan) now stands condemned" (16:11).

My prayer: Thank You for the Holy Spirit's presence in my life and in the whole world. Thank You for the conviction of sin and the cleansing result after repenting.

Day 2: Faith Sight

Read JOHN Chapters 19-21

Faith is believing without seeing something through physical sight. The Apostle Thomas missed seeing Jesus after He was resurrected. He had a hard time developing his "Faith Sight." When the other disciples said, "We have seen the Lord...then Thomas said, "Unless I see the nail marks in His hands and put my finger where the nails were, and put my hand into His side, I will not believe" (20:25). When Thomas did finally see Jesus he cried out, "My Lord and My God!" (20:28). Jesus stated that those with "Faith Sight" would be blessed. He said, "Because You have seen Me, You have believed; blessed are those who have not seen and yet have believed" (20:29).

Only the Holy Spirit working through God's Word is able to give anyone "Faith Sight." The jailer got it when an earthquake released Paul and Silas from their prison cell. The jailor asked, "Sirs, what must I do to be saved?" (Acts 16:30-31). That belief included Jesus' death, burial and Resurrection.

My prayer: It is my prayer that America and the whole world would gain a "Faith Sight."

Day 3: David the Prophet

Read ACTS Chapters 1-3

At Pentecost Peter preached that death could not hold Jesus in the grave. He said, "...God raised Him from the dead, freeing Him from the agony of death, because it was impossible for death to keep its hold on Him" (2:24). He then let the people know that King David had prophesied Christ's Resurrection. Peter quoted David and reminded them that he said God "...will not let Your Holy One see decay" (2:27) from (Psalms 16:10).

Peter authenticated David's prophetic status when he said, "But he was a prophet and knew God had promised him (David) on oath that He would place one of his descendants on his throne. Seeing what was ahead, he spoke of the Resurrection of the Christ, that He was not abandoned to the grave, nor His body see decay" (2:30-31).

David saw his descendant, Jesus, sitting on the throne in heaven. David was referring to Jesus when he wrote, "The Lord said to My Lord: Sit at My right hand until I make Your enemies a footstool for Your feet, for David did not ascend to heaven..." (2:34). David could not go to heaven until after Christ's crucifixion and resurrection.

My prayer: I bow before You with the knowledge that You know the future and control every aspect of history. I praise You for the truth of the Resurrection.

Day 4: Religious Denial

Read ACTS Chapters 4-5

When someone's loved one dies suddenly there can be a period of denial for a while. Many times it is hard for a person to grasp the reality of a situation. A person who is an alcoholic or a drug addict can be in denial In spite of their obvious habits and problems. A person can deny many things that are true but that doesn't change reality.

Many people can deny there is a God and that Jesus was born of a virgin, crucified and resurrected. But that doesn't change the truth nor does it shock God. The thing that no one can deny is the reality of a person becoming sober or drug free after receiving Jesus as their personal Savior. No one can deny when a person changes from a life of degradation to a productive life that honors God. The Pharisees and Sadducees could not deny the work of God through the Apostles. They said, "Everybody living in Jerusalem knows they have done an outstanding miracle, and we cannot deny it" (4:16). We as believers should live so that the lost world cannot deny an "outstanding miracle" has happened in our lives.

My prayer: I yield to the control of the Holy Spirit and seek to live Christ's life so people will know that God is alive and at work in my life.

Day 5: Growing Pains

Read ACTS Chapters 6-8

A growing church will always have growing pains that people call problems. What seems like problems are really opportunities to see God work. There are good problems and bad problems in a church. Good problems can be the result of rapid growth in the church. When a church runs out of space to put people, that is a good problem. There could be many different kinds of good problems. The church at Jerusalem was no exception. Luke reported that, "In those days when the number of disciples was increasing, the Grecian Jews among them complained against the Hebraic Jews because their widows were being overlooked in the daily distribution of food" (6:1).

The church responded appropriately. They recognized the problem, determined a plan to solve the problem, assigned people to deal with it and then continued doing the most important aspect of church ministry. The Apostles said, "We...will give attention to prayer and the ministry of the Lord" (6:4). Instead of having a church fight, the church fixed the problem in a way that glorified the Lord.

My prayer: Dear Lord, help me see problems as an opportunity to glorify You instead of problems that can't be fixed.

Day 6: Blinded to Gain Sight

Read ACTS Chapters 9-11

Saul was convinced he was serving God by persecuting Christians. He was trained and commissioned to imprison torture or kill Christians. He believed Christians blasphemed God. He was a brilliantly educated Rabbi that had memorized much of the Old Testament. He was bathed in what he believed was the truth. He had a problem though. He had missed the truth about the Messiah and had developed his own opinion of how God was going to bring the Messiah to the world. God's plan for Israel was to bring all nations to worship Jehovah-God by bringing God's Word and Son into the world.

God had to blind him with Christ's glory. He had to blind Saul to all he believed before he could see God's purpose for Israel and himself. "As he neared Damascus on his journey, suddenly a light from heaven flashed around him..." Jesus said to him, "Saul, Saul, why do you persecute Me?" (9:3-4) When he encountered Christ he was blinded to everything in this world. "For three days he was blind, and did not eat or drink anything" (9:9). If we see Christ's glory we will be blinded to the world's attractions.

My prayer: Open my eyes to Christ's glory so I can close out the world from my heart.

Day 7: Stand Up Faith

Read ACTS Chapters 12-14

God does all the work in Salvation. The Scriptures state, "For by grace are ye saved through faith; and that not of yourselves: it is the gift of God: not of works, lest any man should boast" (Ephesians 2:8-9). Whenever God blesses someone it is always an act of mercy and kindness. Every person deserves to be sent to hell but God stands ready to bless anyone who will place their faith in Him.

For example: "In Lystra there sat a man crippled in his feet, who was lame from birth and had never walked. He listened to Paul as he was speaking. Paul looked directly at him, saw that he had faith to be healed and called out, 'Stand up on your feet! That man jumped up and began to walk" (14:8-10). This man was like every person without Christ. Everyone is crippled by sin and cannot walk to please the Lord. When he heard about Jesus he had faith that appropriated salvation and his healing. His faith allowed him to stand up and walk in the power of Jesus. When a person has a genuine faith in the Lord Jesus he will be able to stand up and walk in a Godly manner. Without faith he would have been unable to access God's healing.

My prayer: It is my desire to grow in faith and to be able to access all of God's gifts and grace He has ready to share with me.

Yearly Devotions – Week 45

Day 1: God's Shut Door

Read ACTS Chapters 15-17

Disappointment comes many times in life when an opportunity is canceled or closed. In his book *Life Without Limits*, Nick Vujicic talks about his move from Australia to America. He was born with no legs or arms. When he was moved by his parents to America he was petrified to face new class mates as a teenager. As an adult he relates how that change in his life was a blessing. He said, "We often resist change, but really, who would want a life without it? Some of our greatest experiences, growth and rewards came to us as the result of moving to a new place, switching jobs, following a different course of study, or moving into a better relationship."[10]

The Apostle Paul experienced a detour in his missionary journeys. His plan was to preach the gospel in Asia. God had other plans for him and closed that door. "...having been kept by the Holy Spirit from preaching the word in the province of Asia...the Spirit of Jesus would not allow them to..." then "During the night Paul had a vision of a man of Macedonia standing and begging him, 'Come over to Macedonia and help us...'" (16:6-9). God closed one door and opened another one He chose.

My prayer: Help me to accept closed doors and look forward to the open doors You chose, Lord.

---

[10] Vujicic, Nicholas, *Life Without Limits*, 2010, Waterbrook Press, Colorado Springs, CO 80921.

Day 2: Close Encounter of the Spiritual Kind

Read ACTS Chapters 18-19

There is a movie entitled "Close Encounter of the Third Kind" where an alien ship lands and takes people into outer space. Satan's demons have landed on earth to deceive people so they can take them to hell not outer space.

Paul knew of the evil spirit's presence on earth. Through the power of the Holy Spirit and the name of Jesus he set many people free from their power. True believers in Christ have power over evil spirits and can cast them out. Luke illustrates this in Acts. "Some Jews who went around driving out evil spirits tried to invoke the name of the Lord Jesus over those who were demon-possessed. They would say, 'In the name of Jesus whom Paul preaches, I command you to come out. Seven sons of Sceva, a Jewish chief priest, were doing this. One day, the evil spirit answered them, "Jesus I know, and I know about Paul, but who are you?" ... "He gave them such a beating that they ran out of the house naked and bleeding." (19:13-16). The only protection from an encounter of this kind is the Lord Jesus and the presence of the Holy Spirit.

My prayer: Again, I ask for what Jesus taught us to pray in His model prayer, "...deliver us from the evil one."

Day 3: Changing Times

Read ACTS Chapters 20-22

Everyone can become comfortable with conditions they are accustomed to. The Apostle Paul had been trained in Judaism and defended it. While on that mission God changed the course of his life. On the road to Damascus he met the risen Lord. Jesus transformed the purpose of his life from being a persecutor to being the persecuted. After his conversion Jesus told Paul, "Quick, leave Jerusalem immediately, because they will not accept your testimony about Me" (22:18). God changed him from serving the Jews to ministering to the lowly Gentiles. "...then the Lord said, '...Go, I will send you far away to the Gentiles" (22:21). That was a drastic change for Paul.

God rescued Paul from the Jews early in his ministry. God again changes His plans for Paul. God rescued Paul when he entered the ministry but now has an assignment for him to be imprisoned. "...a prophet named Agabus came down from Judea...he took Paul's belt, tied his own hands and feet with it and said, 'The Holy Spirit says, 'In this way the Jews of Jerusalem will bind the owner of this belt..." (21:11). Like Paul, a believer's life will be a series of changes.

My prayer: *Thank You for the truth that no matter how drastic the changes in my life are, You are overseeing every detail of the change.*

Day 4: Safe Until God Wills Otherwise
Read ACTS Chapters 23-25

A believer's soul is safe forever. His body on the other hand is safe until God wills otherwise. God had a specific purpose for Paul. He was God's spiritual delta force to drop in on the enemy directed by Satan. Jesus said to Paul, "Go; I will send you far away to the Gentiles" (22:21). After Paul is arrested God prepared him to go to Satan's headquarters at that time in history. Jesus' orders came through at night and ordered him to "Take courage! As you have testified about Me in Jerusalem, so you must also testify in Rome" (23:11).

Satan immediately ordered his troops to assassinate Paul. "The next morning the Jews formed a conspiracy and bound themselves with an oath not to eat or drink until they had killed Paul" (23:12). God protected Paul at this time. "But when the son of Paul's sister heard of this plot, he went into the barracks and told Paul" (23:16). Paul got to Rome safely and lived there many years. God kept Paul safe until He chose otherwise. He was eventually executed in Rome.

My prayer: Thank You for the many times You have kept me safe while driving, flying and traveling all over the world. Help me to remain faithful until You choose to take me home.

Day 5: Good's Reward

Read ACTS Chapter 26 – ROMANS Chapter 2

Jesus said, "Why callest thou Me good? There is none good but one, that is, God..." (Matthew 19:17 KJV). How is it possible for a man to do good if there are none that are good? Paul said, "...there is no one who does good, not even one" (Romans 3:12). Paul also said, "To those who by persistence in doing good seek glory, honor and immortality, He will give eternal life" (Romans 2:7). That is good's reward – eternal life!

So, how do men do good if there are none that are good? They must be transformed by the power of God into a righteous person. Paul said, "I am not ashamed of the gospel, because it is the power of God for the salvation of everyone who believes...for in the gospel a righteousness from God is revealed, a righteousness that is by faith from first to last..." (Romans 1:16-17). To do good a person must have Jesus dwelling in him through the presence of the Holy Spirit. Jesus said, "If a man remains in Me and I in him, he will bear much fruit, apart from Me You can do nothing" (John 15:5). The only way a person can do good is to let Jesus do it through him.

My prayer: I yield and surrender all that I am to the control of the Holy Spirit to let the Holy Spirit do God's good work through me. I ask to be filled with the Holy Spirit.

Day 6: The Great Exchange

Read ROMANS Chapters 3-6

Paul states that Jesus made a costly transaction for men's souls. They were sold into sin's slavery. One man betrayed all of mankind. Adam followed Satan and believed his lies rather than following God and the truth. "...many died by the trespass of one man..." (5:15). Every descendant of Adam has been condemned to submit to sins enslavement. "Therefore, just as sin entered the world through one man, and death through sin, and in this way death came to all men, because all sinned..." (5:12). Adams rebellious act caused all of mankind to be condemned to hell. Mankind needed someone to rescue them.

The Great Exchange took place when the "Last Adam" (Jesus) exchanged His heavenly position for an earthly one. He donated His life to die on the cross so men could live. "And so it is written the First man Adam was made a living soul; the last Adam (Jesus) was made a quickening Spirit (A life-giving Spirit – restoring the dead to life) (I Corinthians 15:45 AMP). Every person who trusts Jesus has his sins covered by Christ's blood. "...while we were still sinners Christ died for us" (5:8).

My prayer: I praise You and worship You for Your sacrificial death to pay for my sins and the sins of the whole world.

Day 7: Christians Can Celebrate

Read ROMANS Chapters 7-9

During Rome's rule of the world conquering generals celebrated after defeating the opposing army. They were not content to win the war. They wanted to celebrate the victory. They would have parades with the conquered army in chains and their loot displayed on carts showing the riches they had won.

Paul alluded to the Roman process of celebrating their victories when he said we are more than conquerors. Paul is encouraging the Roman believers to realize they have won over life and death. They should celebrate their victory like the conquering Roman army. They should celebrate even though they were being persecuted, tortured and killed. Paul told them they were the winners. "No, in all things we are more than conquerors through Him who loved us. For I am convinced that neither death nor life, neither angels nor demons, neither the present nor the future, nor any powers, neither height nor depth, nor anything else in all creation, will be able to separate us from the love of God that is in Christ Jesus our Lord" (Romans 8:37-39).

My prayer: *Again I praise You for making everything that I have experienced into something good. Your care for each of us is a tremendous blessing to me.*

Yearly Devotions – Week 46

Day 1: Only Brag on Jesus

Read ROMANS Chapters 10-13

Salvation is a gift from God whether a person is a Jew or a Gentile. "For there is no difference between Jew and Gentile – the same Lord is Lord of all and richly blesses all who call on Him, for, 'everyone who calls on the name of the Lord will be saved" (10:12-13). No one can boast how they saved themselves. A person will be humble when he understands salvation is a gift from God and that only Jesus can remove a person's sin.

When a person receives a new nature from God through Jesus his character will conform to Paul's description of an humble person. Paul describes a saved person's new nature. "Love must be sincere. Hate what is evil; cling to what is good. Be devoted to one another in brotherly love. Honor one another above yourselves…" (12:9-10). He said true believers will "live in harmony with one another. Do not be proud, but be willing to associate with people of low position. Do not be conceited" (12:16). A true believer won't brag on what he has done. He will only brag on Jesus.

My prayer: It is my desire to lift up Jesus at all times. Please keep His love and sacrifice before my eyes.

Day 2: Respect the Convictions of Others

Read ROMANS Chapters 14-16

Every home is different and has its own dynamics and behavior. Paul urged believers not to lose respect for each other because of different convictions and lifestyles. They were not to judge people because of different convictions. He said, "Accept him whose faith is weak, without passing judgment on disputable matters" (14:1).

A Christian community should develop an atmosphere of kindness, patience and understanding. A church should be a place where people feel accepted without sacrificing a person's Biblical convictions. Every person's convictions should be accepted without condemnation. Paul said, "For none of us lives to himself alone and none of us dies to himself alone" (14:7). God designed man to be connected to each other emotionally, intellectually and spiritually. How we treat each other is critical in receiving God's blessings. "For we will all stand before God's judgment seat...every knee will bow before Me; every tongue will confess to God" (14:10).

My prayer: Help me stand for the truth and live for the Lord without a judgmental attitude.

Day 3: Qualifications For Ministry

Read I CORINTHIANS Chapters 1-4

Many people have the erroneous idea that only scholars and special people are qualified for ministry. What is miraculous is that God uses ordinary people to do extraordinary things. God does not bless laziness. However, He does use people who are feeble and weak. He is using Nick Vujicic who has no arms or legs. God has used Joni for years who is paralyzed from the neck down. God can use anyone He chooses. In spite of moral indiscretions God uses Jimmy Swaggart and other pastors after they repent and are restored. God will use anyone who yields whole heartedly to Him.

The Apostle Paul declared that God used people that the world did not place much value on. "But God chose the foolish things of the world to shame the wise; God chose the weak things of the world to shame the strong. He chose the lowly things of this world and the despised things – and the things that are not – to nullify the things that are, so that no one may boast before Him" (1:27-29).

My prayer: Thank You for the privilege of being called to share the gospel and pastor Your people. Please help me to yield to Your will and way in serving others.

Day 4: Stumbling Block Christians

Read I CORINTHIANS Chapters 5-9

The Christian who says, "It's my business how I live my life" is a candidate to be a stumbling block. A stumbling block is a Christian who offends other believers by their actions. If a Christian lives in a manner that brings shame to Jesus' name, the Christian becomes a stumbling block. It makes a difference how Christians behave in front of the world. A true born again believer is sensitive to how he lives his life in public as well as in private. Francis of Assisi said something like this, "preach the gospel at all times and if necessary use words."

Weak Christians in Paul's time were those who had been saved out of idolatry where animals sacrificed to pagan gods were eaten to have their gods become a part of them through the meat. Paul said then Christians knew that was not so and could eat the meat unless it caused other believers to be offended. He said, "Therefore, if what I eat causes my brother to fall into sin, I will never eat meat again, so that I will not cause him to fall (8:13).

My prayer: Lord, keep me from being a stumbling block.

Day 5: New Testament Advantage

Read I CORINTHIANS Chapters 10-12

The knowledge of God and His mystery of providing salvation for all mankind is explained for all to see and know in the New Testament. The New Testament explains the Old Testament and the Old Testament illuminates the New Testament.

The stories recorded in the Old Testament are actual historical events. The Holy Spirit recorded these events and explained their significance and the spiritual lessons in the New Testament. Paul wrote, "Now these things occurred as examples to keep us from setting our hearts on evil things as they did...these things happened to them as examples and were written down as warnings for us, on whom the fulfillment of the ages has come" (10:6, 11). The New Testament lets us see God's overview of mankind's existence and destiny. The only way to understand one's life and purpose is to see it through the advantage of the knowledge found in God's Word.

My prayer: Thank You for Your word and letting us know why we were put on this earth. Your graciousness is overwhelming and praise You for allowing me to learn and teach Your word.

Day 6: The Elements of a Spiritual Church

Read I CORINTHIANS Chapters 13-15

The most important part of a church is the foundation. To build a church building men use concrete and rebar for strength. It must be placed on the solid part of the earth. If possible it should be on solid rock. The spiritual foundation is Christ. "For no one can lay any foundation other than the one already laid which is Jesus Christ" (I Corinthians 3:11). Jesus said, "Therefore everyone who hears these words of mine and puts them into practice is like a wise man who built his house on the rock" (Matthew 7:24).

The frame of a church building should be solidly nailed together. The nails that hold a church together are forged in the love of Christ. Paul said, "And now these three remain: faith, hope and love. But the greatest of these is love" (13:13). The rooms in God's church are designed by the Holy Spirit and provide order. "For God is not a God of disorder but of peace" (14:33). The covering for a church is the roof which is the hope found in the promise of the Resurrection. "But Christ has indeed been raised from the dead, the firstfruits of those who have fallen asleep" (15:20).

My prayer: Please bring these elements into our church and to our nation. You are our only hope.

Day 7: You Have to Have It Before You Can Give It

Read I CORINTHIANS Chapter 16 – II CORINTHIANS Chapter 3

There are people who claim to be Christians who say they can't forgive someone. Jesus let His followers know that if they wanted forgiveness they had to forgive. Jesus said, "For if You forgive men when they sin against You, Your heavenly Father will also forgive You. But if You do not forgive men their sins, Your Father will not forgive Your sins" (Matthew 6:14). When we forgive others it lets us out of the prison of bitterness. Forgiveness is vital to spiritual health and growth.

Paul states that God allows us to go through difficult times so we can help others. When God forgives a person of all their sins it fills that person with a spirit of forgiveness. When a person has been forgiven he has the ability to forgive because he has experienced God's grace. Since he has received forgiveness he can give it. Paul wrote, "Praise be to the God and Father of our Lord Jesus Christ, the Father of compassion and the God of all comfort, who comforts us in all our troubles, so that we can comfort those in any trouble with the comfort we ourselves have received from God" (1:3). When You have forgiveness and comfort from God You can give forgiveness and comfort.

My prayer: Lord, let me be a channel of comfort and grace so others can receive Your forgiveness and comfort.

Yearly Devotions – Week 47

Day 1: The Peace Treaty

Read II CORINTHIANS Chapters 4-8

It takes at least two nations to have a war. It also takes at least two nations to agree to a peace treaty. The Korean War was not a declared war. No War was declared in Korea but two armies fought and thousands died. At the conclusion of the conflict peace was declared but the two armies continue to face each other.

A War has been raging for ages between God and man. War was declared when Adam sinned. Adam rebelled against the Commander-in-Chief of the universe. God prepared a peace treaty and offered peace to anyone who would sign it by accepting His terms of repenting of sin and accepting Jesus as Lord and Savior. "Therefore, if anyone is in Christ, he is a new creation...all this is from God, who reconciled us to Himself through Christ and gave us the ministry of reconciliation: that God was reconciling to Himself Christ, not counting men's sins against them" (5:17-19). To receive Christ means the war is over. Reconciliation is a diplomatic term referring to the harmony established between enemies by peace treaties.

My prayer: I praise You for the peace found in Jesus Christ. I plead for peace in America and especially in Israel. I ask that Christ would return soon because He is the Prince of Peace.

Day 2: Spiritual Warriors

Read II CORINTHIANS Chapters 9-12

The Christian life is not one that always goes smoothly and peacefully. The Christian is in a battle as long as he lives on earth. The believer can't see the enemy nor know the enemies location except for one. The enemy is a spiritual force dedicated to kill and destroy all Godly spiritual life. The three enemies are Satan, the world and the flesh.

The most persistent enemy that attacks every day is the flesh. The flesh is the indwelling sinful nature. God describes the flesh in Genesis 6:5 He said, "...the thoughts of his (man's) heart was only evil continually." We know that the enemy is sin, identified as the fallen nature received from Adam. This enemy is not removed after salvation. The fallen nature wars against the Holy Spirit in the Christians heart. Paul said, "For though we live in the world, we do not wage war as the world does. The weapons we fight with are not the weapons of the world...On the contrary, they have divine power to demolish strongholds...we take captive every thought to make it obedient to Christ..." (10:3-5). Every Christian receives the divine nature that forces him from the power of sin called the Holy Spirit.

My prayer: Thank You for the indwelling of the Holy Spirit and I ask to be controlled completely by Him.

Day 3: There is Only One Gospel

Read II CORINTHIANS Chapter 13 - Galatians Chapter 3

To add anything to what Jesus did for man's salvation is an attack on the truth. Satan attempts to distort the truth that Jesus death, burial and resurrection was not enough to pay for man's sin. Satan always tries to add to God's Word. Truth is a person. The Lord Jesus said, "I am the way and the truth and the life" (John 14:6).

What other gospel is there? The other gospel states that You can earn part of Your salvation by Your works. Jesus plus anything is a distortion of the gospel. Any gospel that demands someone to earn part of their salvation by being baptized, join a specific church and submit to certain requirements to attain salvation is another gospel.

The true gospel is the good news that God has provided a way of redemption through His Son Jesus Christ. The gospel is the message that salvation is a gift that cannot be earned. "For by grace (a gift) are ye saved through faith..." (2:8). Paul said, "But even if we or an angel from heaven should preach a gospel other than the one we preached to You, let him be eternally condemned" (Galatians 1:8).

My prayer: *Again, I praise You for the gift of salvation!*

Day 4: You Can Only Harvest What You've Planted

Read GALATIANS Chapters 4-6

Paul states that a person will either use his life to satisfy his flesh or he will live to satisfy the Holy Spirit. He said, "Do not be deceived: God cannot be mocked. A man reaps what he sows. The one who sows to please his sinful nature, from that nature will reap destruction; the one who sows to please the Spirit, from the Spirit will reap eternal life" (6:7-8).

What seeds are used to sow to the "sinful nature"? Paul lists some of the seeds: "...sexual immorality, impurity and debauchery; idolatry and witchcraft; hatred, discord, jealousy, fits of rage, selfish ambition, dissensions, factions and envy; drunkenness, orgies, and the like" (5:19-21).

What seeds are sown to satisfy the Holy Spirit? Paul reveals what the Holy Spirit sows and grows in a believer's life:

"...love, joy, peace, patience, kindness, goodness, faithfulness, gentleness and self-control" (5:22-23). Jesus said, "By their fruit you will recognize them" (Matthew 7:16).

My prayer: Thank You for revealing what I should sow in this world with my life. Give me the strength, wisdom and vision to plant my life where it will produce Your fruit for Your glory.

Day 5: People Who Belong

Read EPHESIANS Chapters 1-4

As a child growing up I never felt like I belonged to a particular town or place as a home. My father was a pipe-line welder and we moved many times a year during one period of my life. Whenever we moved to a new town there were always people who had lived there all their life. It seemed to me that they had a sense of belonging to the community. It appeared to me that I was an outsider and they belonged there with insights about people in the town that I could not comprehend. A Christian is truly an outsider to this world and does not belong to this life.

Christians do belong to another world. God determined from eternity that anyone who placed their faith in Jesus as their Savior was predestined to become like Jesus and belong with Him in heaven forever. "In love He predestined us to be adopted as His sons through Jesus Christ, in accordance with His pleasure and will – to the praise of His glorious grace, which He has freely given us in the One He loves" (1:5-6). Now, I belong.

My prayer: Thank You for adopting me into Your eternal family and home.

Day 6: God Keeps His Work Going

Read EPHESIANS Chapter 5 - Chapter Philippians 1

In the 1940's our family visited an abandoned town in the West Texas desert one Sunday afternoon. One of the abandoned buildings looked like it was meant to be a courthouse. The town had been started in the late 1800's during the cowboy era. It was a moving experience to think that a number of people in covered wagons had come to West Texas with high hopes of establishing a town and for some reason couldn't finish the job.

It is glorious to know that when God starts a job He completes it every time. When He begins something it's assured to get done. Paul told the Philippians, "In all my prayers for all of You, I always pray with joy because of Your partnership in the gospel from the first day until now, being confident of this, that he who began a good work in you will carry it on to completion until the day of Christ Jesus" (Philippians 1:4). That means Christian's are "...strong in the Lord and in His mighty power" (Ephesians 6:10).

My prayer: Your faithfulness is my strength and I rejoice that You will finish Your work in my life. I pray for my church and those who have started their journey of life with You.

Day 7: Every Christian Should Work Out

Read PHILIPPIANS Chapters 2-4

When the term "work out" is used, people think of physical exercise. That is not the kind of work out Paul is talking about. He told the Philippians to work out the spiritual weaknesses in their lives. He said to them, "therefore, my dear friends, as You have always obeyed – not only in my presence, but now much more in my absence – continue to work out Your salvation with fear and trembling for it is God who works in You to will and to act according to His good purpose" (2:12-13).

"The words "work out" are the translation of a Greek word which means 'to carry out to the goal, to carry to its ultimate conclusion.' We say, 'the student worked out a problem in arithmetic.' That is, he carried the problem to its ultimate conclusion. That is the way it's used here. The Philippians are exhorted to carry their salvation to its ultimate conclusion, namely, Christlikeness."[11] If the Christian life was a football game, the believer would take the ball, Christlikeness, for a touchdown.

My prayer: Help me work out my salvation by sharing Christ's love, forgiveness and longsuffering.

---

[11] Wuest, Kenneth S., _Wuest's Word Studies from the Greek New Testament, Volume 3_, 1973, 1989, Wm. B. Eerdman's Pub Co., Grand Rapids Michigan 49502.

Yearly Devotions – Week 48

Day 1: Blocked Carotids

Read COLOSSIANS Chapters 1-4

According to a dictionary a carotid is defined as "each of the two main arteries carrying blood to the head and neck." The head and brain will be damaged if they become blocked. A doctor will have to insert a stint or repair the blockage. The Apostle Paul wrote that there can be a spiritual blockage to the head of the church. That blockage is to preach salvation by works or the worship of anything other than Jesus. That blockage doesn't hurt the head, Jesus, but it does damage the body, the church.

What blocks the flow of love, mercy, kindness and forgives between the body and the head. Paul said, "Therefore do not let anyone judge you by what you eat or drink, or with regard to a religious festival, a new moon celebration or a Sabbath day...the worship of angels..." Why? Because "He has lost connection with the head, from the whole body, supported and held together by its ligaments and sinews, grows as God causes it to grow" (2:16, 18, 19). To make anything essential to salvation other than faith in Jesus alone blocks God's flow of forgiveness to a lost person.

My prayer: Thank You for making salvation so simple. Help me present the simplicity of the gospel so others can receive forgiveness and salvation.

Day 2: The Drive That Thrives

Read I THESSALONIANS Chapters 1-5

Over the fifty four years I've been in the ministry there has been in every church where I've served a person or persons that have been faithful and fruitful. What drove them to be faithful through the ups and downs of the church's life? It couldn't have been for glory or wealth or power. They did not appear to seek praise or to be noticed. They just quietly served the Lord.

What was the drive in their Christian walk that made them thrive? Paul gave us a glimpse of what shapes a person's attitude to remain faithful. He said the Thessalonian's work for the Lord was "...produced by faith, your labor prompted by love, and your endurance inspired by hope in our Lord Jesus Christ" (1:2). A big element that made them thrive was their love of God's Word. He said, "And we also thank God continually because, when you received the Word of God, which you heard from us, you accepted it not as the word of men, but as it actually is the Word of God, which is at work in you who believe" (2:13).

My prayer: _Thank You for Your Word, the Holy Spirit and the fellowship of other believers. It is my prayer to thrive until I arrive in Your presence._

Day 3: Everyone is Invited

Read II THESSALONIANS Chapters 1-3

Most everyone has received an invitation to a gathering with the initials RSVP on it. That means the person being invited needs to notify the person sending the invitation that they will attend. Some false teachers in Thessalonica said the church members there didn't get their invitation to the resurrection and the return of Jesus and they missed the event. Many were upset.

Christ's second coming will be made known and no one will be left behind. Everyone who receives Christ as their personal Savior have reservations and have responded to God's RSVP. Paul comforted the Thessalonians with these words: "Concerning the coming of our Lord Jesus Christ and our being gathered to Him, we ask you brothers, not to become easily unsettled or alarmed by some prophecy, report or letter supposed to have come from us, saying the day of the Lord has already come. Don't let anyone deceive you in any way for, that day will not come until the rebellion occurs and the man of lawlessness is revealed…" (2:1-3).

My prayer: Please come quickly, Lord Jesus. Help me give out as many invitations to the lost of this world as I can.

Day 4: Happy and Content While Here
Read I TIMOTHY Chapters 1-6

One of the saddest occurrences is to see a person who has no joy, purpose or enthusiasm for life. Some people live like everyone is against them. That person seems to be wired negative and in the kickative mood.

To receive Christ as Lord and Savior can change a person from being negative to being positive. How? Contentment is experienced when a person realizes his value comes from God loving him so much that He died on the cross for his sins. Happiness will fill his heart when he realizes God created him for a purpose no one else can accomplish. No one can replace him as that unique individual God designed for His purpose. The only thing that will satisfy a person and bring him joy is to discover God's plan for his life. Worldly things do not satisfy that need God put in man. That is why Paul said, "But godliness with contentment is great gain…But if we have food and clothing, we will be content with that…But You, man of

God, flee from this [worldly things], and pursue righteousness, godliness, faith, love, endurance and gentleness...that we may live peaceful and quiet lives in all godliness and holiness" (6:6, 8, 11, 2:2).

My prayer: I cannot thank You enough Lord for loving me and dying for me. I praise You for Your mercy and kindness.

Day 5: Bashful or Bold?

Read II TIMOTHY Chapters 1-4

Timothy had a calling in his life that had been affirmed by Paul. Paul encouraged Timothy to remember this calling and boldly present the gospel. "For this reason I remind you to fan into flame the gift of God, which is in You through the laying on of my hands. For God did not give us a spirit of timidity, but a spirit of power, of love and of self-discipline. So do not be ashamed to testify about our Lord..." (1:6-8).

Where does a Christian get this boldness? That boldness must come from the presence of the Holy Spirit. Every believer is called to be a bold witness. Every believer is to ask to be filled with the Holy Spirit to allow God's boldness to be manifested. A Spirit filled Christian will be a bold witness as recorded in Acts. "After they prayed, the place where they were meeting was shaken. And they were all filled with the Holy Spirit and spoke the word of God boldly" (Acts 4:31). To be filled with the Holy Spirit, ask God to forgive you of your sins and yield your heart to the Holy Spirit so He can control you.

My prayer: Again, today I ask to be filled with the Holy Spirit and I yield my life to Your control.

Day 6: Behavior Reveals Your Beliefs

Read TITUS Chapters 1 - Philemon

A person's actions show what he really believes in spite of what he says. Someone can say they believe traveling on airplanes is safe but refuse to fly when it is needed. Their action demonstrates what they really believe. A person can say they believe in God and live like the Devil. Their actions reveal what they really believe.

Paul said those who worship creation rather than the God of creation will believe all of life is corrupt. He wrote, "To the pure, all things are pure, but to those who are corrupted and do not believe, nothing is pure. In fact, both their minds and consciences are corrupted" (Titus 1:15). Paul told Timothy that those who taught You had to eat special foods to be spiritual corrupt minds. He said that "...everything God created is good, and nothing is to be rejected if it is received with thanksgiving, because it is consecrated by the Word of God and prayer" (I Timothy 4:4). A person who really believes in the holiness of God will live a holy life.

My prayer: I lift up my plea to You and ask that You convict me when I'm hypocritical and fail to practice what I say I believe. Help me to look at the world through Your holy, pure eyes.

Day 7: Angels Attendance on Earth

Read HEBREWS Chapters 1-6

One great event the angels attended was God's presentation of the law. Psalms indicates there were many angels present when Moses received the Law. "The chariots of God are tens of thousands and thousands of thousands; the Lord has come from Sinai into His sanctuary" (Psalms 68:17). Paul states that the "Law was put into effect through angels by a mediator" (Galatians 3:19). Stephen said to the Jews, "...You who have received the Law that was put into effect through angels, but have not obeyed it" (Acts 7:53). This important event was attended by many angels.

There was a greater event than the giving of the Law. Peter said, "Even angels long to look into these things" (I Peter 1:12). The greatest event on earth was the birth of Jesus. It is the most important event of all creation and the history of man. Instead of going to Mt. Sinai the angels came to Mt. Zion where believers receive salvation through the cross of Christ. Hebrews says to believers, "...You have come to Mt. Zion, to the heavenly Jerusalem, the city of the living God. You have come to thousands upon thousands of angels in joyful assembly..." (12:22). "For if the message spoken by angels was abiding, and every violation and disobedience received its just punishment, how shall we escape if we ignore such a great salvation" (2:2-3)?

My prayer: *I praise You again that Your love for mankind is demonstrated by the giving of Your law and then You're Son.*

Yearly Devotions – Week 49

Day 1: Christ's Blood Brings Life

Read HEBREWS Chapters 7-10

Any part of the body that is cut off from the flow of blood will die and cease functioning. Blood is essential for life. The Bible says, "For the life of the flesh is in the blood..." (Leviticus 17:11). The body will remain healthy as long as the blood continues to flow freely. Without blood the body dies. When God required Israel to sacrifice animals and sprinkle their blood on the altar the blood signified that a death had taken place as demanded by God for the judgment of sin. "In fact, the Law requires that nearly everything be cleansed with blood and without the shedding of blood there is no forgiveness" (9:22).

Why did God require blood to be shed? His holiness demands that all sin must be punished. "For the wages of sin is death" (Romans 6:23). No sin can be overlooked. Since God loves mankind He chose a way they could escape punishment. He sent His Son to shed His innocent, sinless blood as payment for everyone's sin. "But now He has appeared once for all at the end of the ages to do away with sin by the sacrifice of Himself" (9:26). "...the blood of Jesus, His Son, purifies us from all sin" (I John 1:7).

My prayer: I praise You for Your mercy and grace in giving us salvation through Jesus' shed blood.

Day 2: The Finish Line Is In Heaven

Read HEBREWS Chapters 11-13

The old saying, "A woman's work is never done," has reminded people of the responsibility of a wife and mother. A woman probably originated that saying to remind husbands of all they do. These chapters in Hebrews remind believers that the Christian life is never done until we arrive in our "long home" called heaven. A Christian is always on spiritual duty until furloughed to that "long home."

Hebrews lists an honor roll of believers and their deeds done by faith. The writer reminds us that these Old Testament saints did not see the completion of their work while on earth. They faithfully followed God's will and "...through faith conquered kingdoms, administered justice, and gained what was promised..." (11:33). not while on earth but when they went to heaven. What they gained they received when they entered God's presence. "These were all commended for their faith, yet none of them received what had been promised" (11:39). They did not receive it while on earth but they did receive their rewards in heaven.

My prayer: Help me to keep my eyes on Jesus and serve for the rewards in heaven.

Day 5: The Two Kinds of Wisdom

Read JAMES Chapters 1-5

There is earthly wisdom and there is heavenly wisdom. Each wisdom has a different result. Wisdom is the ability to understand facts and use that knowledge to benefit oneself and others.

Earthly wisdom is described by James and accurately reveals its fruit. "Such 'wisdom' does not come down from heaven but is earthly, unspiritual, of the devil. For where You have envy and selfish ambition, there You find disorder and every evil practice" (3:15-16).

Heavenly wisdom can only come from God through His Son, the Holy Spirit and the Word of God. "But the wisdom that comes from heaven is first of all pure; then peace-loving, considerate, submissive, full of mercy and good fruit, impartial and sincere" (3:17). Heavenly wisdom is to obey the Lord and His instructions even when the world thinks that it is unwise. Noah was laughed at for building the Ark when there appeared to be no need for it. His wisdom was evident when he saved his family and the human race by obeying God's instructions.

My prayer: Lord, I lack wisdom and You said, "if any of You lacks wisdom, he should ask God..." So I am asking for Your wisdom in order to live to glorify You.

Day 4: Silence Your Critics

Read I PETER Chapters 1-3

The lost world watches Christians very closely to see if they are living what they say they believe and to see if they are going to stumble and sin. If a believer falls into sin it gives non-believers an excuse to say there is nothing to Christianity and discredits the Christian witness. It gives a non-believer false hope. They convince themselves that faith in Christ has no validity and that they won't be judged by God. It gives them the opportunity to say, "I am as good as any Christian, therefore, I don't need a Savior. When a believer sins, it brings shame on the name of Jesus. He is identified with every professing Christian.

The Apostle Peter directs all believers to keep before them the terrible results sin brings to a believer and the disillusionment to unbelievers. Peter stated, "For it is God's will that by doing good You should silence the ignorant talk of foolish men. Live as free men, but do not use your freedom as a cover-up for evil; live as servants of God" (2:15-16).

My prayer: Lead me not into temptation.

Day 5: Why Believe the Bible

Read I PETER Chapters 4 – II PETER 2

Men have tried to discount and destroy the Bible ever since it was written. Why do they want to destroy it? They want to destroy it because it reveals a holy God who holds men accountable for their behavior and tells of a judgment day. Only the God of the Bible declares Himself to be holy without sin and that He is all powerful. Men rebel at the absolute holiness and power of God. Men believe God overlooks our sin. The Bible is unbending and absolute in demanding that men live according to God's standards. "...For God cannot be tempted with evil, neither tempteth He any man" (James 1:13 KJV).

Why should we believe the Bible? I believe the Bible because the men who God used to write it experienced God's presence and saw Him do many wonderful and mighty things. "We did not follow cleverly invented stories when we told you about the power and coming of our Lord Jesus Christ, but we were eyewitnesses of His majesty..." They heard God say, "...this is My Son, whom I love; with Him I am well pleased...we ourselves heard this voice that came from heaven when we were with Him on the sacred mountain" (II Peter 1:16-18). They were all killed except John rather than deny Jesus. They shared the truth with others who testified of its validity.

My prayer: Lord, I praise You for giving us the truth in Your inerrant, infallible Word. Help me to fill my heart with Your Word.

Day 6: What Is Walking In the Light?
Read II PETER Chapter 3 – I JOHN Chapter 3

Walking in the light is to walk towards God and to attempt to do His will. "…God is light; in Him there is no darkness at all" (I John 1:5). To walk in His light is to acknowledge one's sinfulness and seek His forgiveness and mercy through His grace. Salvation is a gift that cannot be earned. "…if we walk in the light, as He is in the light, we have fellowship with one another, and the blood of Jesus, His Son, purifies us from all sin" (I John 1:7). "This is how we know we are in Him: Whoever claims to live in Him must walk as Jesus did" (I John 2:5-6).

Walking in darkness can easily be identified. "If we claim to have fellowship with Him yet walk in the darkness, we lie and do not live the truth" (I John 1:6). Darkness is described by John. "…it is the man who denies that Jesus is the Christ" (I John 2:22). It is "…the cravings of sinful man, the lust of the eyes and the boasting of what he has and does – comes not from the Father but from the world" (I John 2:16).

My prayer: Help me stay in the light and keep my eyes fixed on Jesus.

Day 7: "Who Is It That Overcomes The World?"
Read I JOHN Chapter 4 – III JOHN

Why do we need to overcome the world and what is the world? The world is opposed to everything that is Godly and that belongs to Him, including man. The world, as God's enemy, hates God and is opposed to everything He does. The world strives to destroy man with sin and His creation with Satan's help. The world so hated God that it crucified His Son.

The world is the educational system that teaches God did not create man. The world is the religious system that preaches that a person must earn salvation by works. The world believes that God's design of marriage between one man and one woman is wrong. The world is for sodomites and perverted women being able to marry and in so doing redefine marriage. The world accepts adultery and fornication as normal behavior. The world seeks possessions, power and privilege.

"Who is it that overcomes the world? Only he who believes that Jesus is the Son of God" (5:5). "You, dear children, are from God and have overcome them, because the one who is in you is greater than the one who is in the world" (4:4).

My prayer: Dear Lord, I rely on Your power to overcome the world and I rejoice that You have overcome all evil through Your precious blood and resurrection. I pray for those who are still in bondage to the world.

Yearly Devotions – Week 50

Day 1: Jesus Knows

Read JUDE - REVELATION Chapters 2

Santa Claus has become the one the world knows as having knowledge about everyone's behavior. The Christmas song goes something like this, "...He knows when you've been bad or good so be good for goodness sake." The only problem with that song is there is no Santa Claus and no one can be good enough for God because His standards of goodness are too high for men to reach. Everyone is born with a sinful nature and their goodness is as "filthy rags" in God's sight.

Jesus is the only one who knows our behavior accurately. John revealed Jesus' knowledge of people's behavior when he wrote Revelation. Jesus knew the bad and the good behavior. He told the churches, "I know your deeds, your hard work and your perseverance.... You have persevered and have endured hardships for My Name, and have not grown weary" (2:2, 3). He then lets them know about their bad behavior. "Yet I hold this against you: You have forsaken your first love...repent and do the things you did at first" (2:4, 5).

My prayer: Thank You for Your grace and may I remember the joy and excitement when I first surrendered to You and return to being an effective witness.

Day 2: Heaven Business

Read REVELATION Chapters 3-7

Heaven is a busy place and will always be a busy place. Its business is to worship the one who created everything and a place where love, compassion and righteousness are practiced perfectly. Since God created all things He has the right to demand His creation to worship Him. God's intention and execution of all His activities is to bless those of His creation and benefit them with His presence.

When everyone who goes to heaven gets there it will be one gigantic worship service around the throne of God. God gave man salvation and prepares them to live with Him for eternity. How can we be sure this is so? John saw it. "After this I looked and there before me was a great multitude that no one could count, from every nation, tribe, people and language, standing before the throne and in front of the Lamb...And they cried out in a loud voice: "Salvation belongs to our God, who sits on the throne, and to the Lamb" (7:9, 10). Everyone can start their worship now.

My prayer: _I praise You and worship You for providing my salvation through Christ's shed blood. Help me broadcast the good news._

Day 3: People in Hell Still Hate God

Read REVELATION Chapters 8-12

The amazing thing about the lost is that they will never love God nor experience God's love in eternity. A lost person would not be happy in heaven. Worship, adoration and praise of God will be the eternal activity in heaven. If a lost person does not enjoy that on earth he wouldn't enjoy it in heaven.

After great pain, plagues of fire, smoke and sulfur during the great tribulation people refused to seek God. "The rest of mankind that were not killed by these plagues still did not repent of the work of their hands; they did not stop worshiping demons, and idols of gold, silver, bronze, stone and wood – idols that cannot see or hear or walk. Nor did they repent of their murders, their magic arts, their sexual immorality or their thefts" (9:20-21). Jesus said, "...men loved darkness instead of light because their deeds were evil. Everyone who does evil hates the light, and will not come into the light for fear that his deeds will be exposed" (John 3:19-20). To live in hell without love and righteousness is unthinkable.

My prayer: I pray for those who still have an opportunity to receive forgiveness and salvation from the Lord. I plead with You to send conviction through Your word and the Holy Spirit that men and women come to Christ now while the door is still open to them.

Day 4: Heaven's Main Activity

Read REVELATION Chapters 13-16

Every creature in heaven continually worships God. They honor God with their obedience and praise. To honor God means we understand His worth and appropriate praise for Him accordingly. Revelation lets us get a peek of heavenly activity where praise is in progress at all times. John wrote of his vision, "Then I saw another angel flying in midair...He said in a loud voice, 'Fear God and give Him glory, because the hour of His judgment has come. Worship Him who made the heavens, the earth, the sea and the springs of water" (14:6, 7).

The angels sing and worship God with musical instruments. Large groups of redeemed people who were persecuted and ridiculed on earth sing with the angels as they all worship God. "They hold harps given them by God and sing the song of Moses the servant of God and the song of the Lamb. 'Great and marvelous are Your deeds, Lord God Almighty. Just and true are Your ways, King of the ages...for You alone are holy..." (15:3, 4).

My prayer: Thank You for letting me see the glorious prospect of what I will experience in heaven. Help me to know how to worship in a way that honors and pleases You.

Day 5: God Will Judge All Nations

Read REVELATION Chapters 17-18

Nations are made up of people. The leaders of Nations either lead their people in a Godly direction or in an ungodly direction. All national leaders and the people of each nation will stand before a holy God and give an account of their actions.

According to the Psalmist there will come a time when every nation will become so corrupt they will join together to fight God. They will be led by the anti – Christ. "Why do the nations conspire and the peoples plot in vain? The kings of the earth take their stand and the rulers gather together against the Lord and against His Anointed One" (Psalms 2:1-2). Jesus said, "When the Son of Man comes in His glory, and all the angels with Him, He will sit on His throne in heavenly glory. All the nations will be gathered before Him...He will put the sheep on His right and the goats on His left" (Matthew 25:31-33). God keeps records of the nation's sin. "...for her sins are piled up to heaven, and God has remembered her crimes" (18:5). We must pray for America.

My prayer: Lord, have mercy on America and send a spiritual awakening.

Day 6: No Bedrooms in Heaven

Read REVELATION Chapters 19-22

There is a glorious time coming for every true born-again believer. It will be an exciting time of experiencing the joys of being in the very presence of God. There will be no need to go to bed because our glorified bodies will be perfectly adapted to heavenly conditions. "The city does not need the sun or the moon to shine on it, for the glory of God gives it light, and the Lamb is its lamp...On no day will its gates ever be shut, for there will be no night there" (21:23, 25).

The city of God will be beyond anything man can imagine. John got to see that city. "...He carried me away in the Spirit...and showed me the Holy City, Jerusalem...it shone with the glory of God, and its brilliance was like that of a precious jewel, like a jasper, clear as crystal" (21:10, 11). "Now the dwelling of God is with men, and He will live with them...there will be no more death or mourning or crying or pain, for the old order of things has passed away" (21:3, 4). A person must make a reservation to be a citizen of the city. "...only those whose names are written in the Lamb's book of life..." can enter this city (21:27). That reservation is made when a person asks Christ to be their Savior.

My prayer: First, I want to thank You, Lord, for letting us see what our future with You will be like. Give me strength and discernment to be able to lead people to accept Jesus as their Savior. Help me to fill Your city with sinners saved by grace.

About the Author

Pat Bullock and his wife Nancy have been in ministry for fifty-seven years and Pat has pastored eight churches. He and Nancy started several churches and two Christian schools. These churches kept Pat busy as a bi-vocational pastor. He taught in public schools throughout Texas in Ackerly, Garden City, and Alpine. He earned his pilot's license and flew for the Department of Agriculture. He had a welding job in Odessa, Texas building oil tanks. He did carpentry work and pastored a new church. His last full time pastorate was with Annaville Baptist Church in Corpus Christi, Texas where he served for eighteen years.

Pat served as the Director of Missions for the Heart of Kansas Southern Baptist Association in Wichita, Kansas for over ten years. He presently serves as Associate Pastor at Summit Church in Wichita, Kansas. www.summitchurchkansas.com

Pat Bullock has served as a trustee with the International Mission Board of the Southern Baptist Convention in Richmond, Virginia for seven years. He served as a Trustee of Southwestern Baptist Theological Seminary in Fort Worth, Texas for nine years. He also served as a Regent with the Midwestern Baptist Theological Seminary in Kansas City, Missouri for five years.

Pat has had the privilege of preaching the gospel in Romania and the Ukraine soon after the Iron Curtain was torn down. He held an Evangelistic Meeting in Scotland and saw God move in a wonderful way. He has seen God's faithfulness and has written these devotions from his lifetime of experiences.

Made in the USA
San Bernardino, CA
18 April 2015